D0516833

MARK WAID · PETER KRAUSE
IRREDEEMABLE
VOLUME 3

Ross Richie - Chief Executive Officer

Mark Waid - Editor-in-Chief

Adam Fortier - VP-Publishing

Lance Kreiter - VP-Licensing & Merchandising

Chip Mosher - Marketing Director

Jenny Christopher - Sales Director

Matt Gagnon - Managing Editor

Ian Brill - Editor

Bryce Carlson - Editor

Dafna Pleban - Editor

Aaron Sparrow - Editor

Christopher Meyer - Editor

Shannon Watters - Assistant Editor

Christopher Burns - Assistant Editor

Jason Long - Assistant Editor

Neil Loughrie - Publishing Coordinator

Travis Beatty - Traffic Coordinator

Ivan Salazar - Marketing Assistant

Kate Hayden - Executive Assistant

Brian Latimer - Graphic Designer

Erika Terriquez - Graphic Designer

IRREDEEMABLE V3 — June 2010 published by BOOM! Studios. Irredeemable is copyright © 2010 Boom Entertainment, Inc. BOOM! Studios™ and the BOOM! logo are trademarks of Boom Entertainment, Inc., registered in various countries and categories. All rights reserved. The characters and events depicted herein are fictional. Any similarity to actual persons, demons, anti-Christs, aliens, vampires, face-suckers or political figures, whether living, dead or undead, or to any actual or supernatural events is coincidental and unintentional. So don't come whining to us. Office of publication: 6310 San Vicente Blvd, Ste 404, Los Angeles, CA 90048-5457. For information regarding the CPSIA on this printed material call: 203-595-3636 and provide reference # EAST — 66135

A catalog record for this book is available from OCLC and on our website www.boom-studios.com on the Librarians page.

First Edition: June 2010

10 9 8 7 6 5 4 3 2 1

Printed in U.S.A.

IRREDEEMABLE

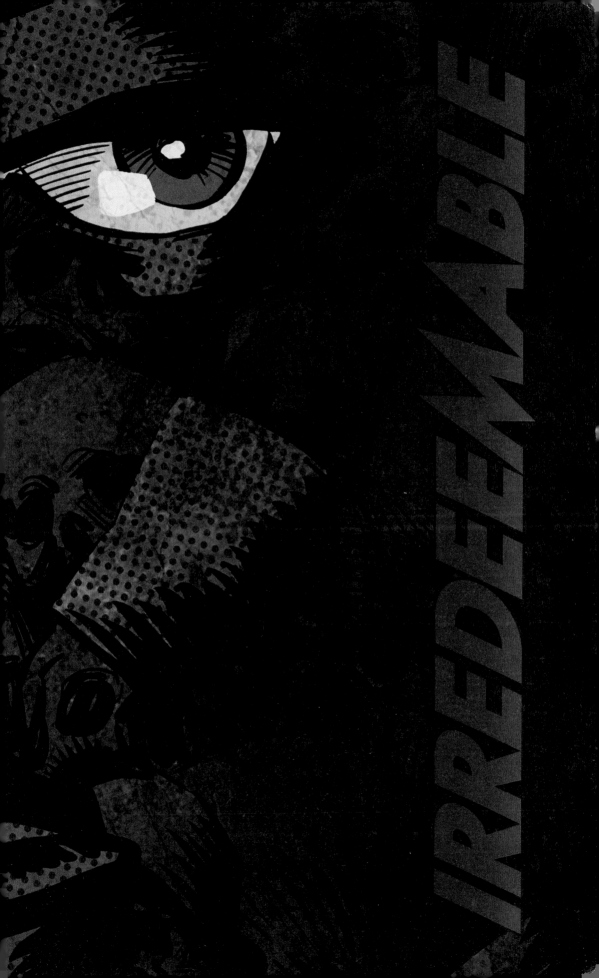

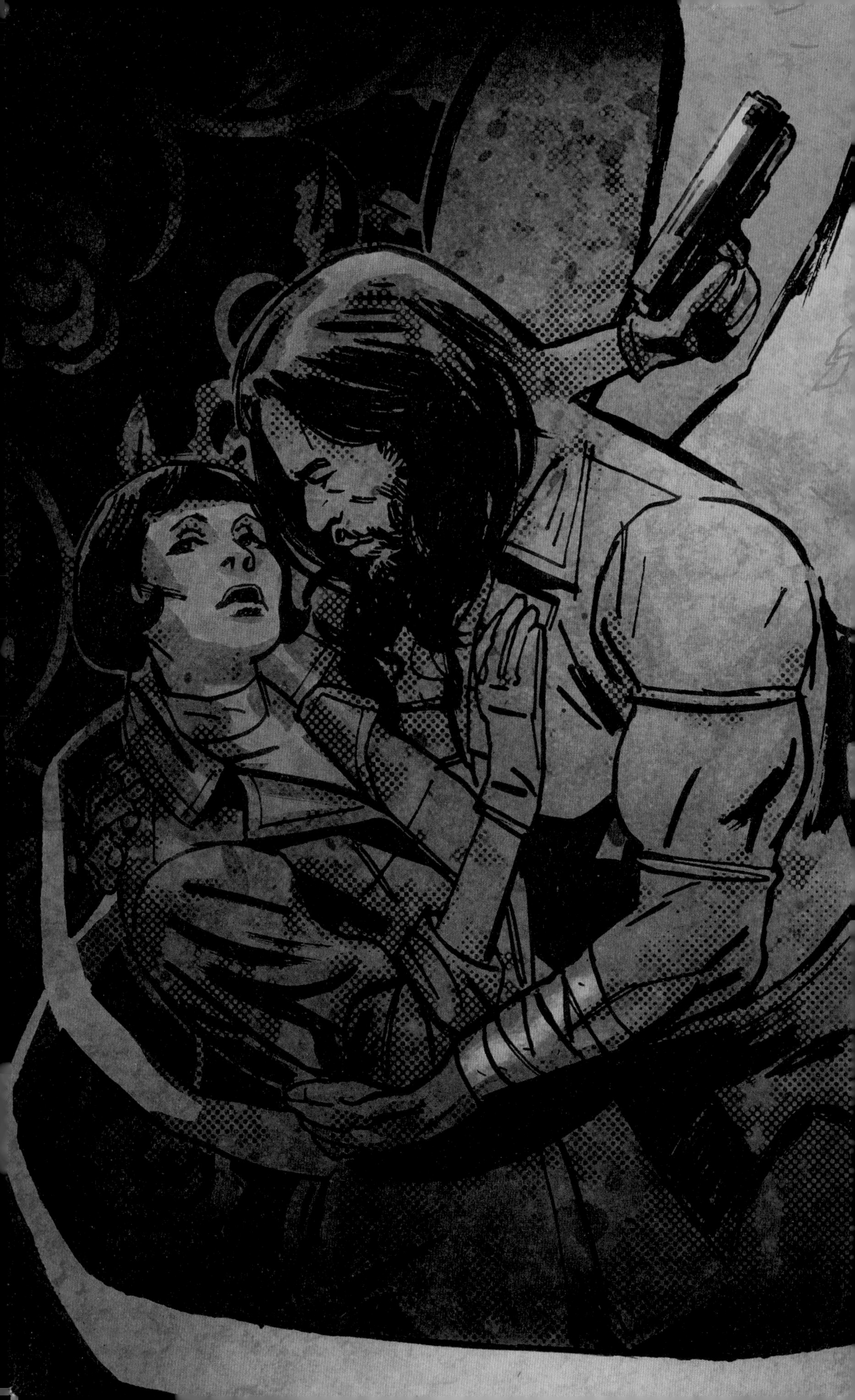

CREATED AND WRITTEN BY:

MARK WAID

ARTISTS:

PETER KRAUSE

ISSUE 9 / ISSUE 10 (PAGES 5-8, 13-19) / ISSUE 11 (PAGES 13-22) / ISSUE 12 (PAGES 12-22)

DIEGO BARRETO

ISSUE 10 (PAGES 1-4, 9-12, 20-22) / ISSUE 11 (PAGES 1-12) / ISSUE 12 (PAGES 1-11)

COLORIST: ANDREW DALHOUSE
LETTERER: ED DUKESHIRE
EDITOR: MATT GAGNON

COVER: BARRY KITSON
COLORS: ANDREW DALHOUSE

PLUTONIAN CHARACTER DESIGN: PAUL AZACETA
GRAPHIC DESIGN: BRIAN LATIMER

CHAPTER 9

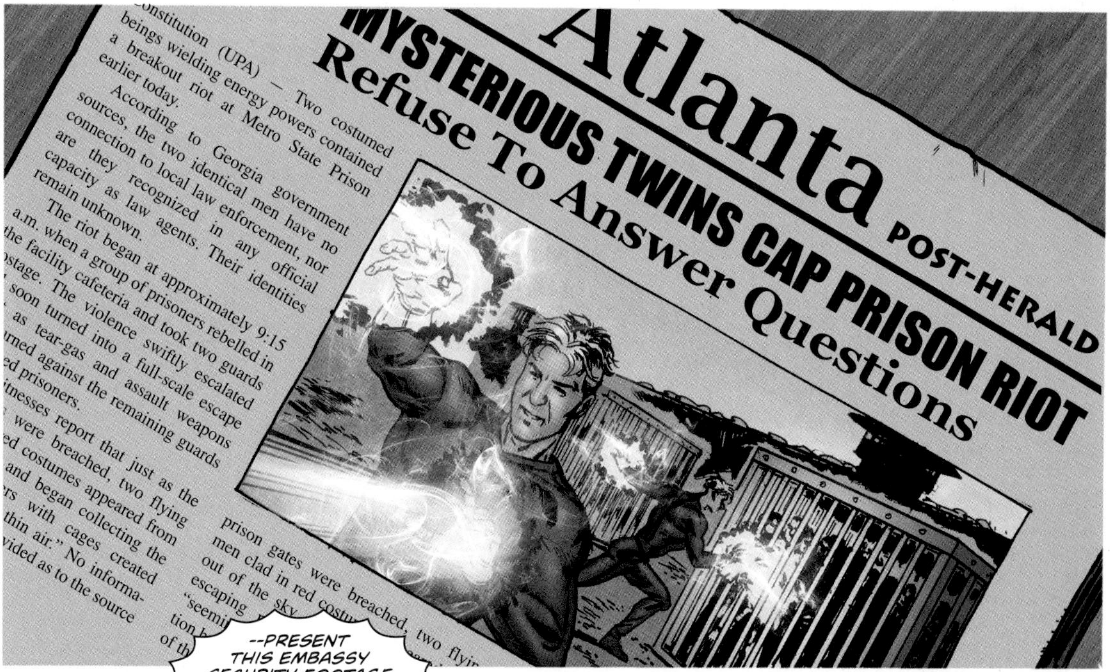
Atlanta POST-HERALD
MYSTERIOUS TWINS CAP PRISON RIOT
Refuse To Answer Questions
onstitution (UPA) – Two costumed beings wielding energy powers contained a breakout riot at Metro State Prison earlier today.
According to Georgia government sources, the two identical men have no connection to local law enforcement, nor are they recognized in any official capacity as law agents. Their identities remain unknown.
The riot began at approximately 9:15 a.m. when a group of prisoners rebelled in the facility cafeteria and took two guards ostage. The violence swiftly escalated soon turned into a full-scale escape as tear-gas and assault weapons rned against the remaining guards ed prisoners.
itnesses report that just as the were breached, two flying ed costumes appeared from and began collecting the rs with cages created thin air." No informa- vided as to the source
prison gates were breached, two flyin men clad in red costu out of the sky escaping "seemi tion of th

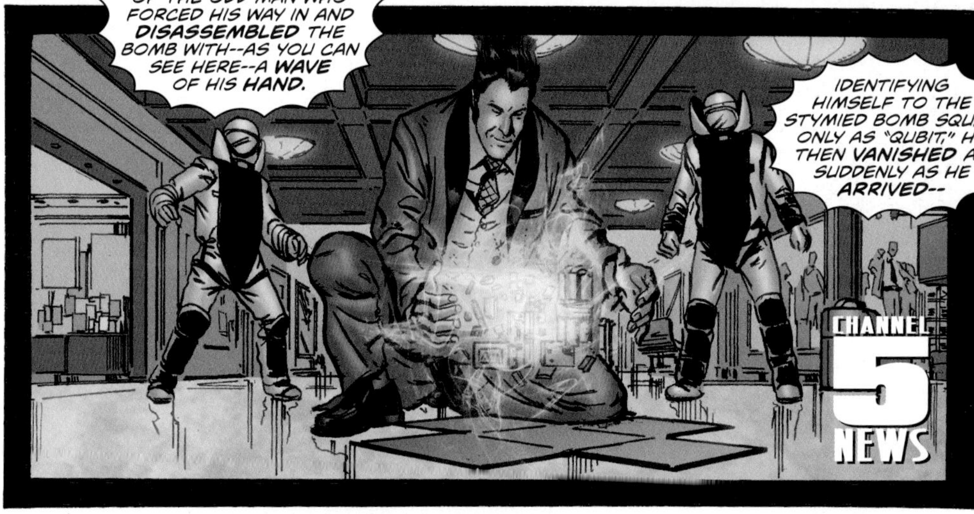
--PRESENT THIS EMBASSY SECURITY FOOTAGE OF THE ODD MAN WHO FORCED HIS WAY IN AND DISASSEMBLED THE BOMB WITH--AS YOU CAN SEE HERE--A WAVE OF HIS HAND.
IDENTIFYING HIMSELF TO THE STYMIED BOMB SQUAD ONLY AS "QUBIT," HE THEN VANISHED AS SUDDENLY AS HE ARRIVED--
CHANNEL 5 NEWS

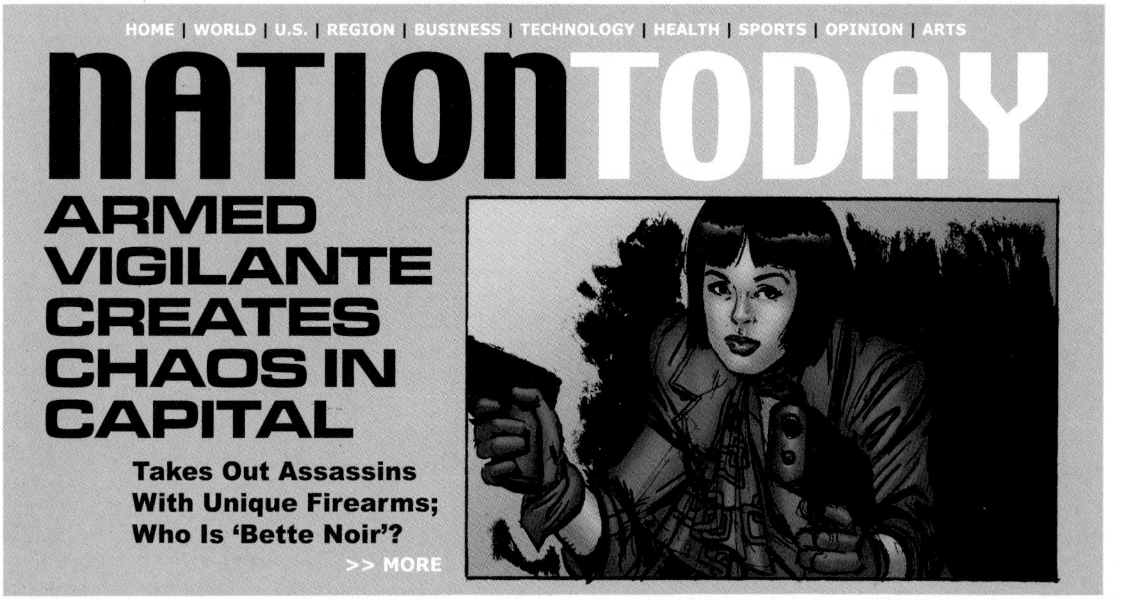
HOME | WORLD | U.S. | REGION | BUSINESS | TECHNOLOGY | HEALTH | SPORTS | OPINION | ARTS
NATION TODAY
ARMED VIGILANTE CREATES CHAOS IN CAPITAL
Takes Out Assassins With Unique Firearms; Who Is 'Bette Noir'?
>> MORE

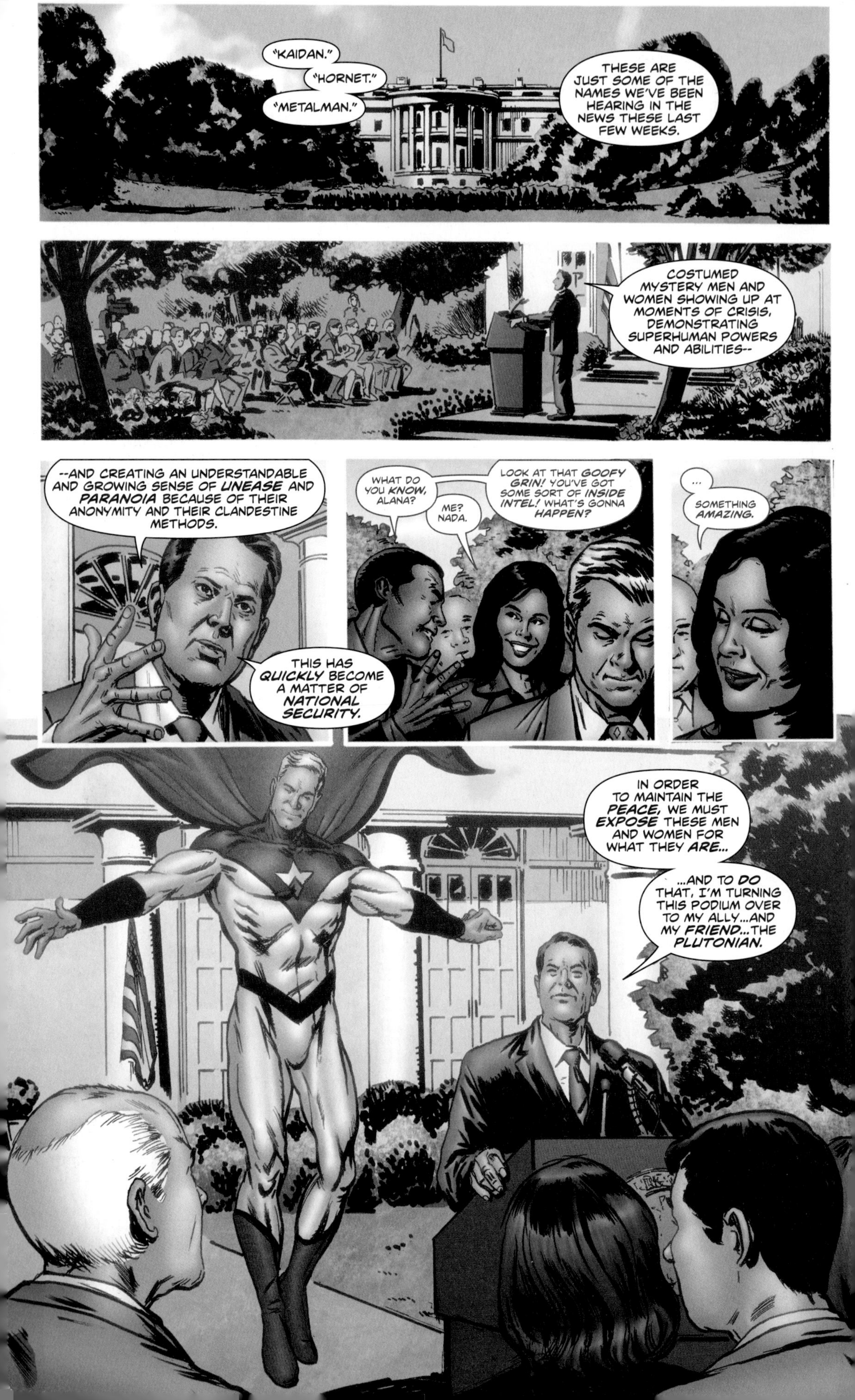
"KAIDAN."
"HORNET."
"METALMAN."
THESE ARE JUST SOME OF THE NAMES WE'VE BEEN HEARING IN THE NEWS THESE LAST FEW WEEKS.
COSTUMED MYSTERY MEN AND WOMEN SHOWING UP AT MOMENTS OF CRISIS, DEMONSTRATING SUPERHUMAN POWERS AND ABILITIES--
--AND CREATING AN UNDERSTANDABLE AND GROWING SENSE OF *UNEASE* AND *PARANOIA* BECAUSE OF THEIR ANONYMITY AND THEIR CLANDESTINE METHODS.
THIS HAS *QUICKLY* BECOME A MATTER OF *NATIONAL SECURITY.*
WHAT DO YOU *KNOW,* ALANA?
ME? NADA.
LOOK AT THAT *GOOFY GRIN!* YOU'VE GOT SOME SORT OF *INSIDE INTEL!* WHAT'S GONNA *HAPPEN?*
...
SOMETHING *AMAZING.*
IN ORDER TO MAINTAIN THE *PEACE,* WE MUST *EXPOSE* THESE MEN AND WOMEN FOR WHAT THEY *ARE...*
...AND TO *DO* THAT, I'M TURNING THIS PODIUM OVER TO MY ALLY...AND MY *FRIEND...*THE *PLUTONIAN.*

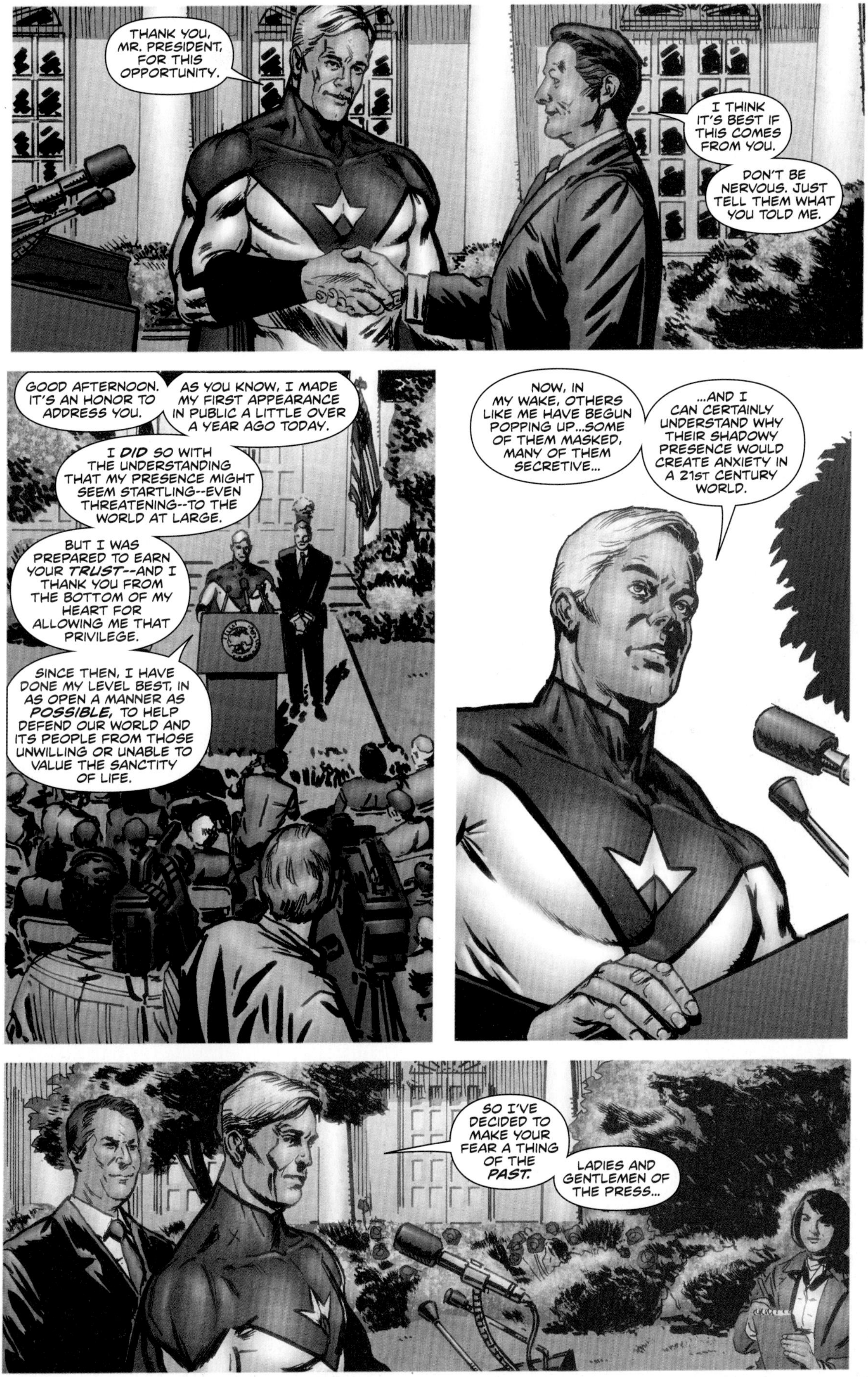
THANK YOU, MR. PRESIDENT, FOR THIS OPPORTUNITY.
I THINK IT'S BEST IF THIS COMES FROM YOU.
DON'T BE NERVOUS. JUST TELL THEM WHAT YOU TOLD ME.
GOOD AFTERNOON. IT'S AN HONOR TO ADDRESS YOU.
AS YOU KNOW, I MADE MY FIRST APPEARANCE IN PUBLIC A LITTLE OVER A YEAR AGO TODAY.
I *DID* SO WITH THE UNDERSTANDING THAT MY PRESENCE MIGHT SEEM STARTLING--EVEN THREATENING--TO THE WORLD AT LARGE.
BUT I WAS PREPARED TO EARN YOUR *TRUST*--AND I THANK YOU FROM THE BOTTOM OF MY HEART FOR ALLOWING ME THAT PRIVILEGE.
SINCE THEN, I HAVE DONE MY LEVEL BEST, IN AS OPEN A MANNER AS *POSSIBLE,* TO HELP DEFEND OUR WORLD AND ITS PEOPLE FROM THOSE UNWILLING OR UNABLE TO VALUE THE SANCTITY OF LIFE.
NOW, IN MY WAKE, OTHERS LIKE ME HAVE BEGUN POPPING UP...SOME OF THEM MASKED, MANY OF THEM SECRETIVE...
...AND I CAN CERTAINLY UNDERSTAND WHY THEIR SHADOWY PRESENCE WOULD CREATE ANXIETY IN A 21ST CENTURY WORLD.
SO I'VE DECIDED TO MAKE YOUR FEAR A THING OF THE *PAST.*
LADIES AND GENTLEMEN OF THE PRESS...

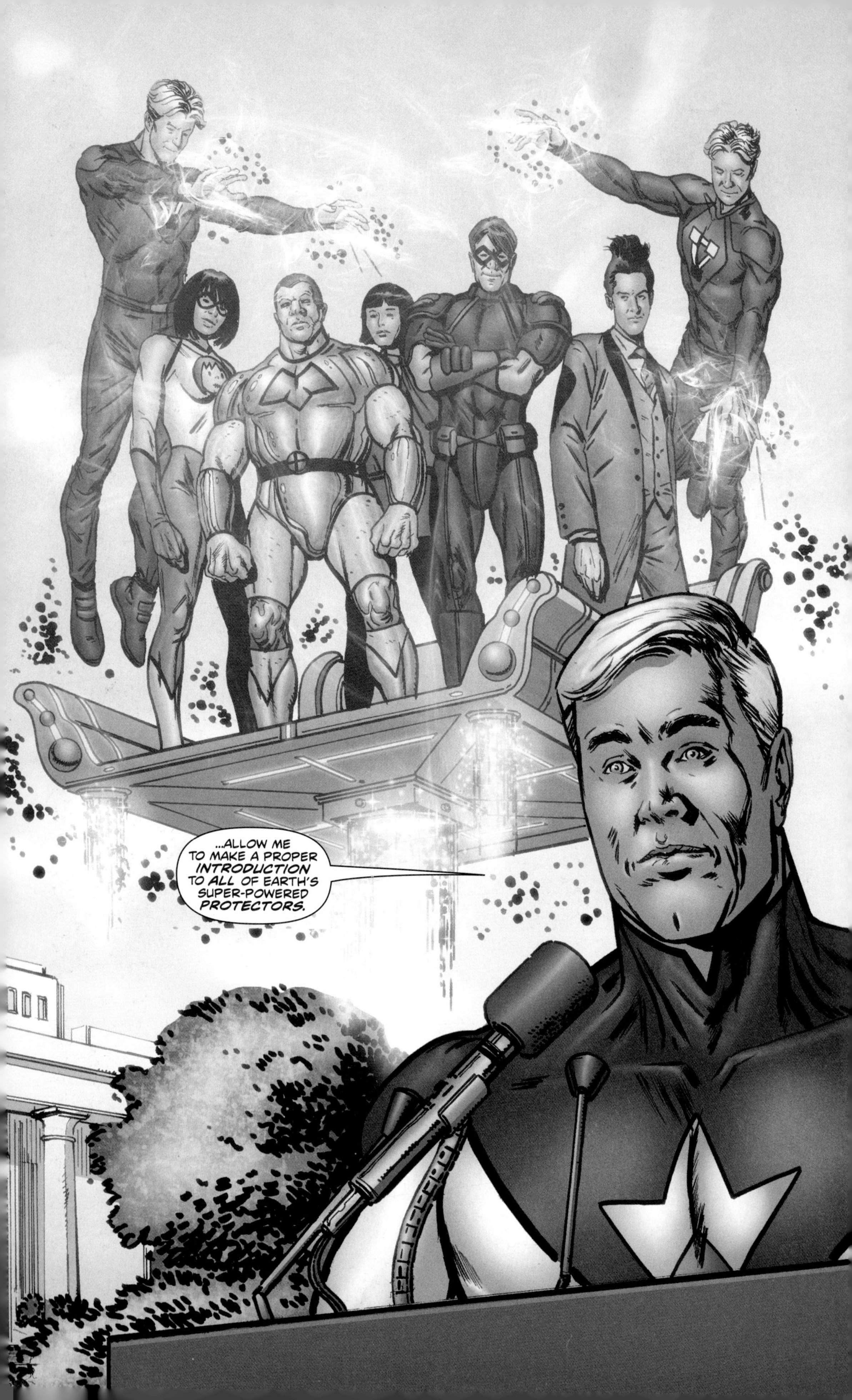
...ALLOW ME TO MAKE A PROPER INTRODUCTION TO ALL OF EARTH'S SUPER-POWERED PROTECTORS.

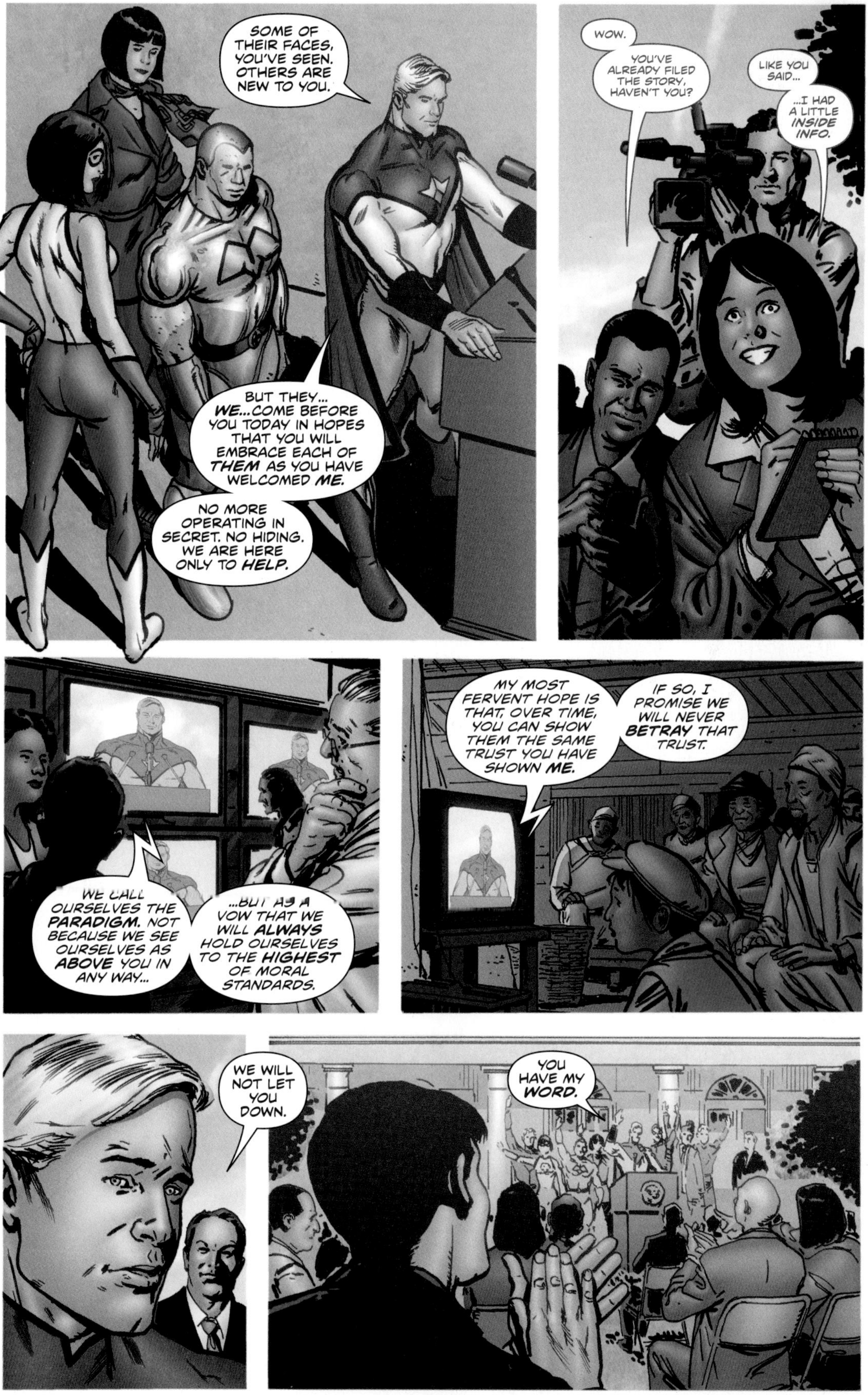
SOME OF THEIR FACES, YOU'VE SEEN. OTHERS ARE NEW TO YOU.
BUT THEY... **WE**...COME BEFORE YOU TODAY IN HOPES THAT YOU WILL EMBRACE EACH OF **THEM** AS YOU HAVE WELCOMED **ME**.
NO MORE OPERATING IN SECRET. NO HIDING. WE ARE HERE ONLY TO **HELP**.
WOW.
YOU'VE ALREADY FILED THE STORY, HAVEN'T YOU?
LIKE YOU SAID...
...I HAD A LITTLE *INSIDE INFO.*
WE CALL OURSELVES THE **PARADIGM**. NOT BECAUSE WE SEE OURSELVES AS **ABOVE** YOU IN ANY WAY...
...BUT AS A VOW THAT WE WILL **ALWAYS** HOLD OURSELVES TO THE **HIGHEST** OF MORAL STANDARDS.
MY MOST FERVENT HOPE IS THAT, OVER TIME, YOU CAN SHOW THEM THE SAME TRUST YOU HAVE SHOWN **ME**.
IF SO, I PROMISE WE WILL NEVER **BETRAY** THAT TRUST.
WE WILL NOT LET YOU DOWN.
YOU HAVE MY **WORD**.

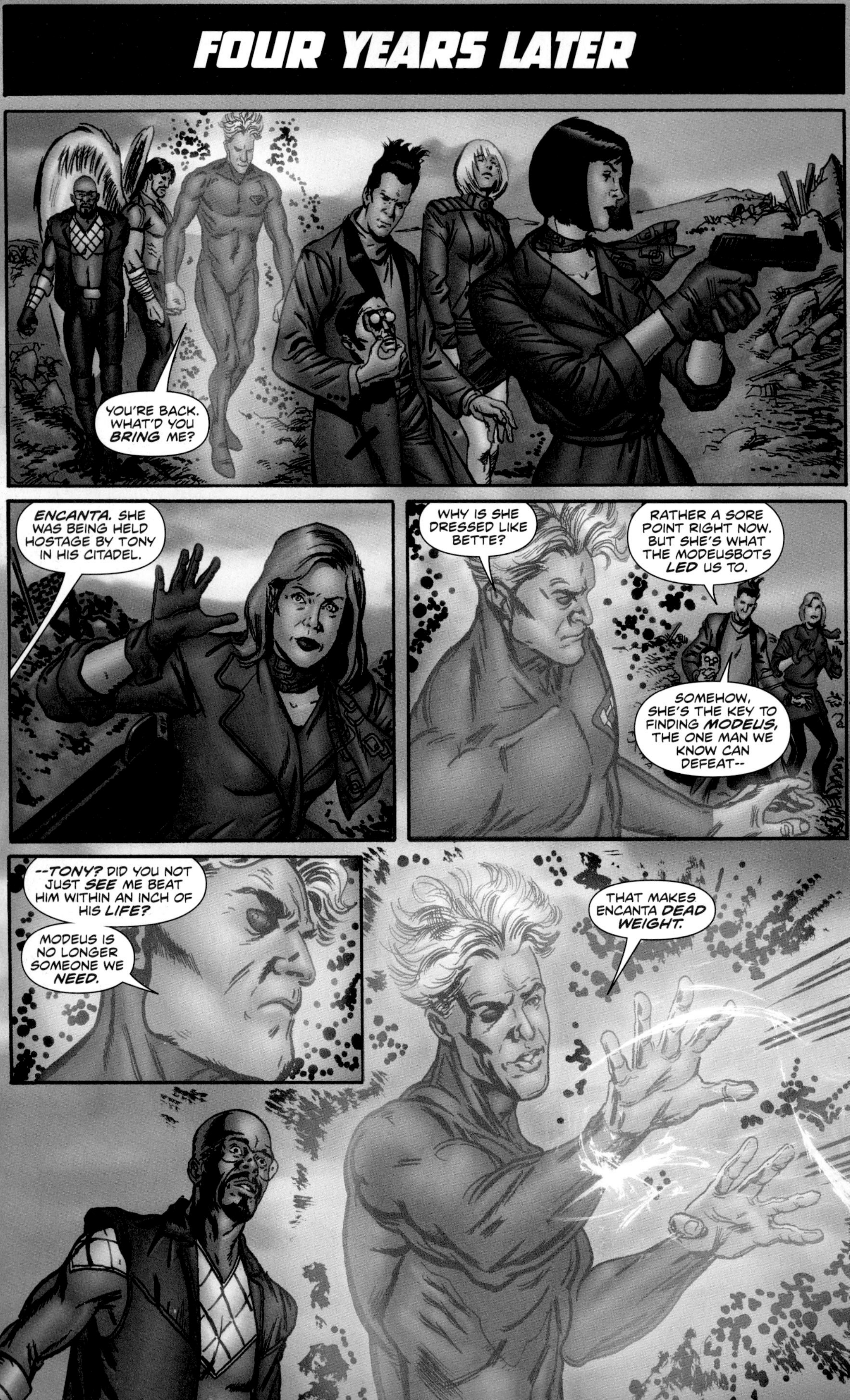
FOUR YEARS LATER
YOU'RE BACK. WHAT'D YOU BRING ME?
ENCANTA. SHE WAS BEING HELD HOSTAGE BY TONY IN HIS CITADEL.
WHY IS SHE DRESSED LIKE BETTE?
RATHER A SORE POINT RIGHT NOW. BUT SHE'S WHAT THE MODEUSBOTS LED US TO.
SOMEHOW, SHE'S THE KEY TO FINDING MODEUS, THE ONE MAN WE KNOW CAN DEFEAT--
--TONY? DID YOU NOT JUST SEE ME BEAT HIM WITHIN AN INCH OF HIS LIFE?
MODEUS IS NO LONGER SOMEONE WE NEED.
THAT MAKES ENCANTA DEAD WEIGHT.

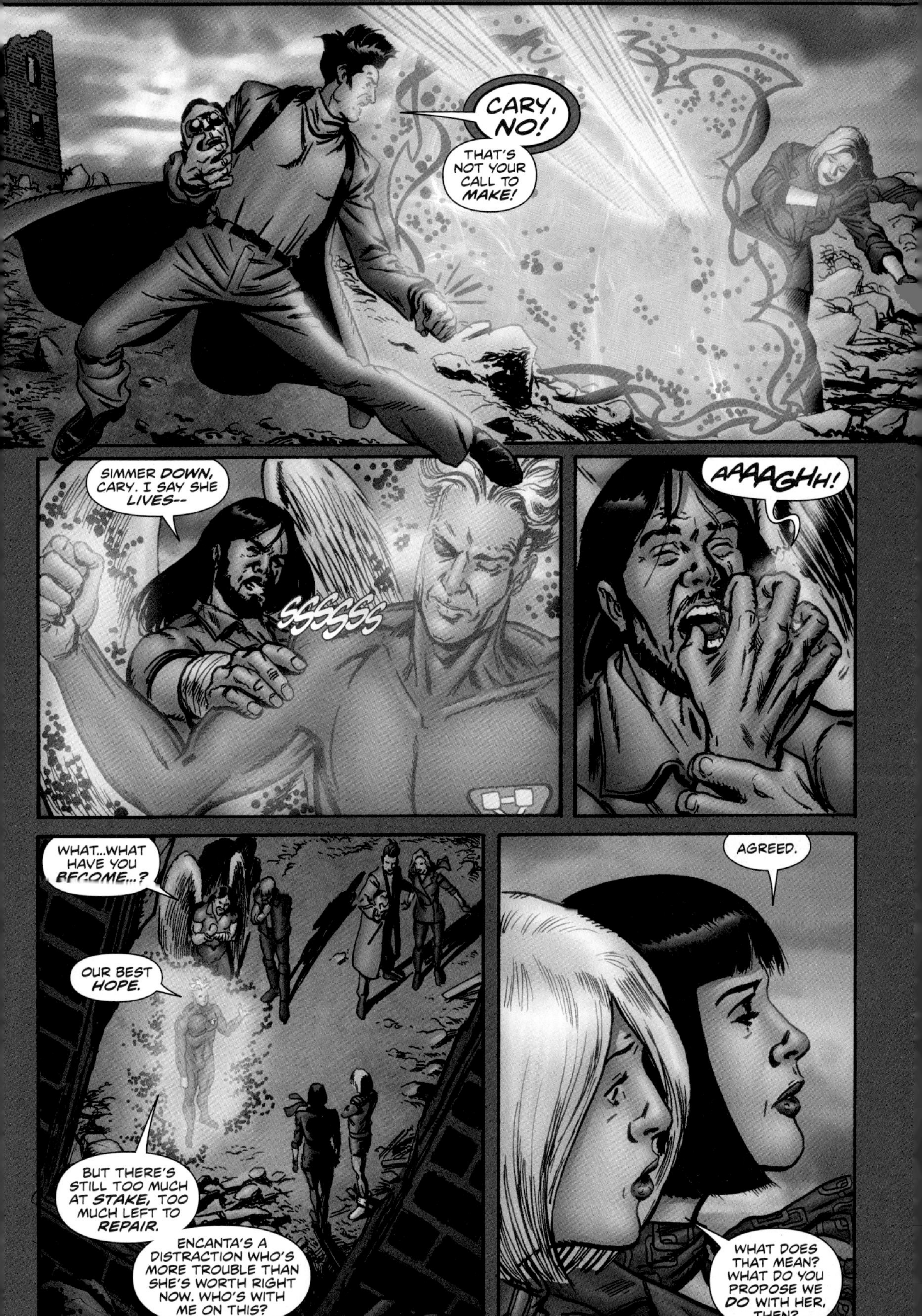
CARY, NO!
THAT'S NOT YOUR CALL TO MAKE!
SIMMER DOWN, CARY. I SAY SHE LIVES--
SSSSSS
AAAAGHH!
WHAT...WHAT HAVE YOU BECOME...?
OUR BEST HOPE.
BUT THERE'S STILL TOO MUCH AT STAKE, TOO MUCH LEFT TO REPAIR.
ENCANTA'S A DISTRACTION WHO'S MORE TROUBLE THAN SHE'S WORTH RIGHT NOW. WHO'S WITH ME ON THIS?
AGREED.
WHAT DOES THAT MEAN? WHAT DO YOU PROPOSE WE DO WITH HER, THEN?

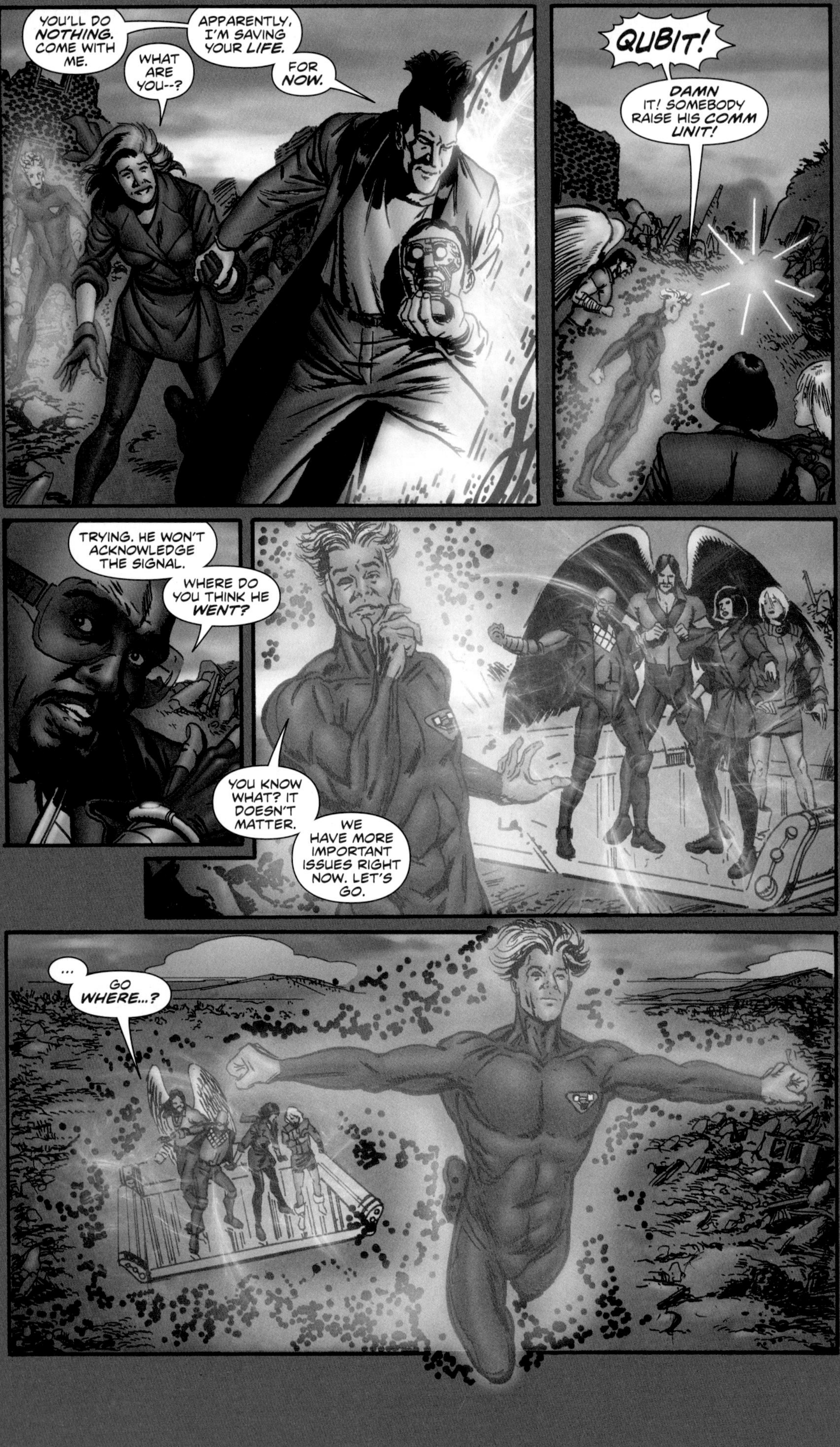

YOU'LL DO NOTHING. COME WITH ME.
APPARENTLY, I'M SAVING YOUR LIFE.
WHAT ARE YOU--?
FOR NOW.
QUBIT!
DAMN IT! SOMEBODY RAISE HIS COMM UNIT!
TRYING. HE WON'T ACKNOWLEDGE THE SIGNAL.
WHERE DO YOU THINK HE WENT?
YOU KNOW WHAT? IT DOESN'T MATTER.
WE HAVE MORE IMPORTANT ISSUES RIGHT NOW. LET'S GO.
...GO WHERE...?

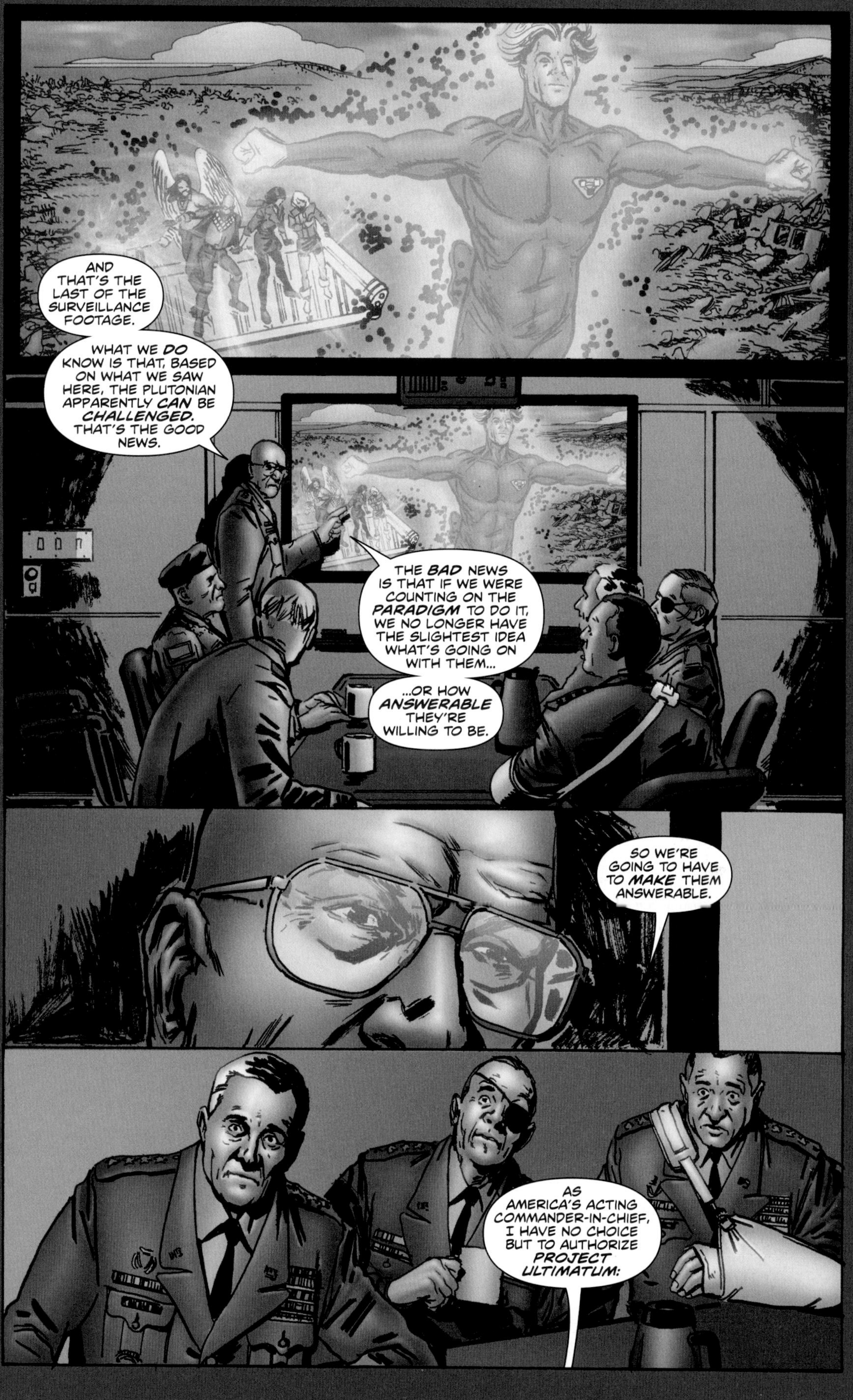
AND THAT'S THE LAST OF THE SURVEILLANCE FOOTAGE.
WHAT WE DO KNOW IS THAT, BASED ON WHAT WE SAW HERE, THE PLUTONIAN APPARENTLY CAN BE CHALLENGED. THAT'S THE GOOD NEWS.
THE BAD NEWS IS THAT IF WE WERE COUNTING ON THE PARADIGM TO DO IT, WE NO LONGER HAVE THE SLIGHTEST IDEA WHAT'S GOING ON WITH THEM...
...OR HOW ANSWERABLE THEY'RE WILLING TO BE.
SO WE'RE GOING TO HAVE TO MAKE THEM ANSWERABLE.
AS AMERICA'S ACTING COMMANDER-IN-CHIEF, I HAVE NO CHOICE BUT TO AUTHORIZE PROJECT ULTIMATUM:

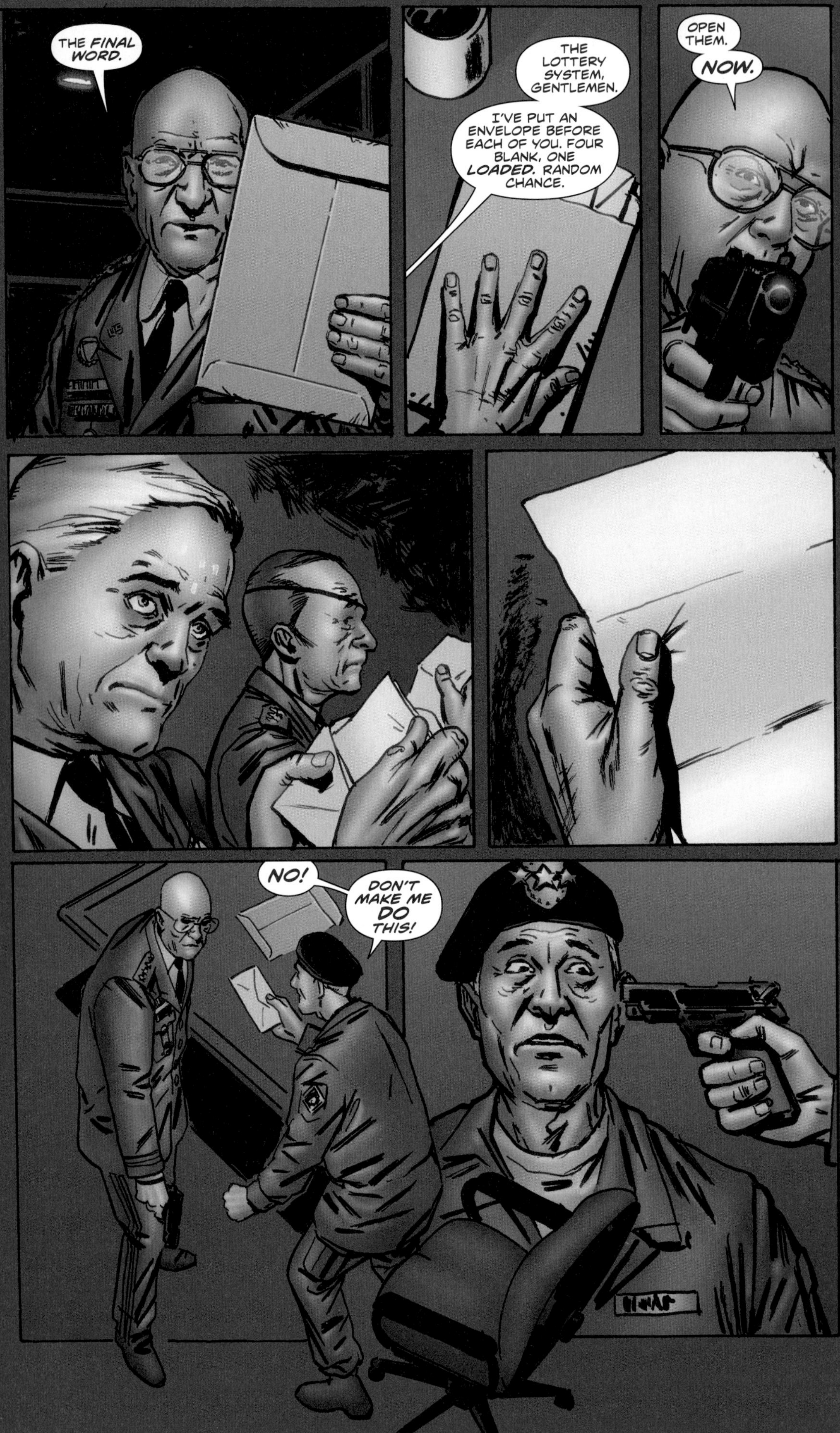
THE FINAL WORD.
THE LOTTERY SYSTEM, GENTLEMEN.
I'VE PUT AN ENVELOPE BEFORE EACH OF YOU. FOUR BLANK, ONE LOADED. RANDOM CHANCE.
OPEN THEM.
NOW.
NO!
DON'T MAKE ME DO THIS!

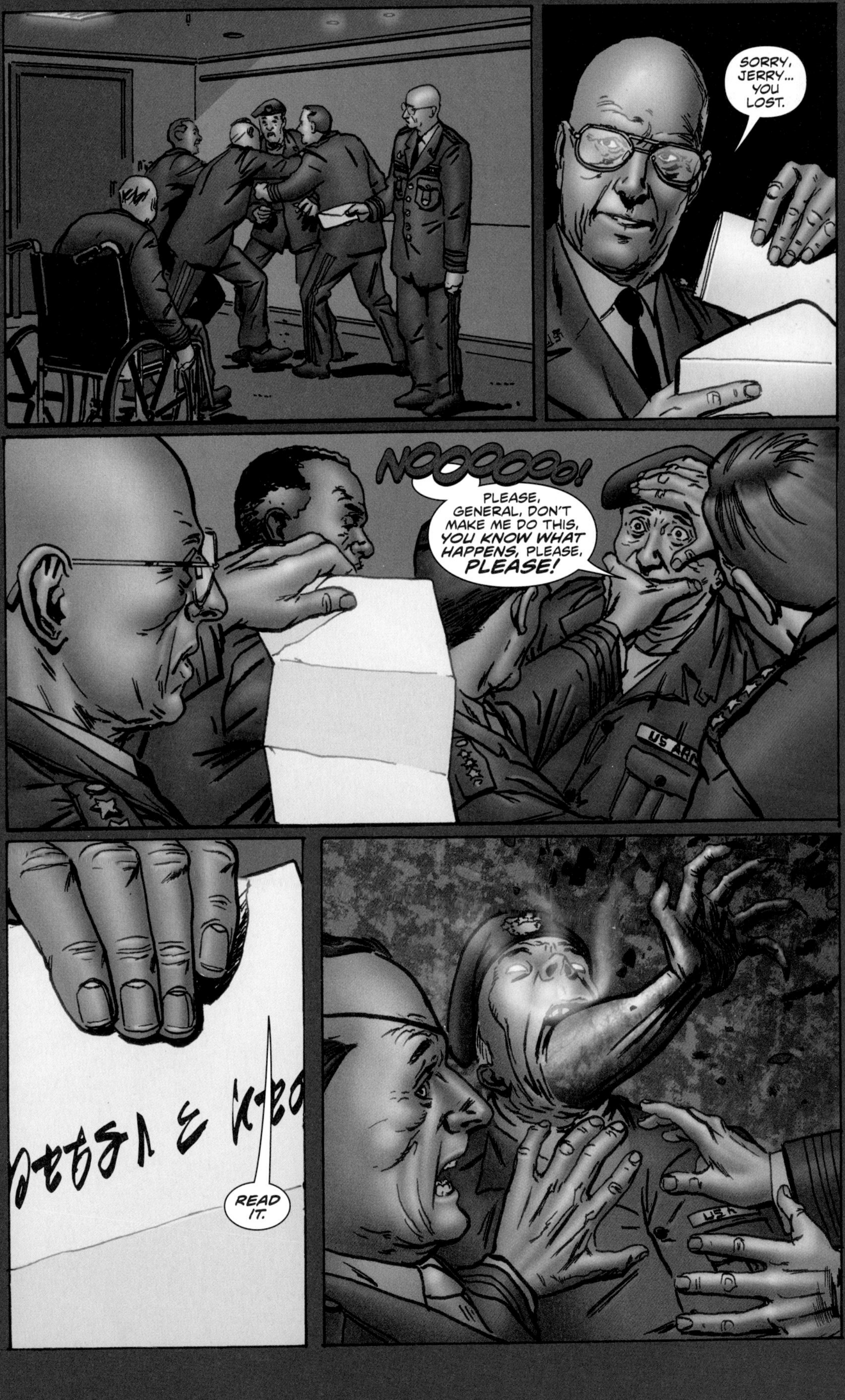
SORRY, JERRY... YOU LOST.
NOOOOOOo!
PLEASE, GENERAL, DON'T MAKE ME DO THIS, *YOU KNOW WHAT HAPPENS*, PLEASE, ***PLEASE!***
READ IT.

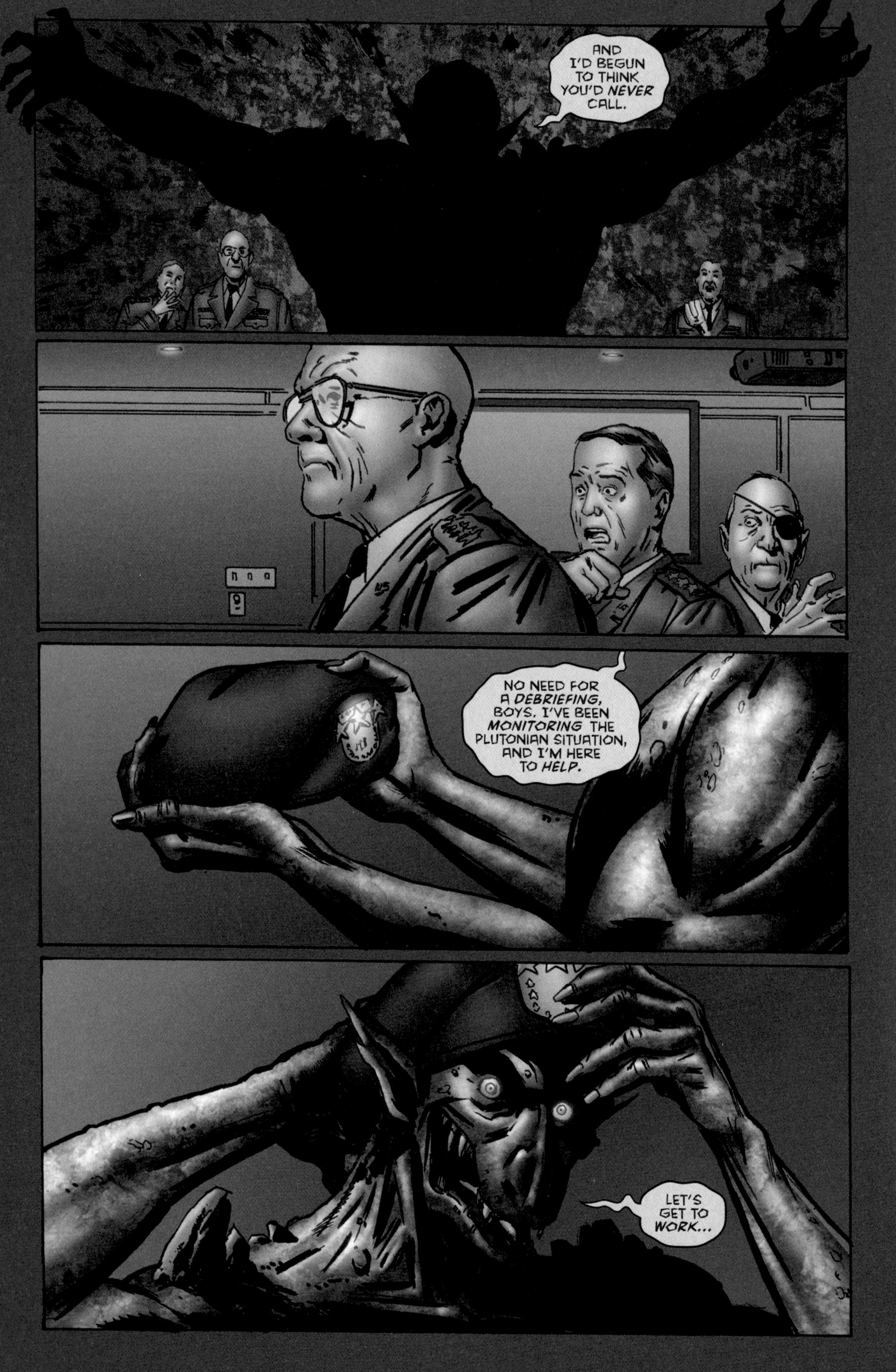
AND I'D BEGUN TO THINK YOU'D NEVER CALL.
NO NEED FOR A DEBRIEFING, BOYS. I'VE BEEN MONITORING THE PLUTONIAN SITUATION, AND I'M HERE TO HELP.
LET'S GET TO WORK...

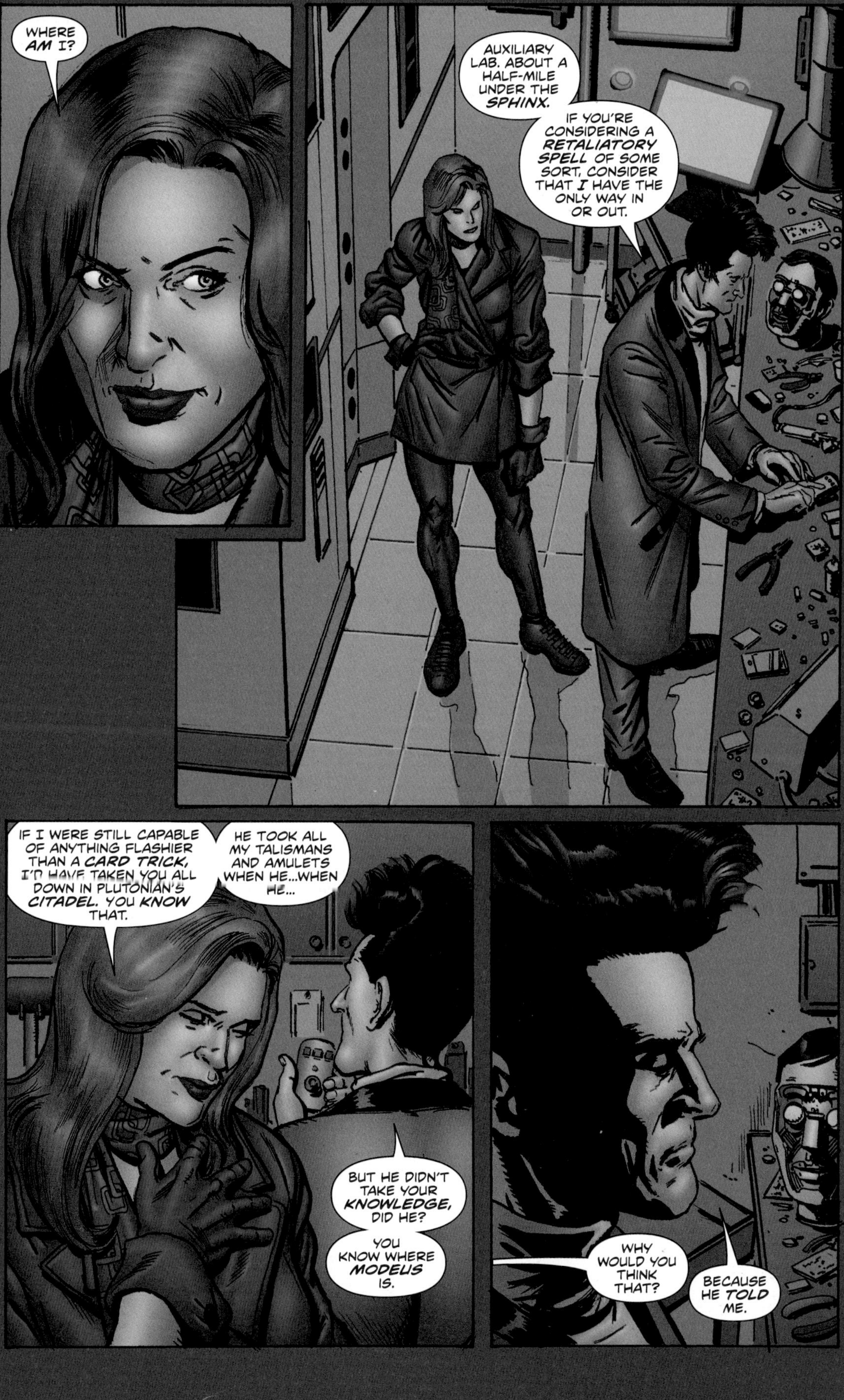

WHERE AM I?
AUXILIARY LAB. ABOUT A HALF-MILE UNDER THE SPHINX.
IF YOU'RE CONSIDERING A RETALIATORY SPELL OF SOME SORT, CONSIDER THAT I HAVE THE ONLY WAY IN OR OUT.
IF I WERE STILL CAPABLE OF ANYTHING FLASHIER THAN A CARD TRICK, I'D HAVE TAKEN YOU ALL DOWN IN PLUTONIAN'S CITADEL. YOU KNOW THAT.
HE TOOK ALL MY TALISMANS AND AMULETS WHEN HE...WHEN HE...
BUT HE DIDN'T TAKE YOUR KNOWLEDGE, DID HE?
YOU KNOW WHERE MODEUS IS.
WHY WOULD YOU THINK THAT?
BECAUSE HE TOLD ME.

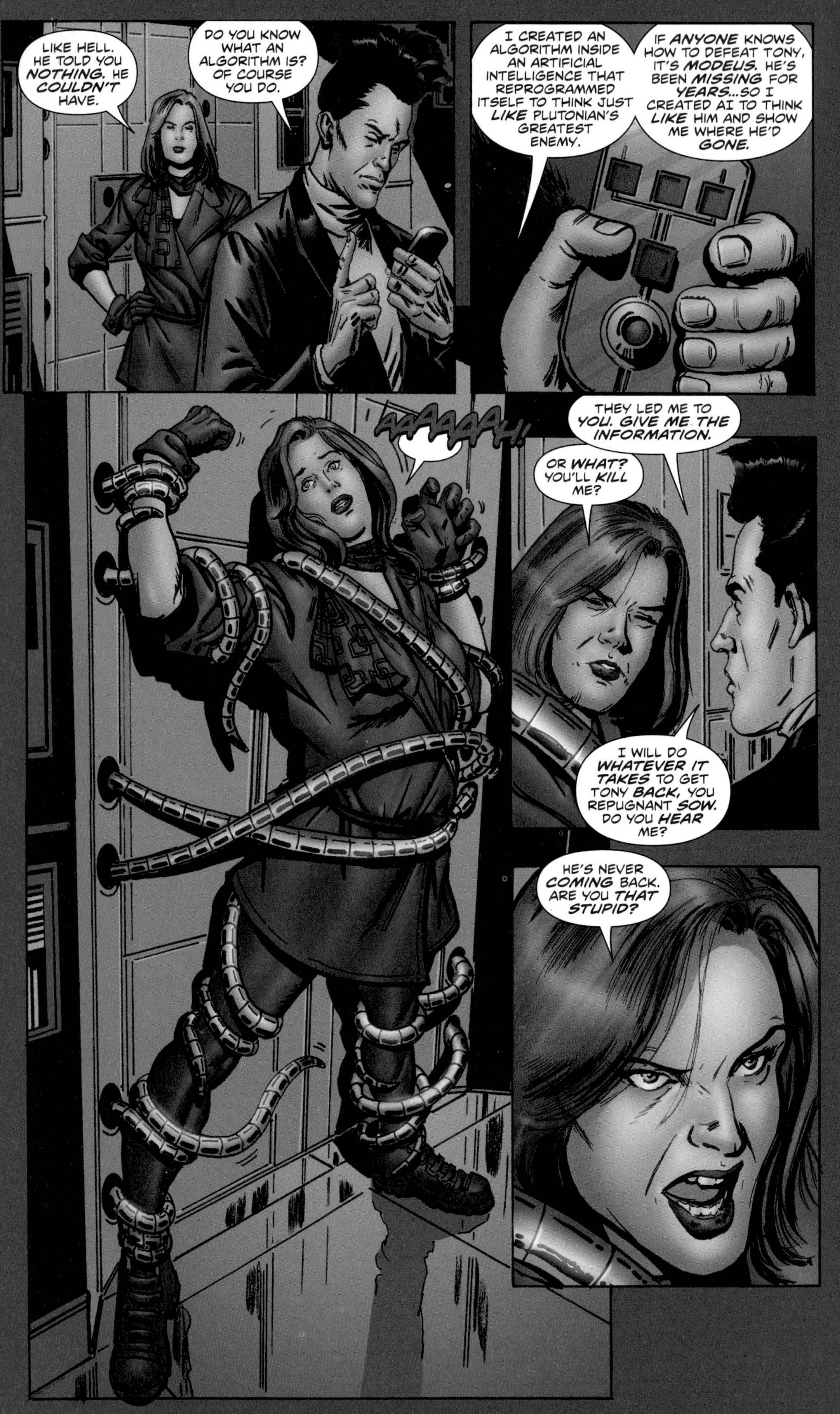
LIKE HELL. HE TOLD YOU NOTHING. HE COULDN'T HAVE.
DO YOU KNOW WHAT AN ALGORITHM IS? OF COURSE YOU DO.
I CREATED AN ALGORITHM INSIDE AN ARTIFICIAL INTELLIGENCE THAT REPROGRAMMED ITSELF TO THINK JUST LIKE PLUTONIAN'S GREATEST ENEMY.
IF ANYONE KNOWS HOW TO DEFEAT TONY, IT'S MODEUS. HE'S BEEN MISSING FOR YEARS...SO I CREATED AI TO THINK LIKE HIM AND SHOW ME WHERE HE'D GONE.
AAAAAAAH!
THEY LED ME TO YOU. GIVE ME THE INFORMATION.
OR WHAT? YOU'LL KILL ME?
I WILL DO WHATEVER IT TAKES TO GET TONY BACK, YOU REPUGNANT SOW. DO YOU HEAR ME?
HE'S NEVER COMING BACK. ARE YOU THAT STUPID?

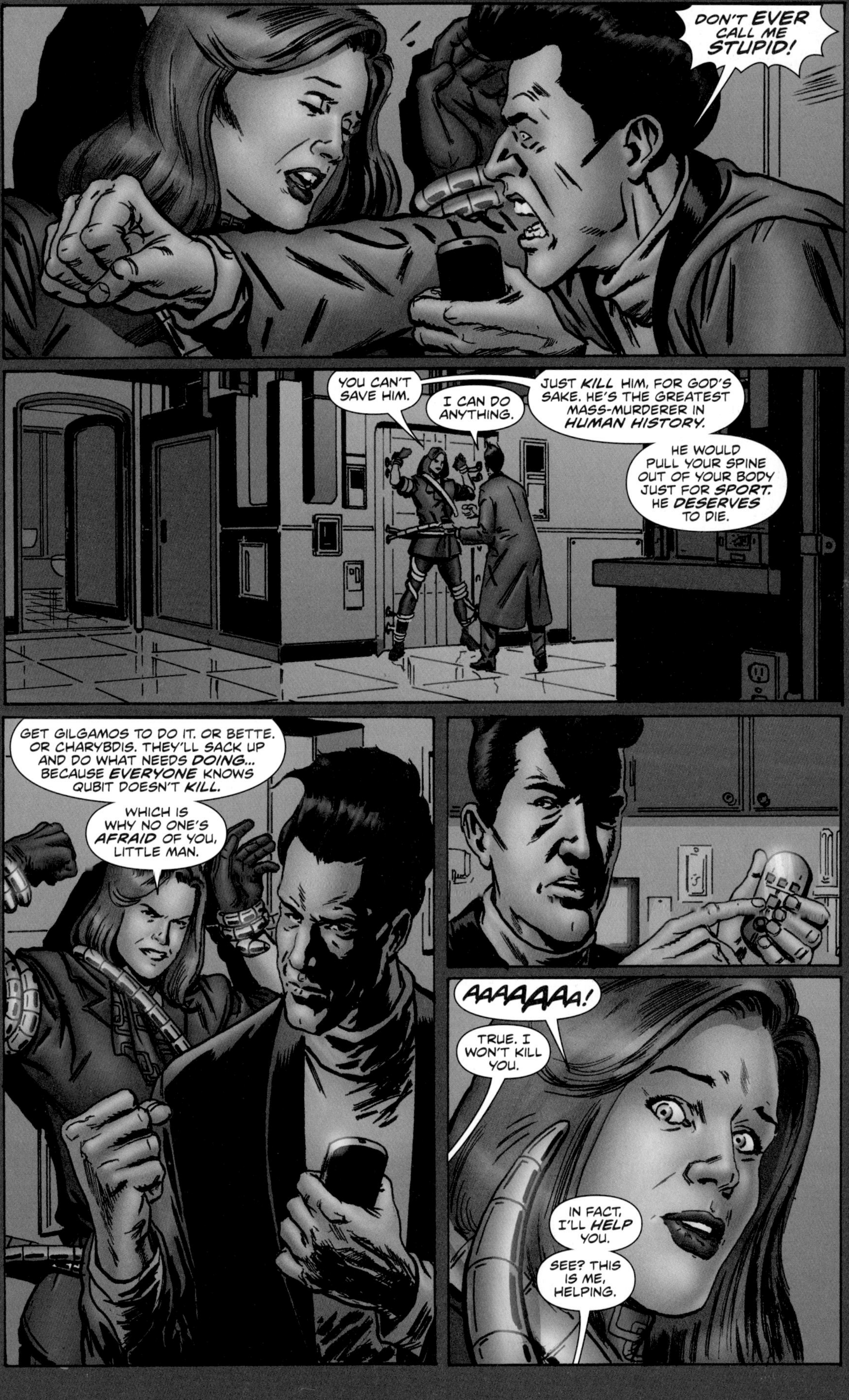
DON'T EVER CALL ME STUPID!
YOU CAN'T SAVE HIM.
I CAN DO ANYTHING.
JUST KILL HIM, FOR GOD'S SAKE. HE'S THE GREATEST MASS-MURDERER IN HUMAN HISTORY.
HE WOULD PULL YOUR SPINE OUT OF YOUR BODY JUST FOR SPORT. HE DESERVES TO DIE.
GET GILGAMOS TO DO IT. OR BETTE. OR CHARYBDIS. THEY'LL SACK UP AND DO WHAT NEEDS DOING... BECAUSE EVERYONE KNOWS QUBIT DOESN'T KILL.
WHICH IS WHY NO ONE'S AFRAID OF YOU, LITTLE MAN.
AAAAAAa!
TRUE. I WON'T KILL YOU.
IN FACT, I'LL HELP YOU.
SEE? THIS IS ME, HELPING.

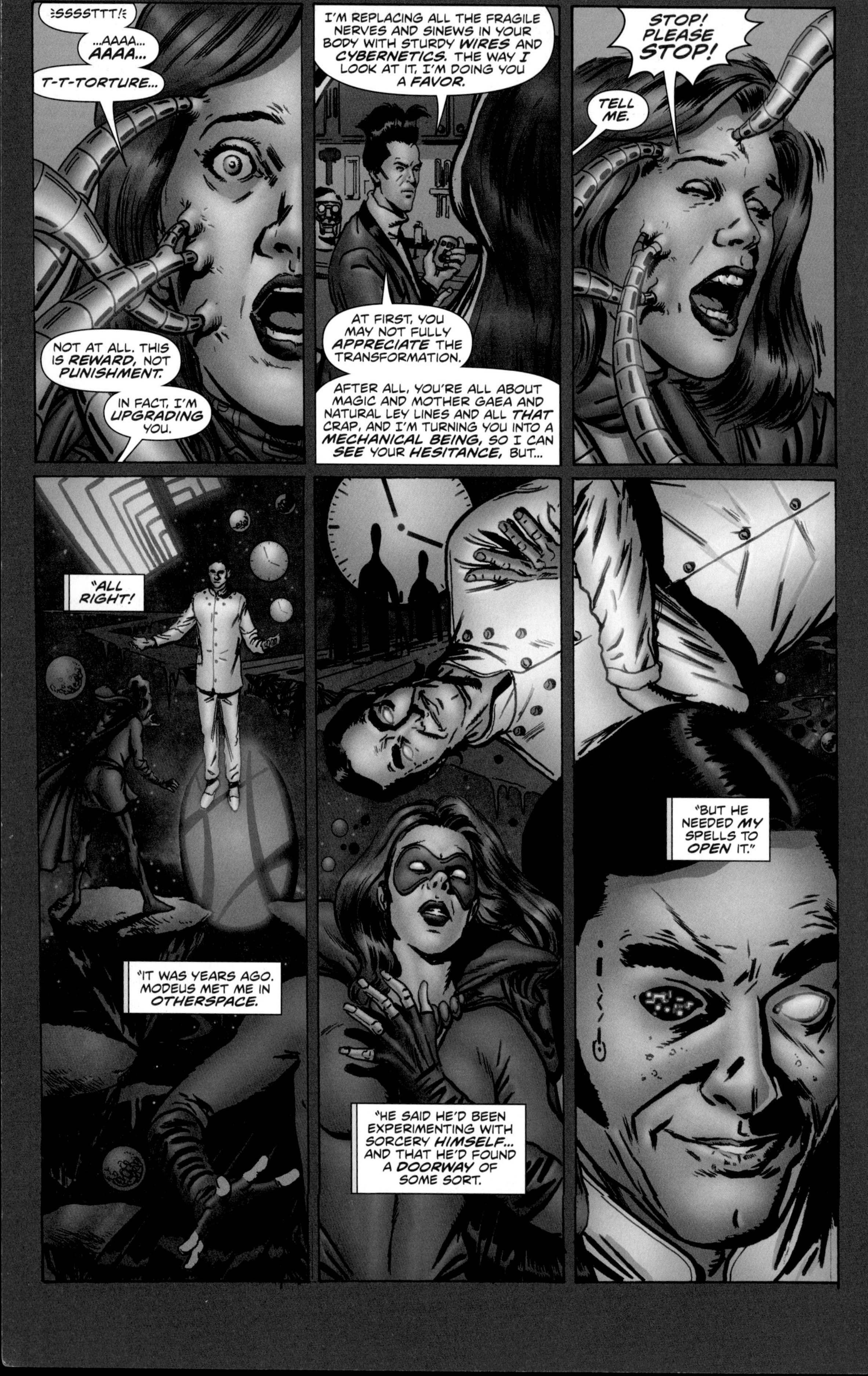

SSSSTTT!
...AAAA... AAAA...
T-T-TORTURE...
NOT AT ALL. THIS IS REWARD, NOT PUNISHMENT.
IN FACT, I'M UPGRADING YOU.
I'M REPLACING ALL THE FRAGILE NERVES AND SINEWS IN YOUR BODY WITH STURDY WIRES AND CYBERNETICS. THE WAY I LOOK AT IT, I'M DOING YOU A FAVOR.
AT FIRST, YOU MAY NOT FULLY APPRECIATE THE TRANSFORMATION.
AFTER ALL, YOU'RE ALL ABOUT MAGIC AND MOTHER GAEA AND NATURAL LEY LINES AND ALL THAT CRAP, AND I'M TURNING YOU INTO A MECHANICAL BEING, SO I CAN SEE YOUR HESITANCE, BUT...
STOP! PLEASE STOP!
TELL ME.
"ALL RIGHT!
"IT WAS YEARS AGO. MODEUS MET ME IN OTHERSPACE.
"HE SAID HE'D BEEN EXPERIMENTING WITH SORCERY HIMSELF... AND THAT HE'D FOUND A DOORWAY OF SOME SORT.
"BUT HE NEEDED MY SPELLS TO OPEN IT."

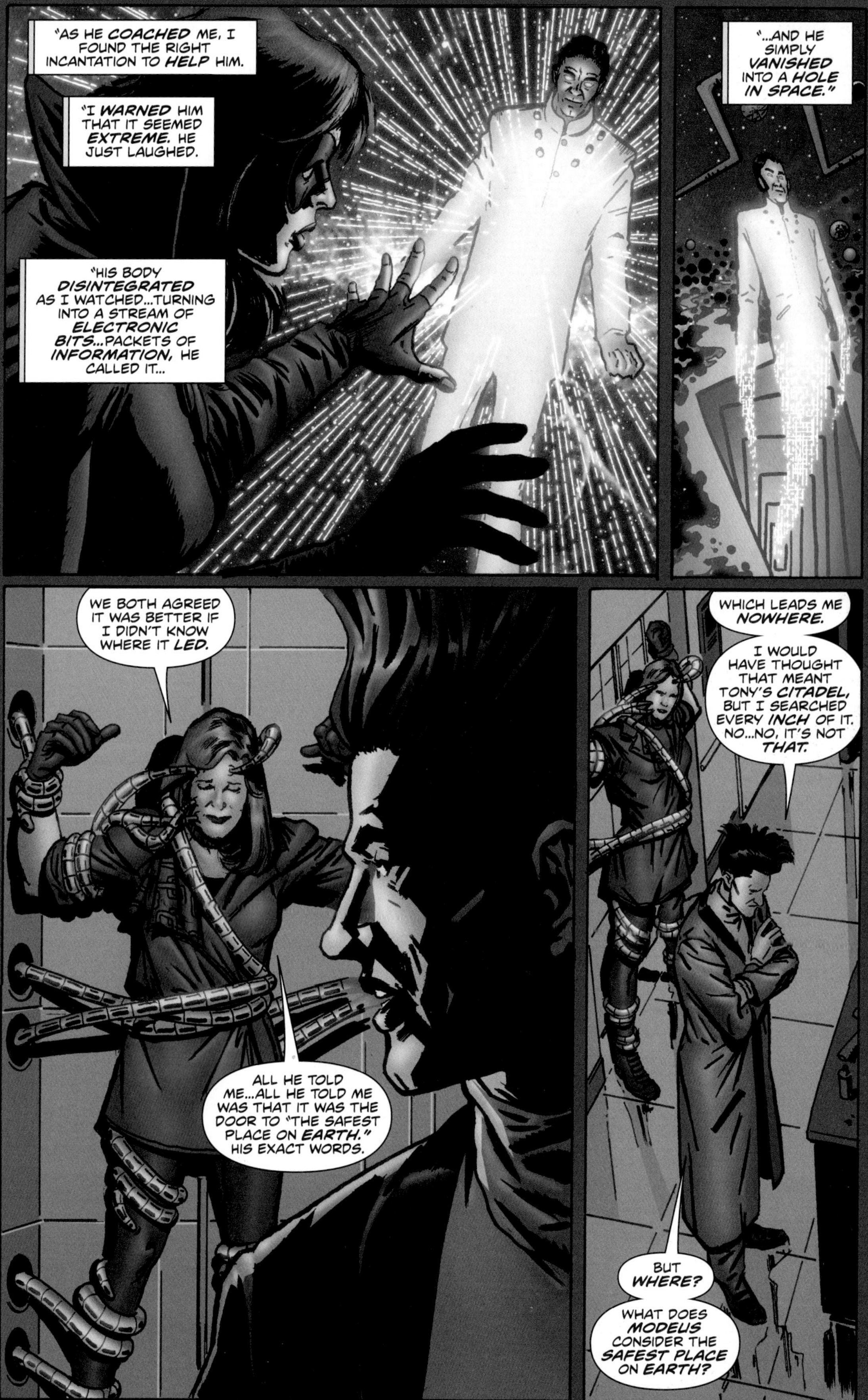
"AS HE COACHED ME, I FOUND THE RIGHT INCANTATION TO HELP HIM.
"I WARNED HIM THAT IT SEEMED EXTREME. HE JUST LAUGHED.
"HIS BODY DISINTEGRATED AS I WATCHED...TURNING INTO A STREAM OF ELECTRONIC BITS...PACKETS OF INFORMATION, HE CALLED IT...
"...AND HE SIMPLY VANISHED INTO A HOLE IN SPACE."
WE BOTH AGREED IT WAS BETTER IF I DIDN'T KNOW WHERE IT LED.
ALL HE TOLD ME...ALL HE TOLD ME WAS THAT IT WAS THE DOOR TO "THE SAFEST PLACE ON EARTH." HIS EXACT WORDS.
WHICH LEADS ME NOWHERE.
I WOULD HAVE THOUGHT THAT MEANT TONY'S CITADEL, BUT I SEARCHED EVERY INCH OF IT. NO...NO, IT'S NOT THAT.
BUT WHERE?
WHAT DOES MODEUS CONSIDER THE SAFEST PLACE ON EARTH?

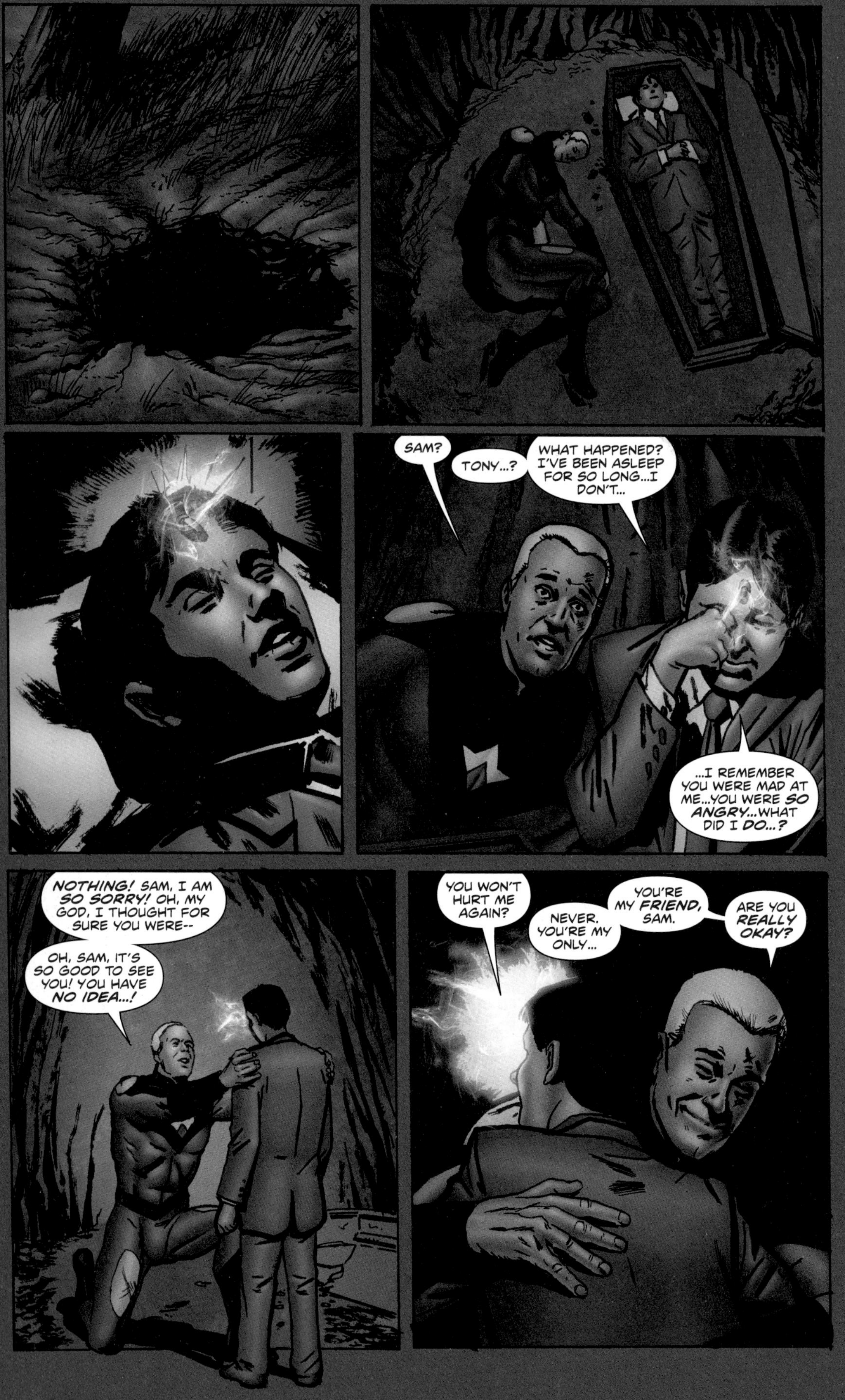
SAM?
TONY...?
WHAT HAPPENED? I'VE BEEN ASLEEP FOR SO LONG...I DON'T...
...I REMEMBER YOU WERE MAD AT ME...YOU WERE SO ANGRY...WHAT DID I DO...?
NOTHING! SAM, I AM SO SORRY! OH, MY GOD, I THOUGHT FOR SURE YOU WERE--
OH, SAM, IT'S SO GOOD TO SEE YOU! YOU HAVE NO IDEA...!
YOU WON'T HURT ME AGAIN?
NEVER. YOU'RE MY ONLY...
YOU'RE MY FRIEND, SAM.
ARE YOU REALLY OKAY?

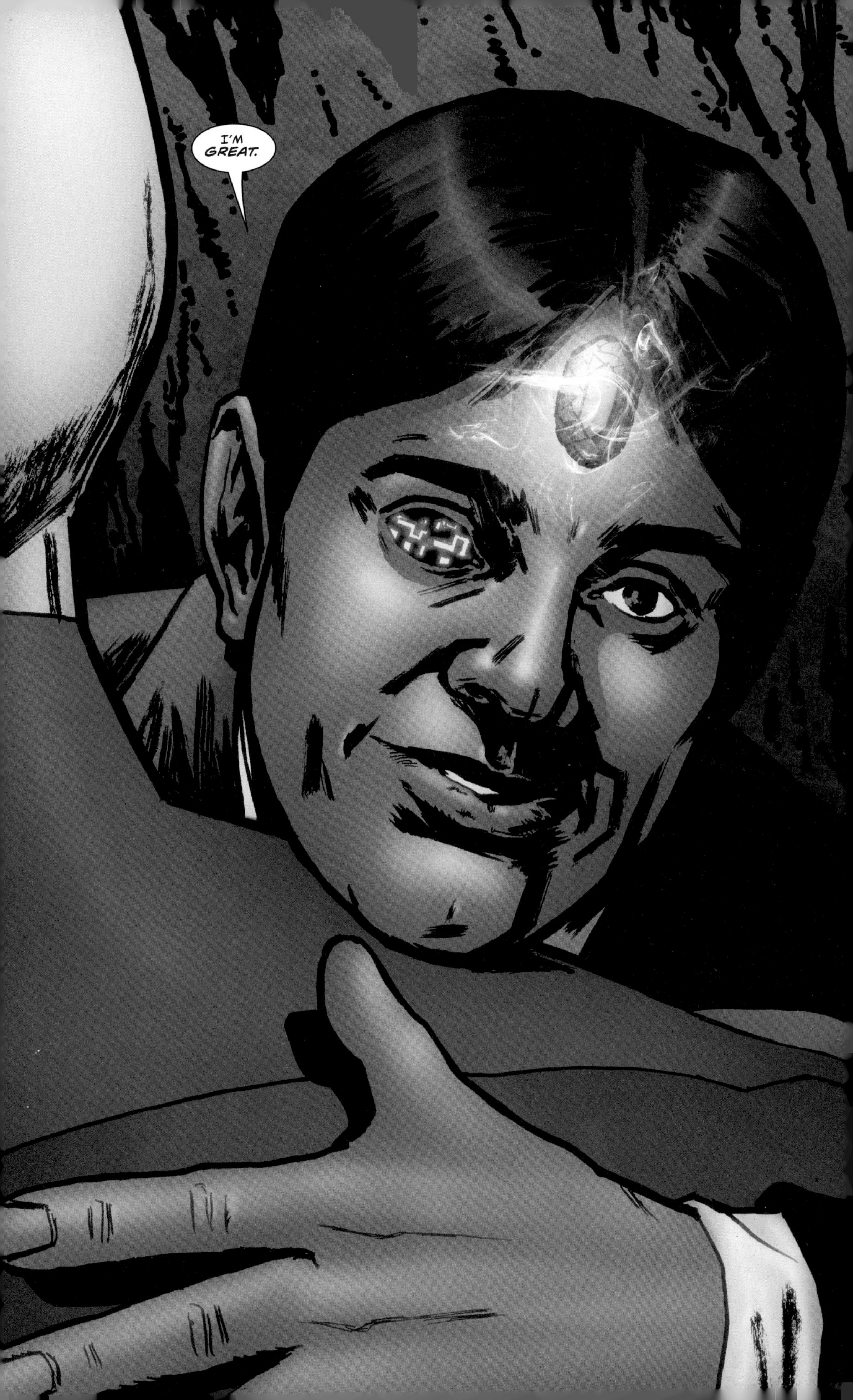
I'M GREAT.

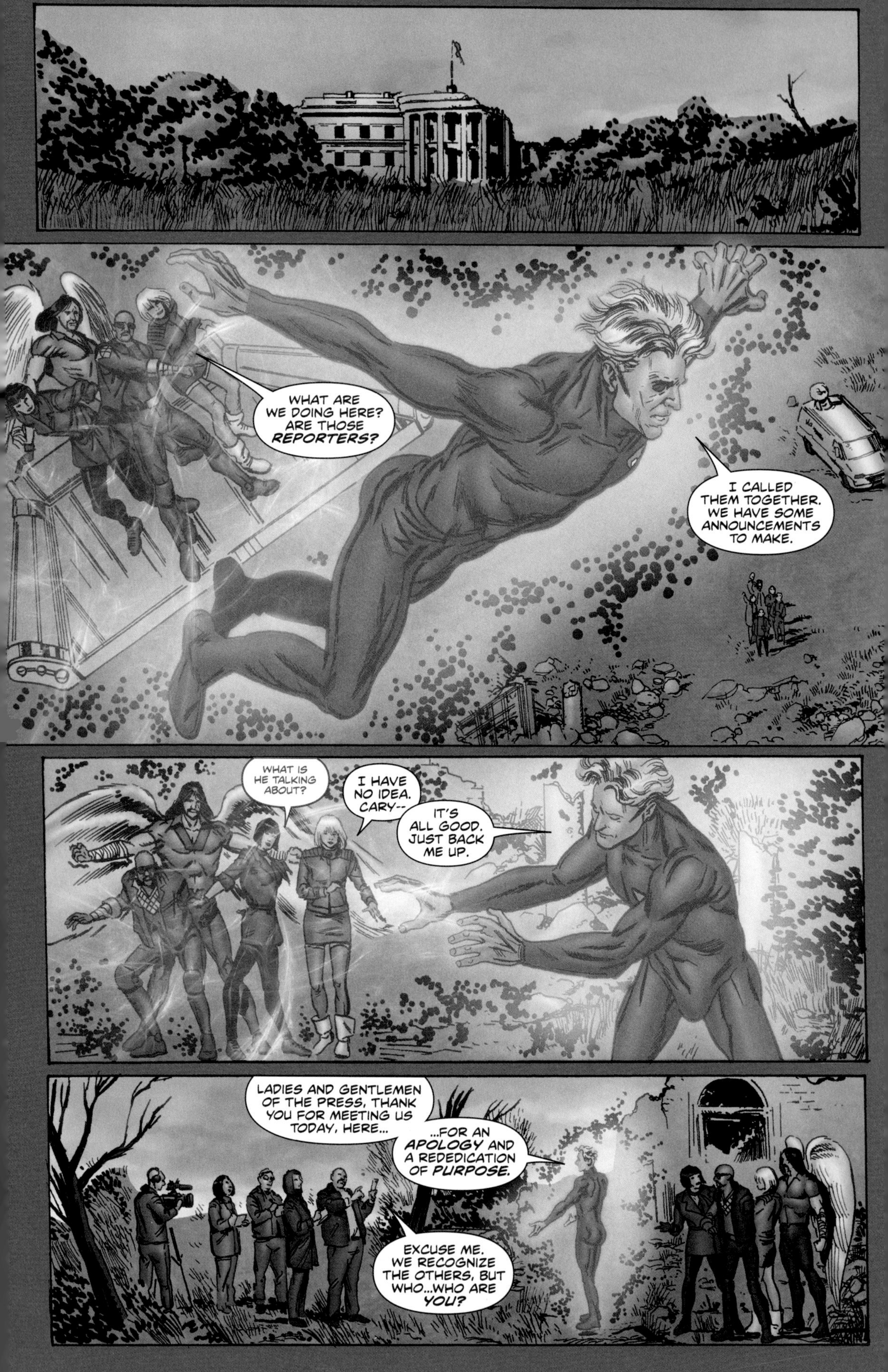
WHAT ARE WE DOING HERE? ARE THOSE *REPORTERS?*
I CALLED THEM TOGETHER. WE HAVE SOME ANNOUNCEMENTS TO MAKE.
WHAT IS HE TALKING ABOUT?
I HAVE NO IDEA. CARY--
IT'S ALL GOOD. JUST BACK ME UP.
LADIES AND GENTLEMEN OF THE PRESS, THANK YOU FOR MEETING US TODAY, HERE...
...FOR AN *APOLOGY* AND A REDEDICATION OF *PURPOSE.*
EXCUSE ME. WE RECOGNIZE THE OTHERS, BUT WHO...WHO ARE *YOU?*

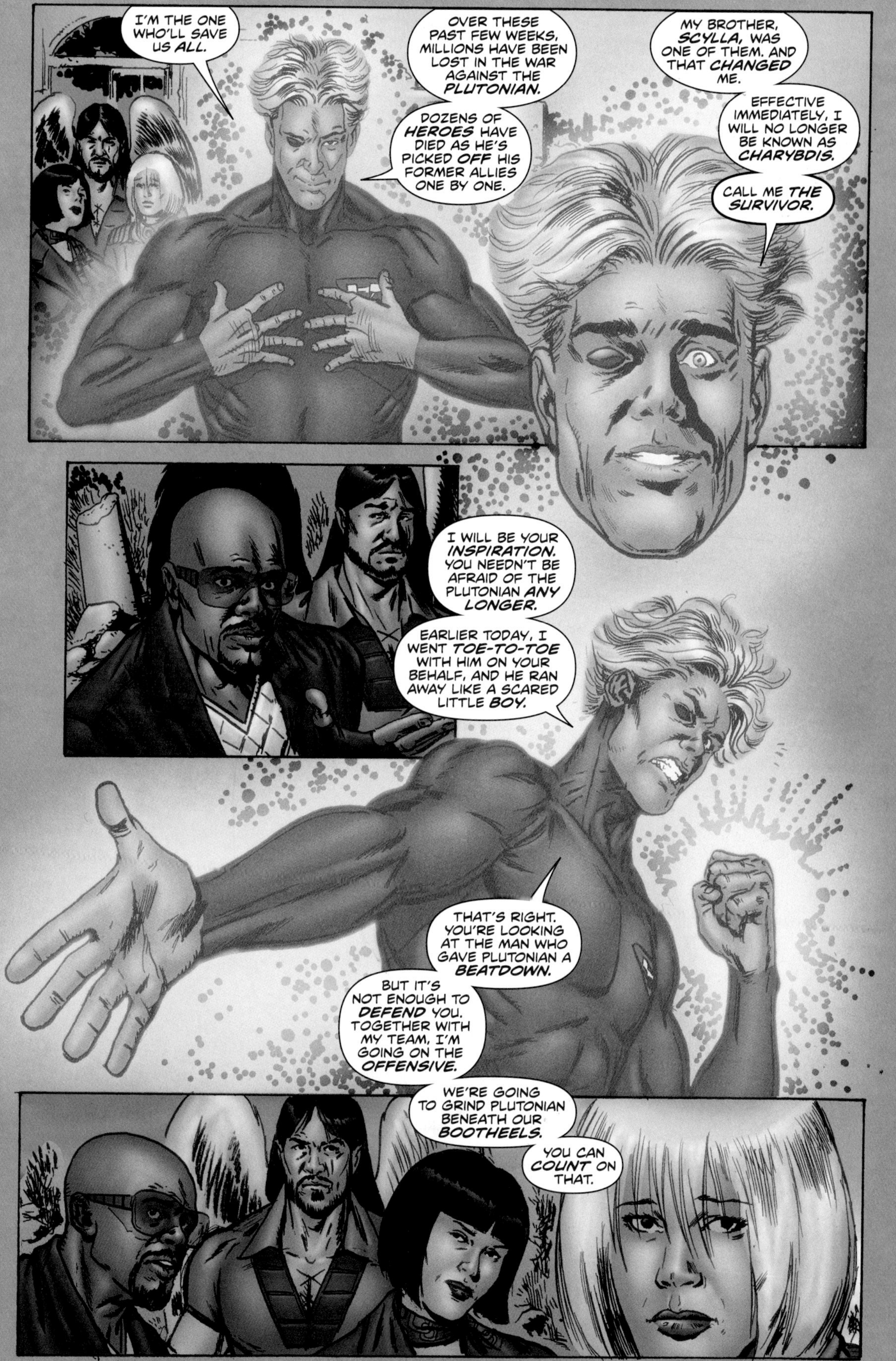
I'M THE ONE WHO'LL SAVE US ALL.
OVER THESE PAST FEW WEEKS, MILLIONS HAVE BEEN LOST IN THE WAR AGAINST THE PLUTONIAN.
DOZENS OF HEROES HAVE DIED AS HE'S PICKED OFF HIS FORMER ALLIES ONE BY ONE.
MY BROTHER, SCYLLA, WAS ONE OF THEM. AND THAT CHANGED ME.
EFFECTIVE IMMEDIATELY, I WILL NO LONGER BE KNOWN AS CHARYBDIS.
CALL ME THE SURVIVOR.
I WILL BE YOUR INSPIRATION. YOU NEEDN'T BE AFRAID OF THE PLUTONIAN ANY LONGER.
EARLIER TODAY, I WENT TOE-TO-TOE WITH HIM ON YOUR BEHALF, AND HE RAN AWAY LIKE A SCARED LITTLE BOY.
THAT'S RIGHT. YOU'RE LOOKING AT THE MAN WHO GAVE PLUTONIAN A BEATDOWN.
BUT IT'S NOT ENOUGH TO DEFEND YOU. TOGETHER WITH MY TEAM, I'M GOING ON THE OFFENSIVE.
WE'RE GOING TO GRIND PLUTONIAN BENEATH OUR BOOTHEELS.
YOU CAN COUNT ON THAT.

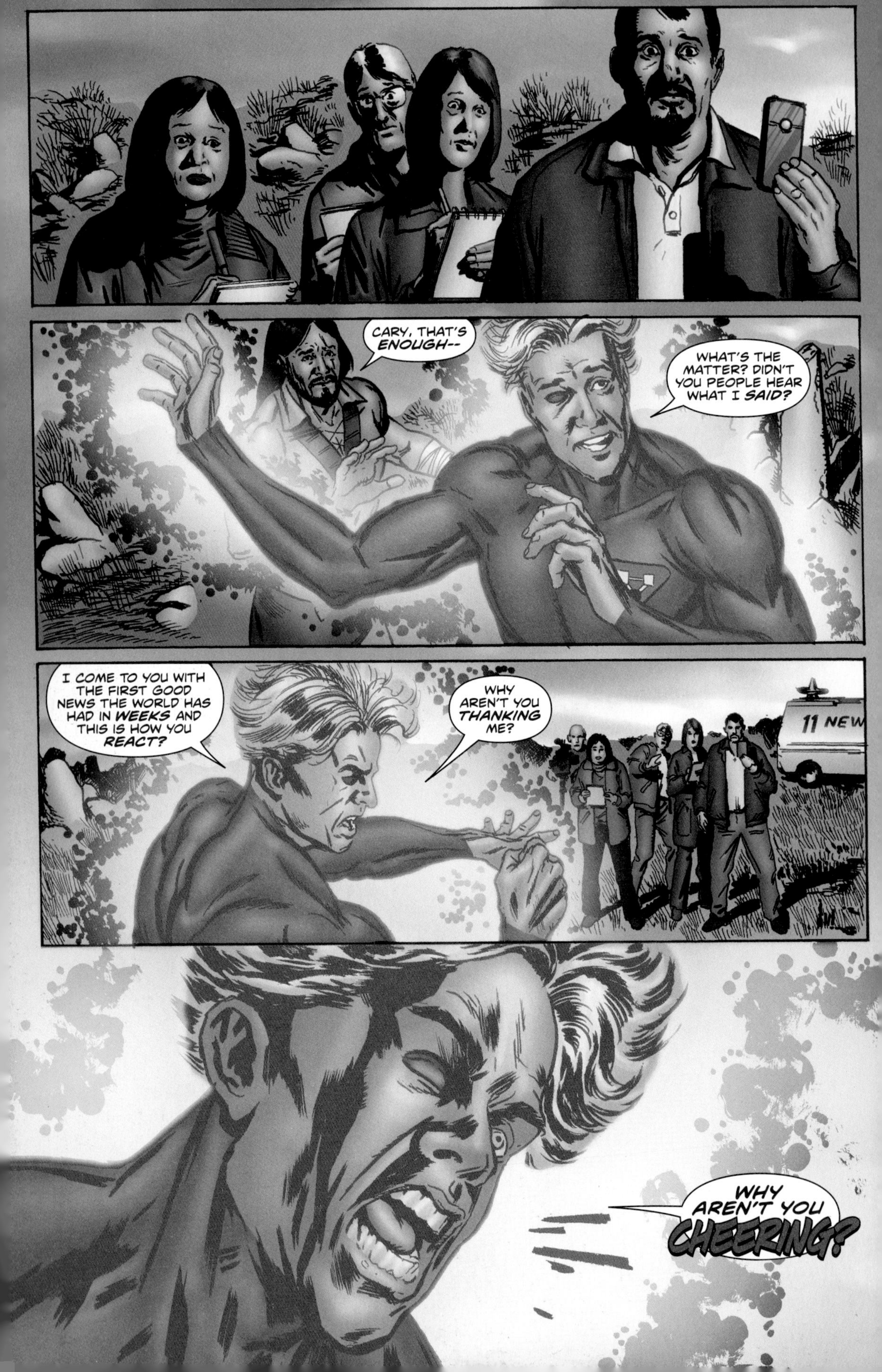
CARY, THAT'S ENOUGH--
WHAT'S THE MATTER? DIDN'T YOU PEOPLE HEAR WHAT I SAID?
I COME TO YOU WITH THE FIRST GOOD NEWS THE WORLD HAS HAD IN WEEKS AND THIS IS HOW YOU REACT?
WHY AREN'T YOU THANKING ME?
11 NEW
WHY AREN'T YOU CHEERING?

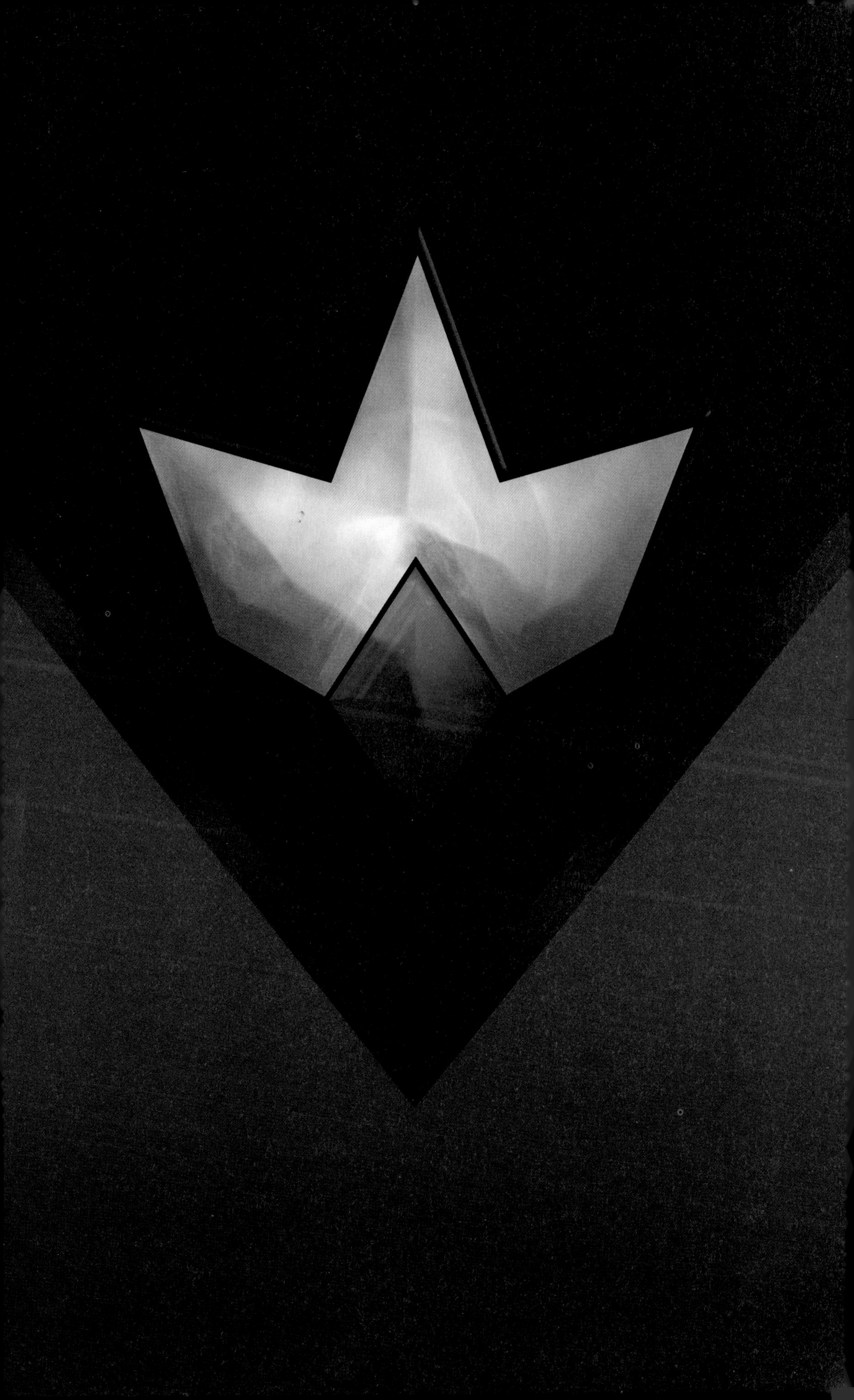

CHAPTER 10

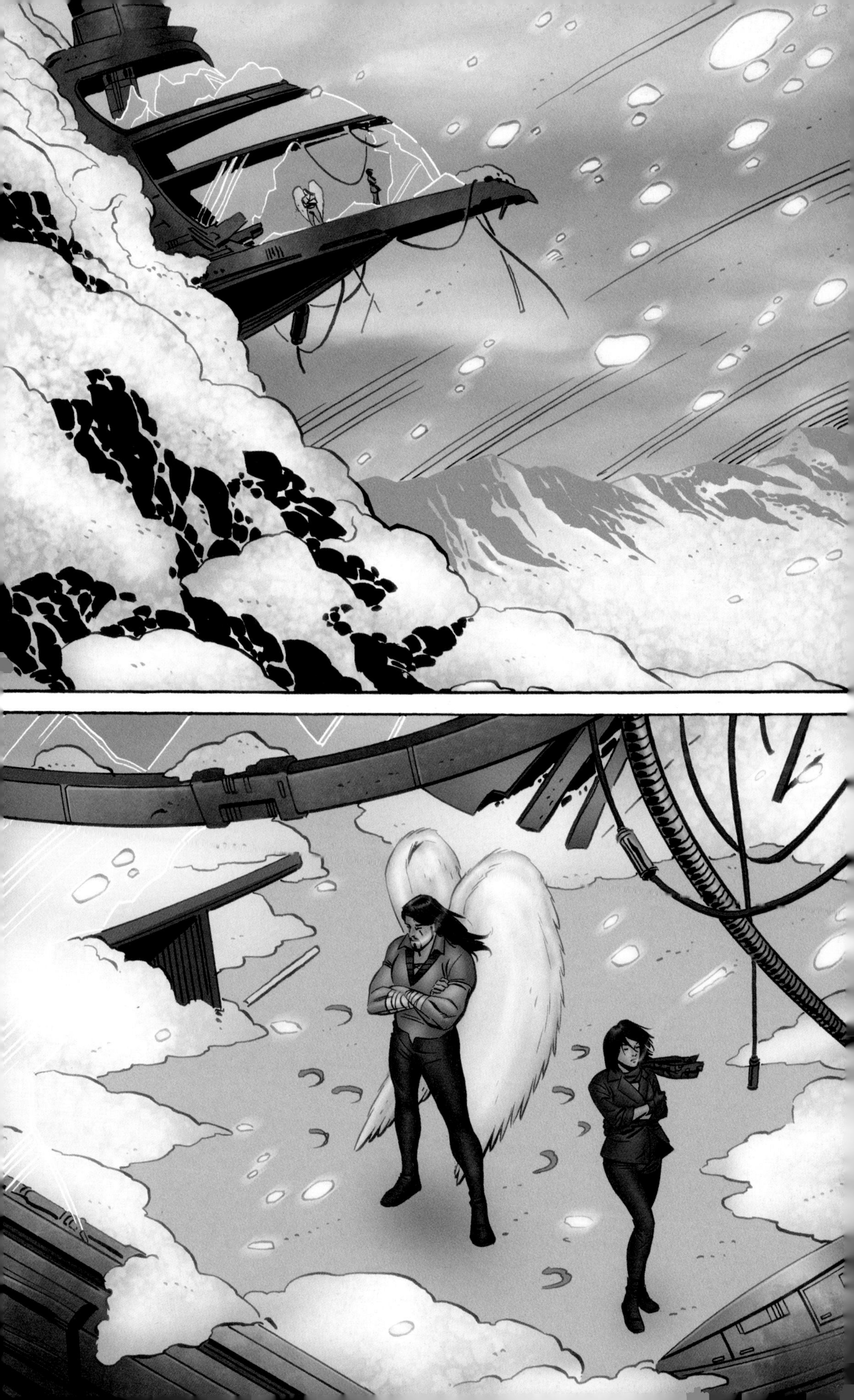

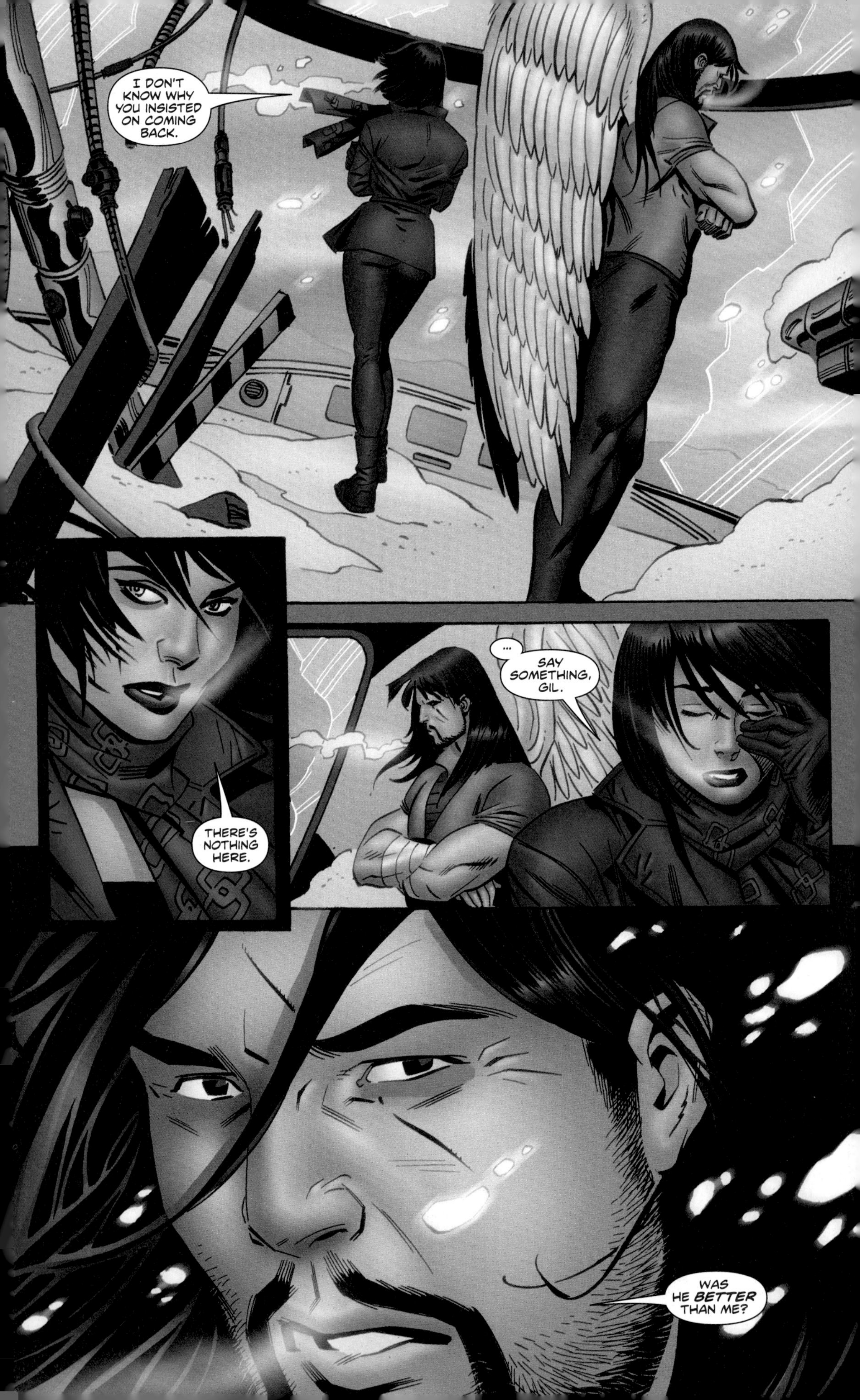
I DON'T KNOW WHY YOU INSISTED ON COMING BACK.
THERE'S NOTHING HERE.
... SAY SOMETHING, GIL.
WAS HE *BETTER* THAN ME?

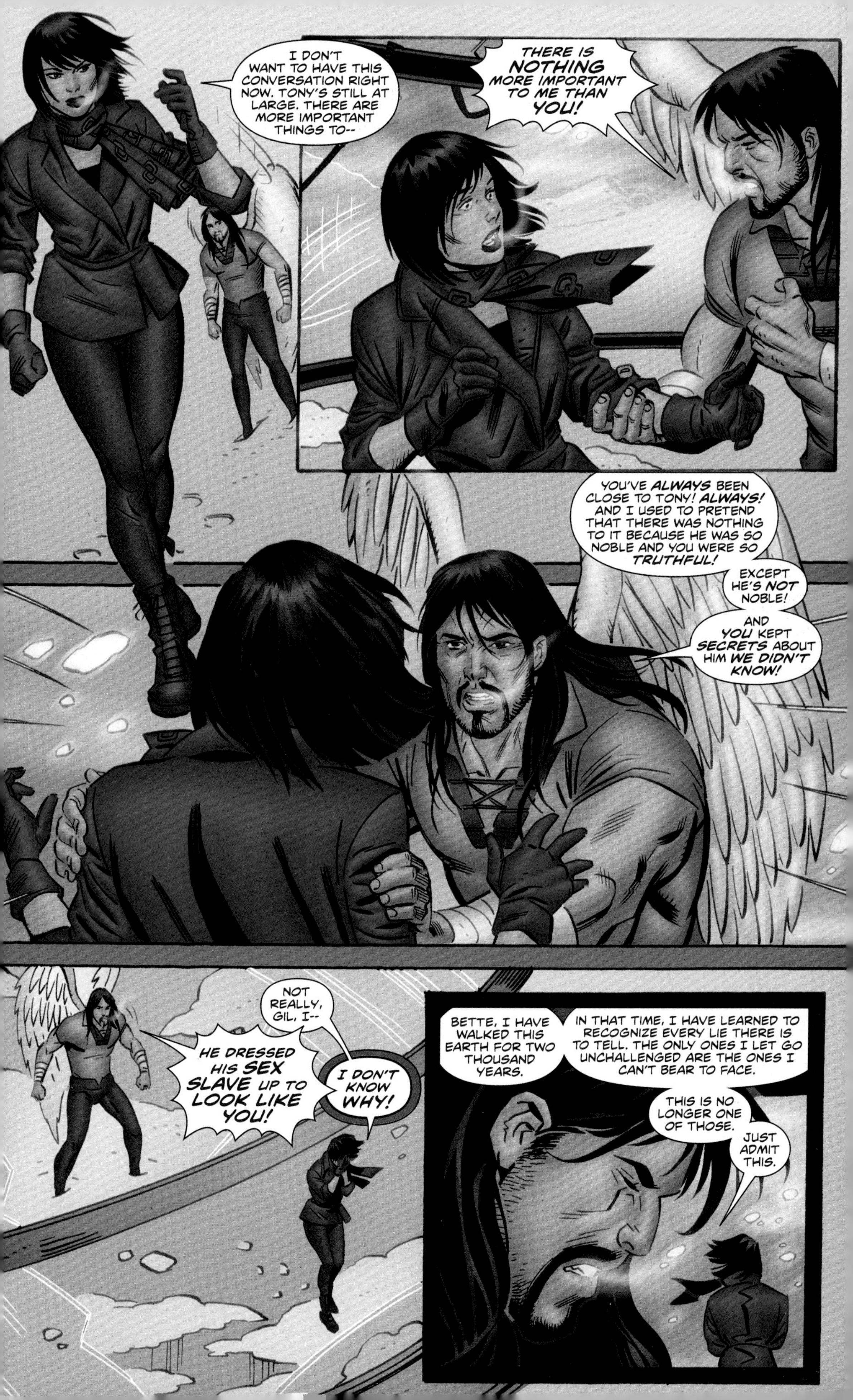
I DON'T WANT TO HAVE THIS CONVERSATION RIGHT NOW. TONY'S STILL AT LARGE. THERE ARE MORE IMPORTANT THINGS TO--
THERE IS NOTHING MORE IMPORTANT TO ME THAN YOU!
YOU'VE ALWAYS BEEN CLOSE TO TONY! ALWAYS! AND I USED TO PRETEND THAT THERE WAS NOTHING TO IT BECAUSE HE WAS SO NOBLE AND YOU WERE SO TRUTHFUL!
EXCEPT HE'S NOT NOBLE!
AND YOU KEPT SECRETS ABOUT HIM WE DIDN'T KNOW!
NOT REALLY, GIL, I--
HE DRESSED HIS SEX SLAVE UP TO LOOK LIKE YOU!
I DON'T KNOW WHY!
BETTE, I HAVE WALKED THIS EARTH FOR TWO THOUSAND YEARS.
IN THAT TIME, I HAVE LEARNED TO RECOGNIZE EVERY LIE THERE IS TO TELL. THE ONLY ONES I LET GO UNCHALLENGED ARE THE ONES I CAN'T BEAR TO FACE.
THIS IS NO LONGER ONE OF THOSE.
JUST ADMIT THIS.

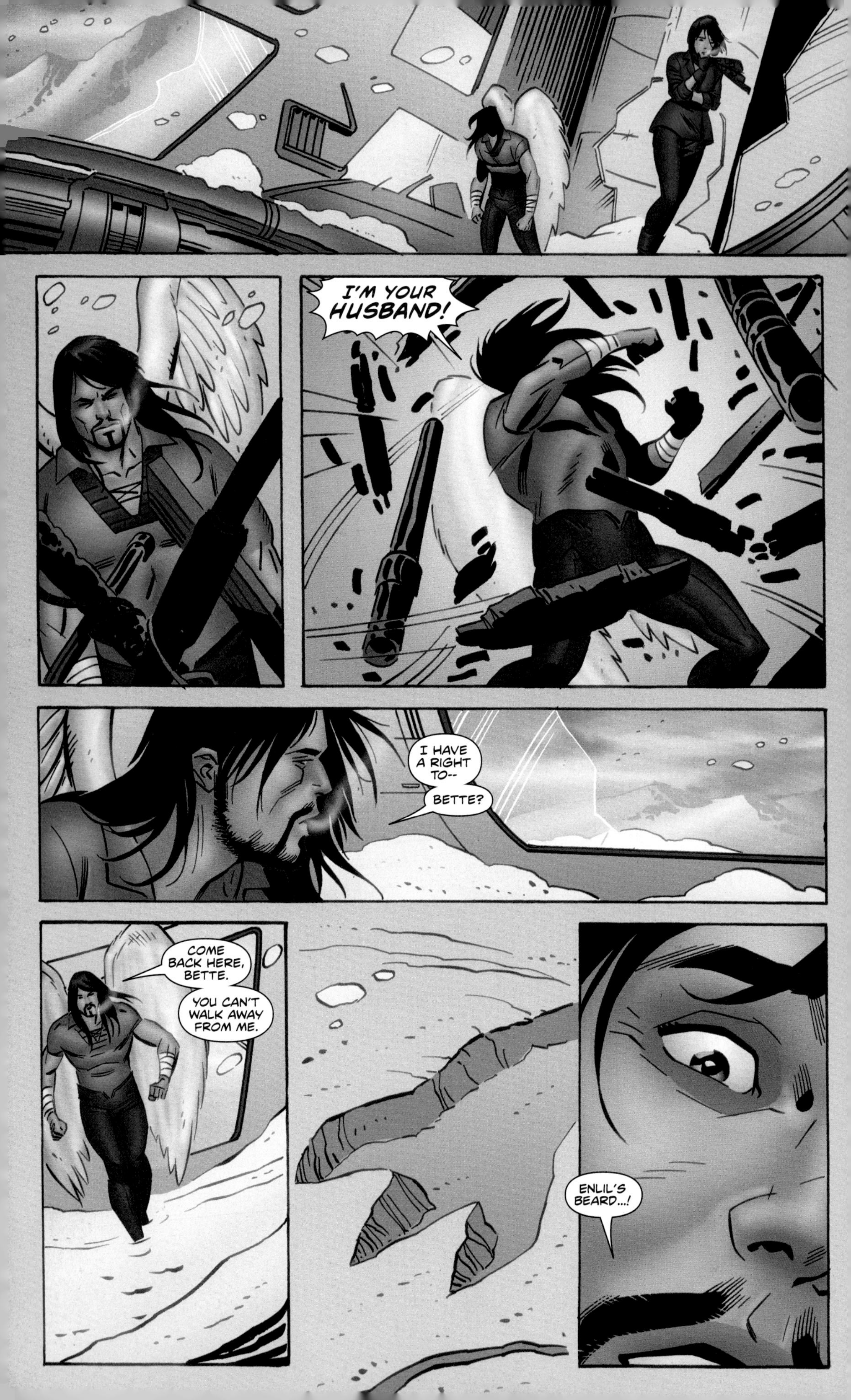
I'M YOUR HUSBAND!
I HAVE A RIGHT TO--
BETTE?
COME BACK HERE, BETTE.
YOU CAN'T WALK AWAY FROM ME.
ENLIL'S BEARD...!

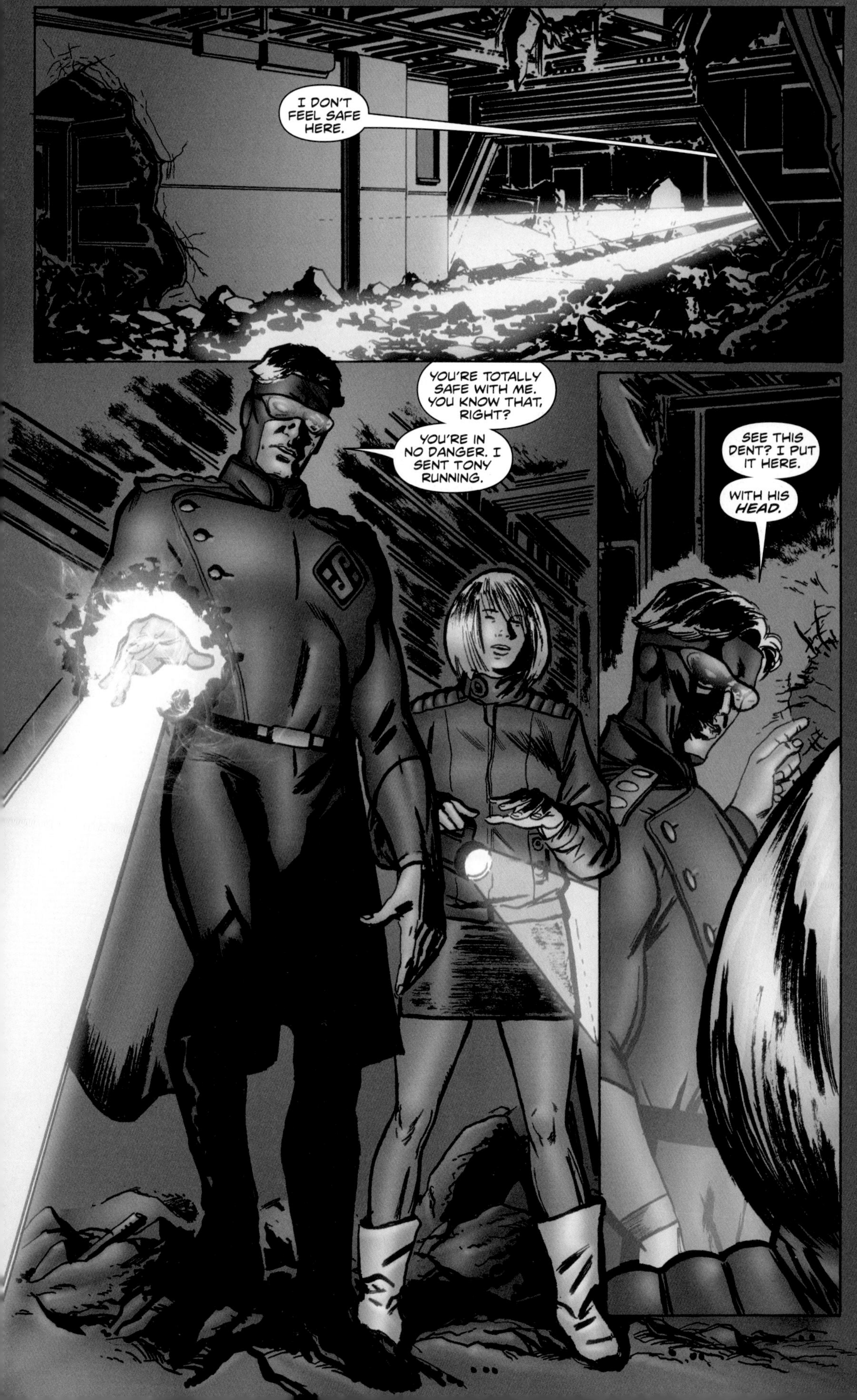
I DON'T FEEL SAFE HERE.
YOU'RE TOTALLY SAFE WITH ME. YOU KNOW THAT, RIGHT?
YOU'RE IN NO DANGER. I SENT TONY RUNNING.
SEE THIS DENT? I PUT IT HERE.
WITH HIS *HEAD.*

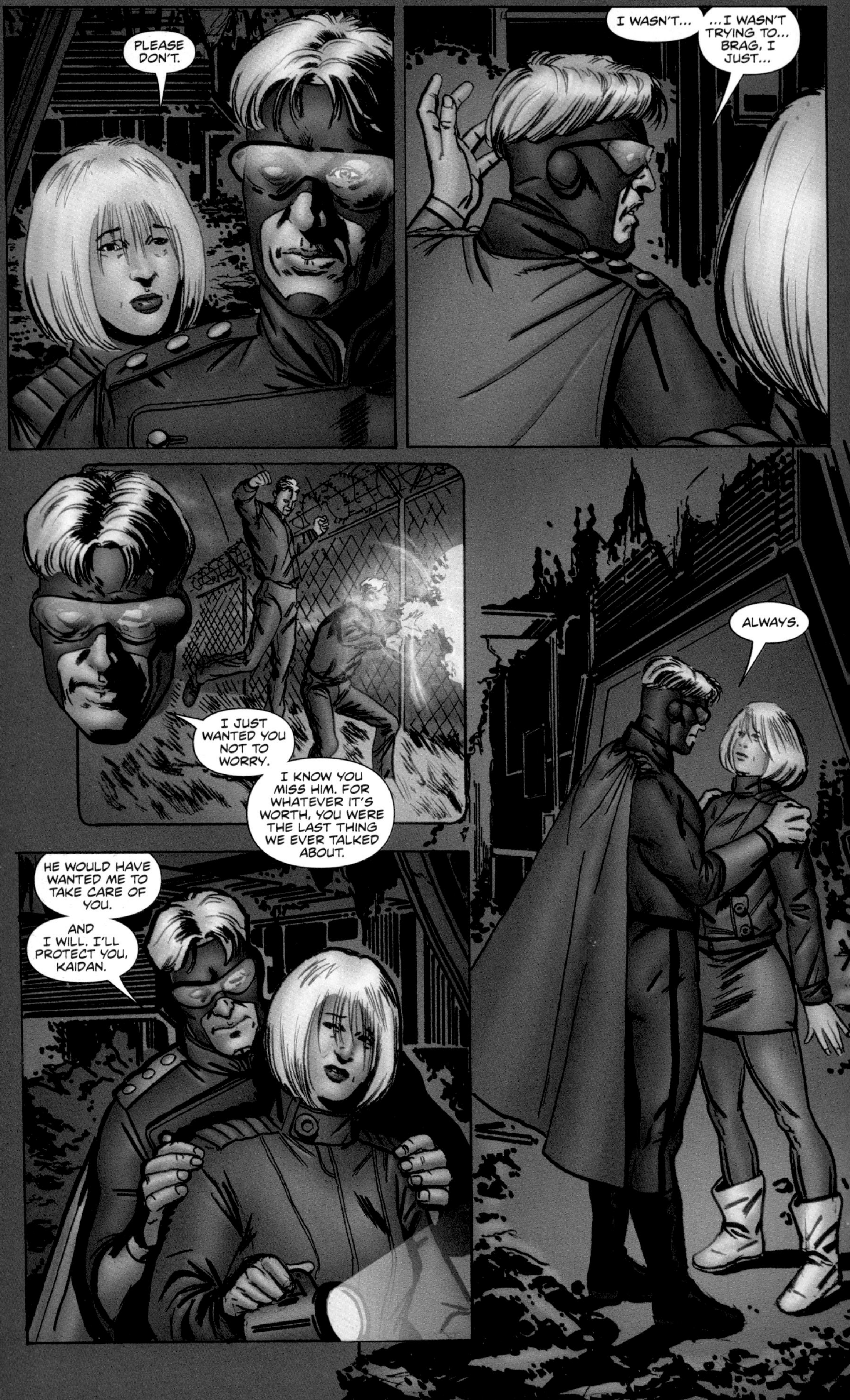
PLEASE DON'T.
I WASN'T...
...I WASN'T TRYING TO... BRAG, I JUST...
I JUST WANTED YOU NOT TO WORRY.
I KNOW YOU MISS HIM. FOR WHATEVER IT'S WORTH, YOU WERE THE LAST THING WE EVER TALKED ABOUT.
HE WOULD HAVE WANTED ME TO TAKE CARE OF YOU.
AND I WILL. I'LL PROTECT YOU, KAIDAN.
ALWAYS.

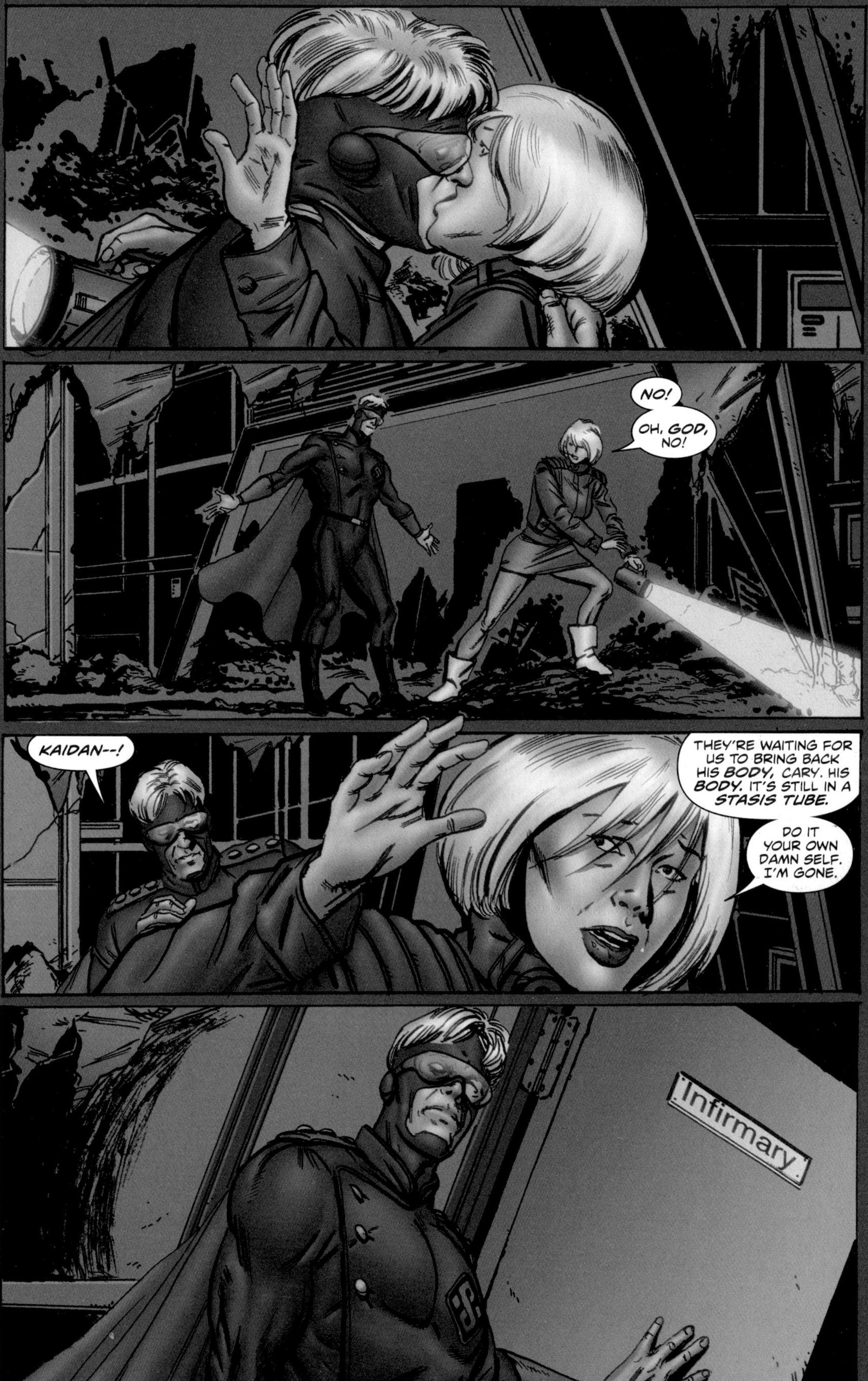
NO!
OH, GOD, NO!
KAIDAN--!
THEY'RE WAITING FOR US TO BRING BACK HIS BODY, CARY. HIS BODY. IT'S STILL IN A STASIS TUBE.
DO IT YOUR OWN DAMN SELF. I'M GONE.
Infirmary.

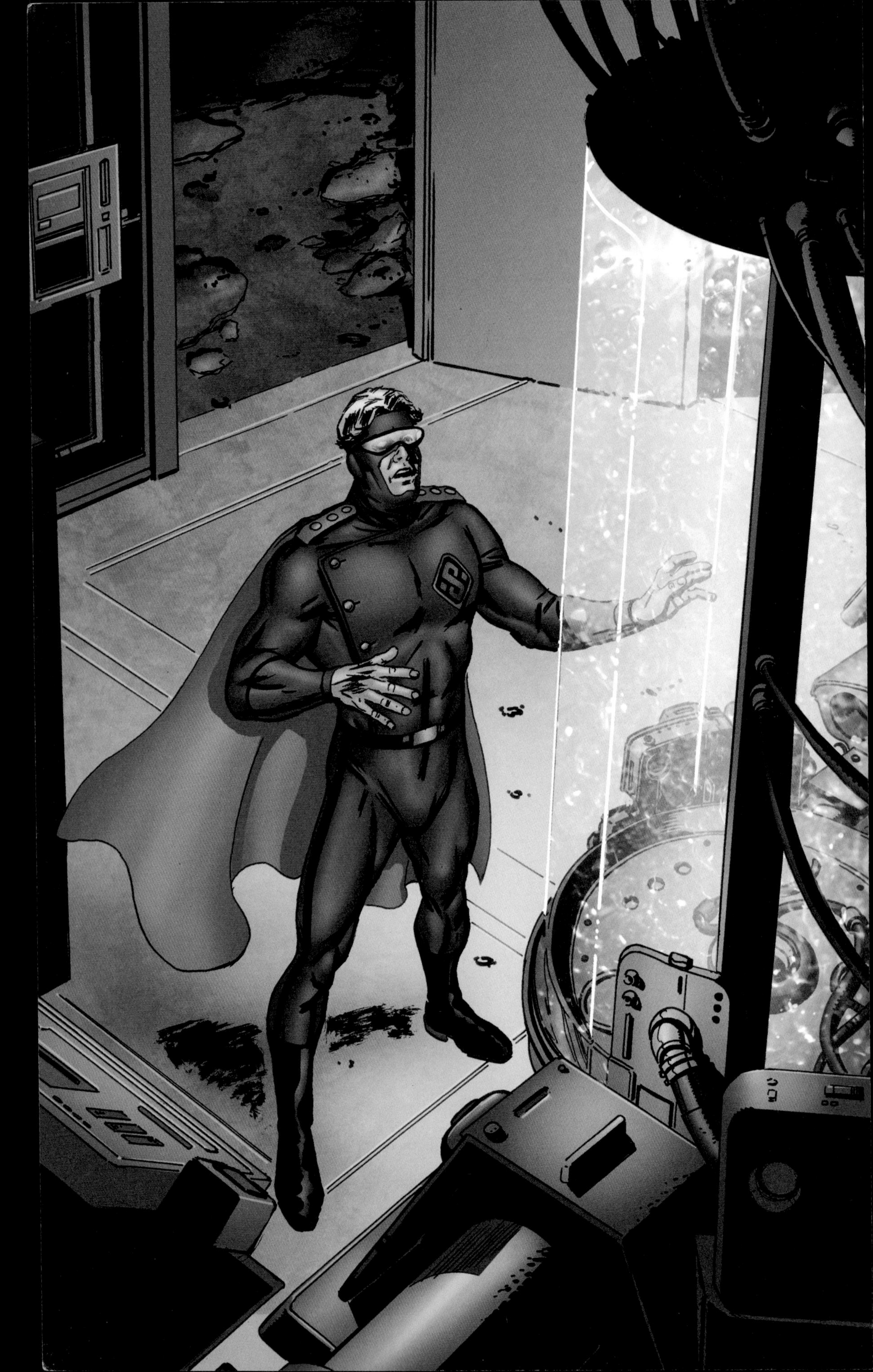

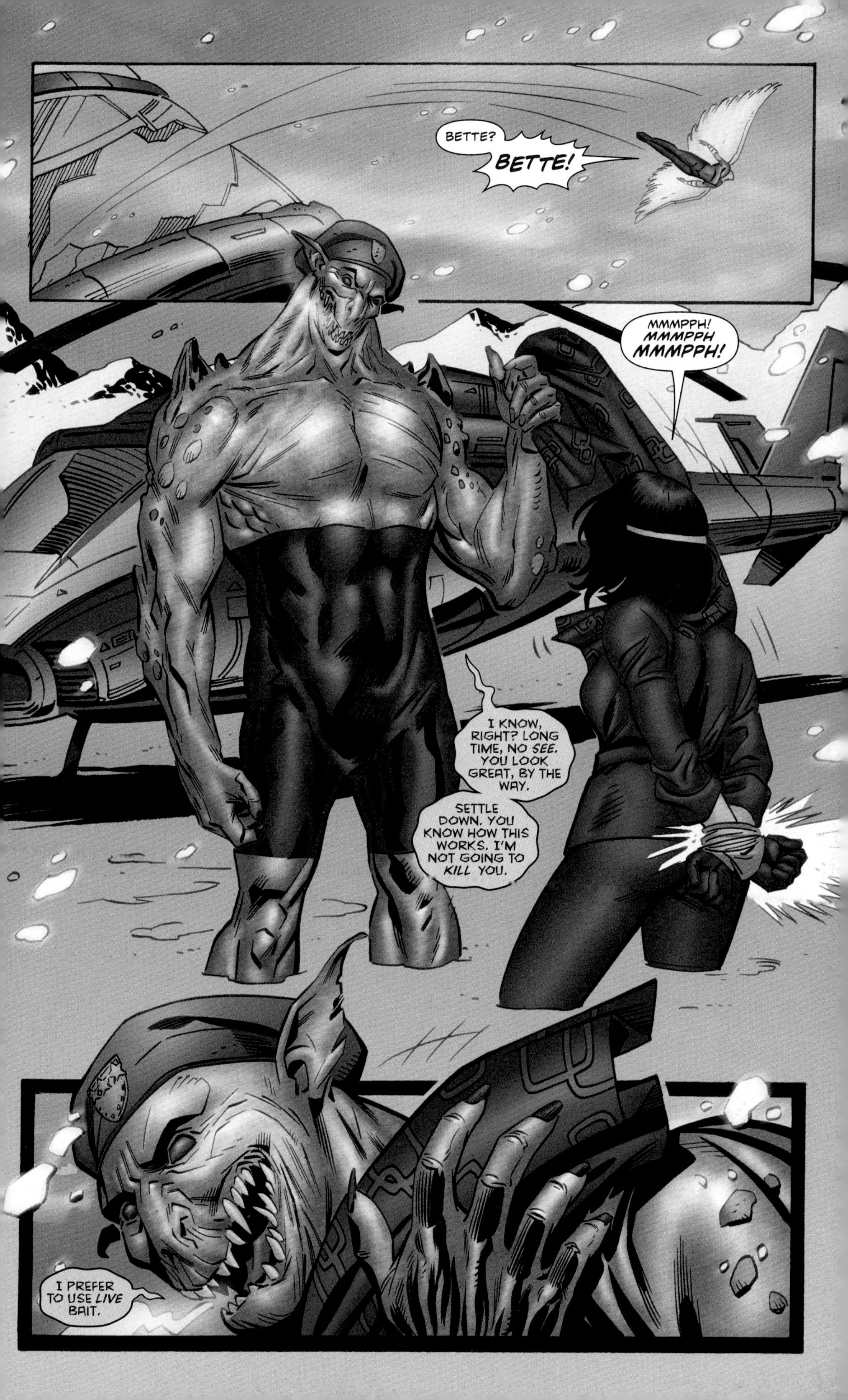
BETTE? BETTE!
MMMPPH! MMMPPH MMMPPH!
I KNOW, RIGHT? LONG TIME, NO SEE. YOU LOOK GREAT, BY THE WAY.
SETTLE DOWN. YOU KNOW HOW THIS WORKS. I'M NOT GOING TO KILL YOU.
I PREFER TO USE LIVE BAIT.

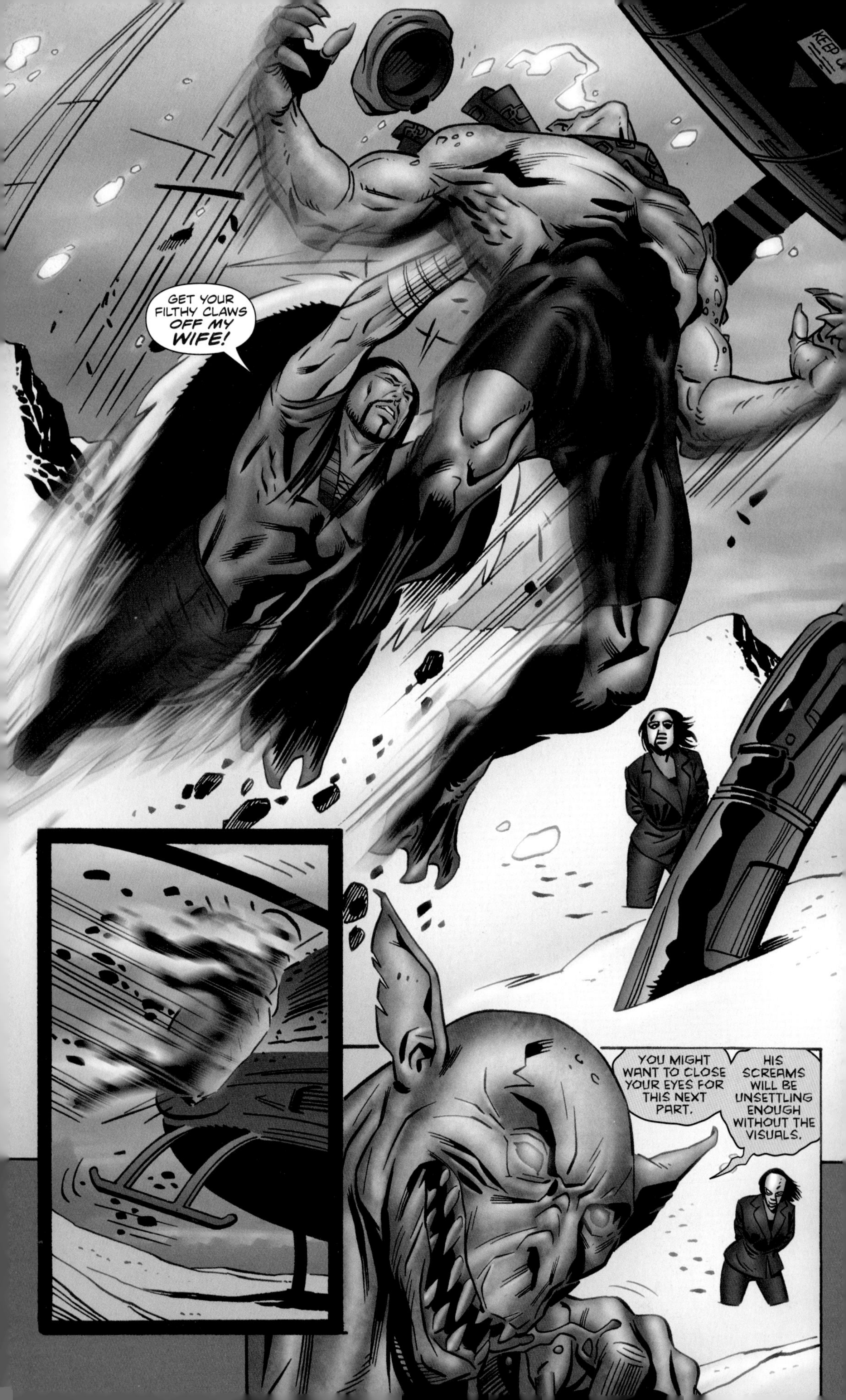
GET YOUR FILTHY CLAWS OFF MY WIFE!
YOU MIGHT WANT TO CLOSE YOUR EYES FOR THIS NEXT PART.
HIS SCREAMS WILL BE UNSETTLING ENOUGH WITHOUT THE VISUALS.

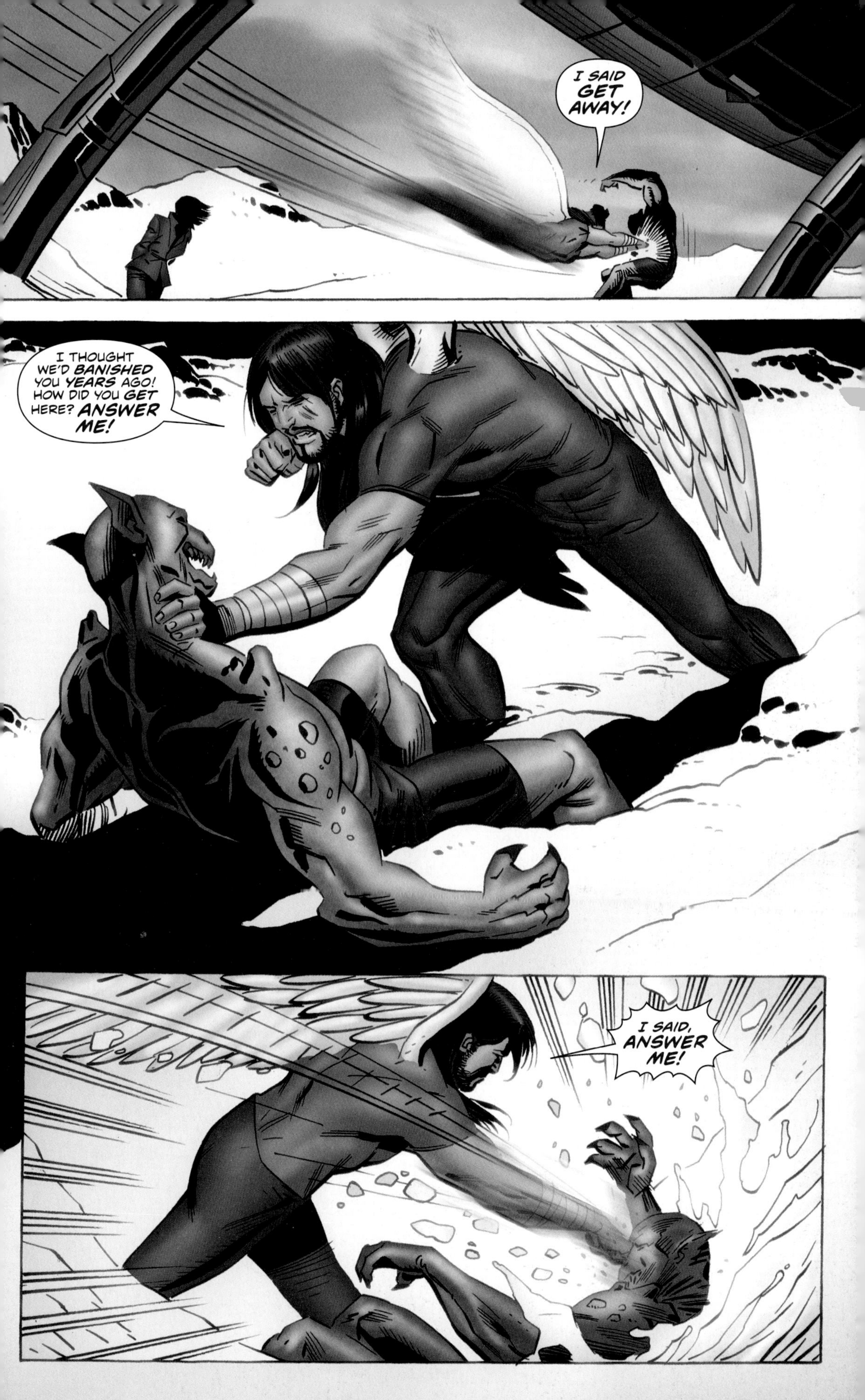
I SAID GET AWAY!
I THOUGHT WE'D BANISHED YOU YEARS AGO! HOW DID YOU GET HERE? ANSWER ME!
I SAID, ANSWER ME!

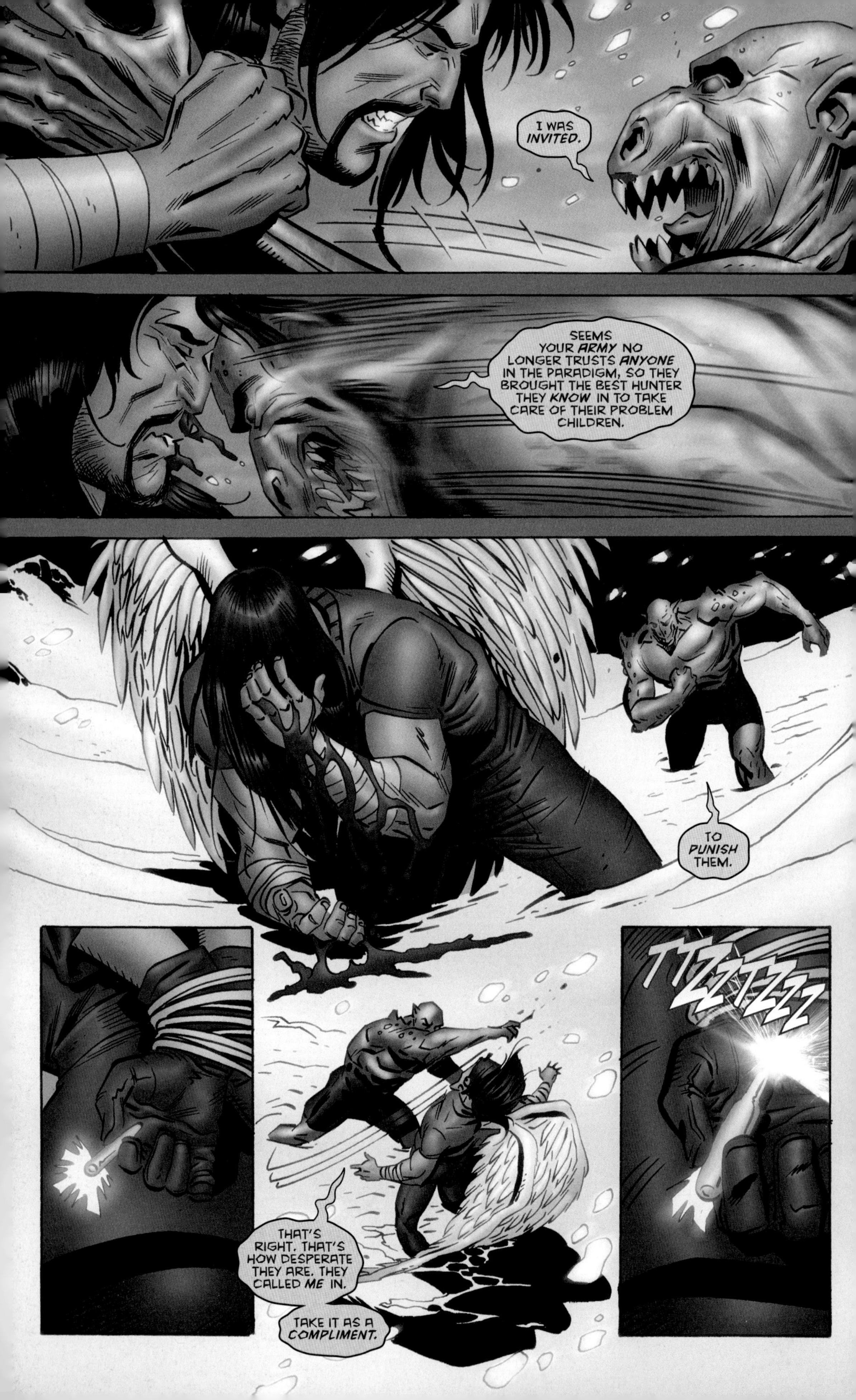
I WAS INVITED.
SEEMS YOUR ARMY NO LONGER TRUSTS ANYONE IN THE PARADIGM, SO THEY BROUGHT THE BEST HUNTER THEY KNOW IN TO TAKE CARE OF THEIR PROBLEM CHILDREN.
TO PUNISH THEM.
THAT'S RIGHT. THAT'S HOW DESPERATE THEY ARE. THEY CALLED ME IN.
TAKE IT AS A COMPLIMENT.
TTZZTZZZ

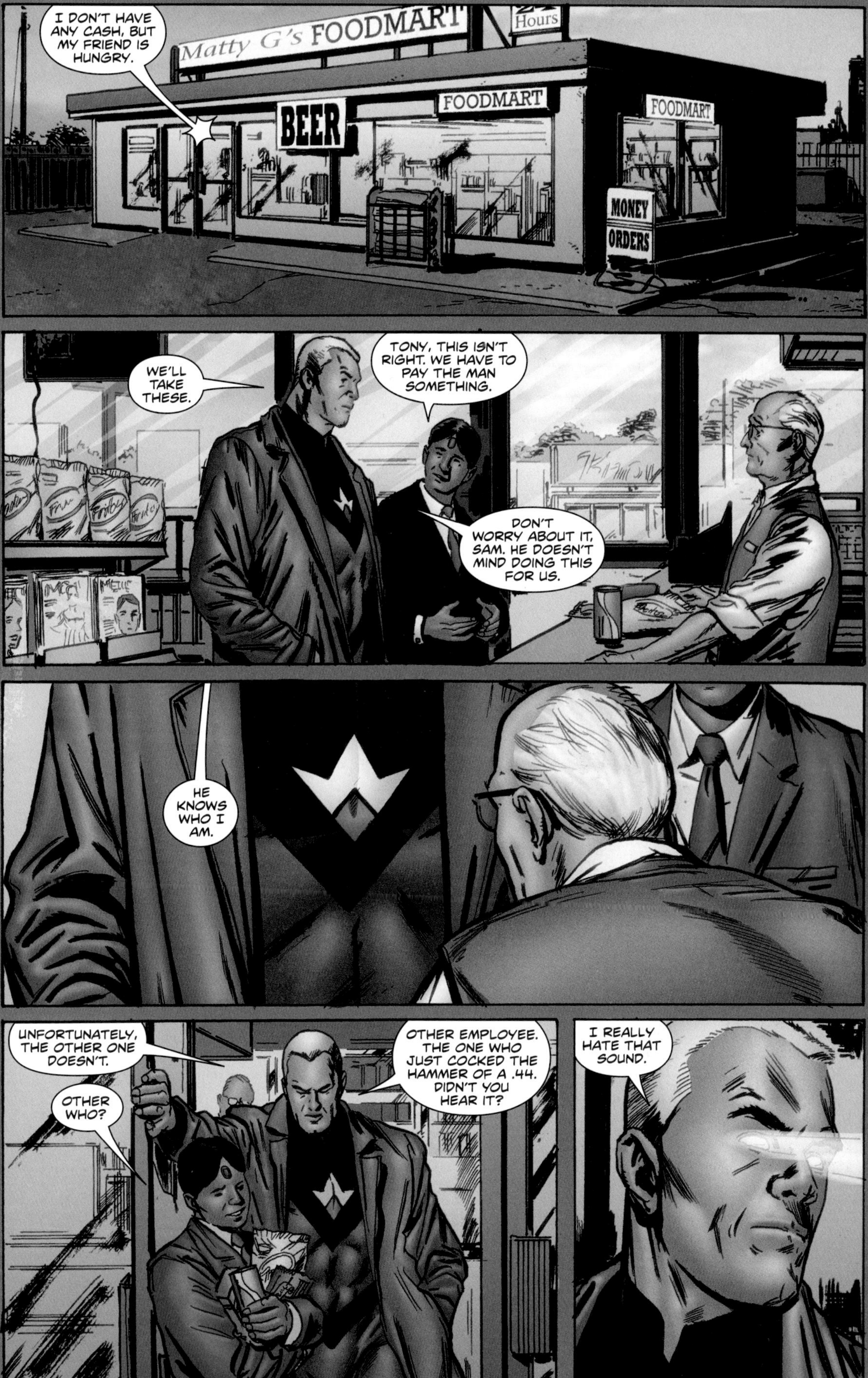

I DON'T HAVE ANY CASH, BUT MY FRIEND IS HUNGRY.
Matty G's FOODMART
24 Hours
BEER
FOODMART
FOODMART
MONEY ORDERS
WE'LL TAKE THESE.
TONY, THIS ISN'T RIGHT. WE HAVE TO PAY THE MAN SOMETHING.
DON'T WORRY ABOUT IT, SAM. HE DOESN'T MIND DOING THIS FOR US.
HE KNOWS WHO I AM.
UNFORTUNATELY, THE OTHER ONE DOESN'T.
OTHER WHO?
OTHER EMPLOYEE. THE ONE WHO JUST COCKED THE HAMMER OF A .44. DIDN'T YOU HEAR IT?
I REALLY HATE THAT SOUND.

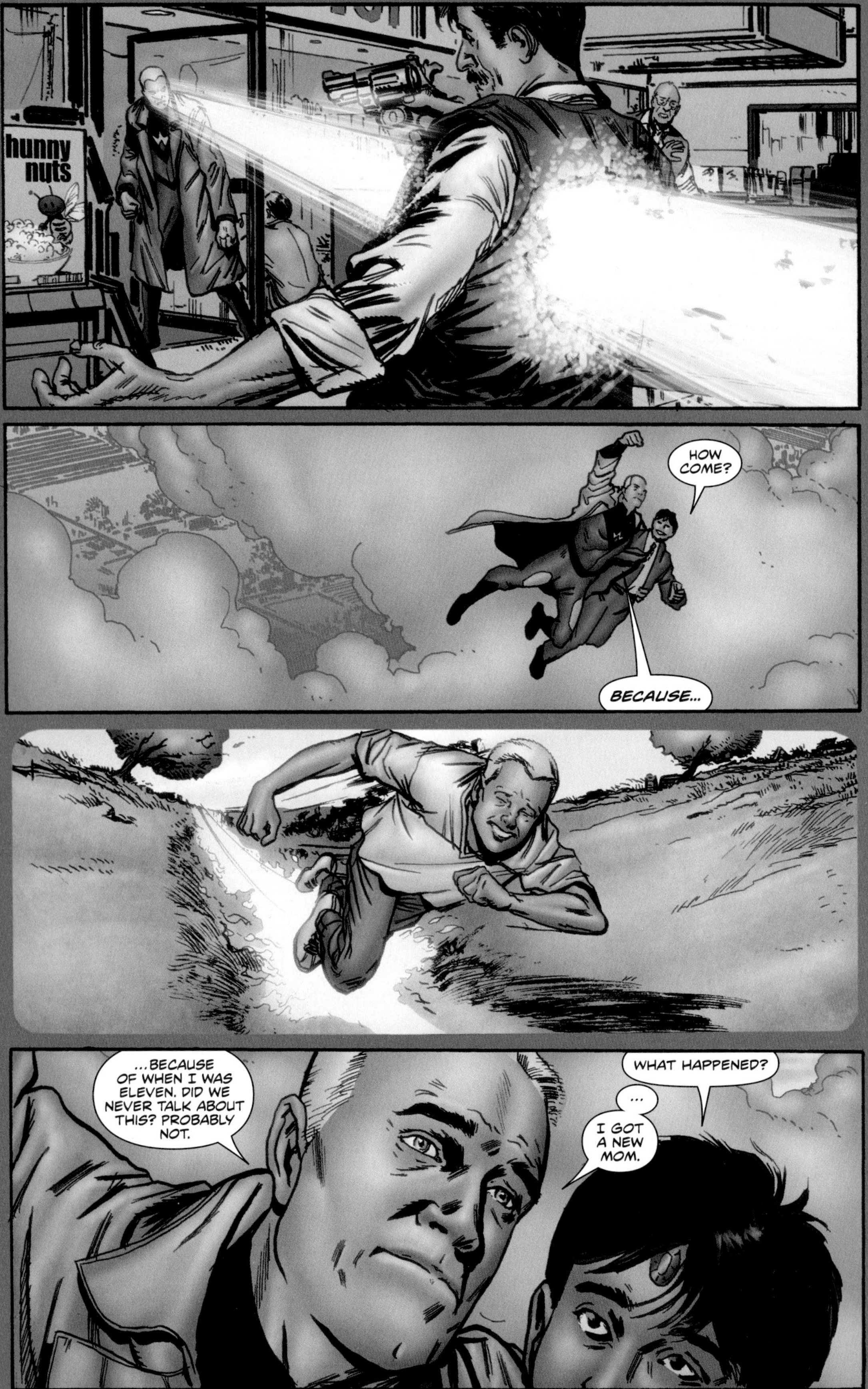
hunny nuts
HOW COME?
BECAUSE...
...BECAUSE OF WHEN I WAS ELEVEN. DID WE NEVER TALK ABOUT THIS? PROBABLY NOT.
WHAT HAPPENED?
...
I GOT A NEW MOM.

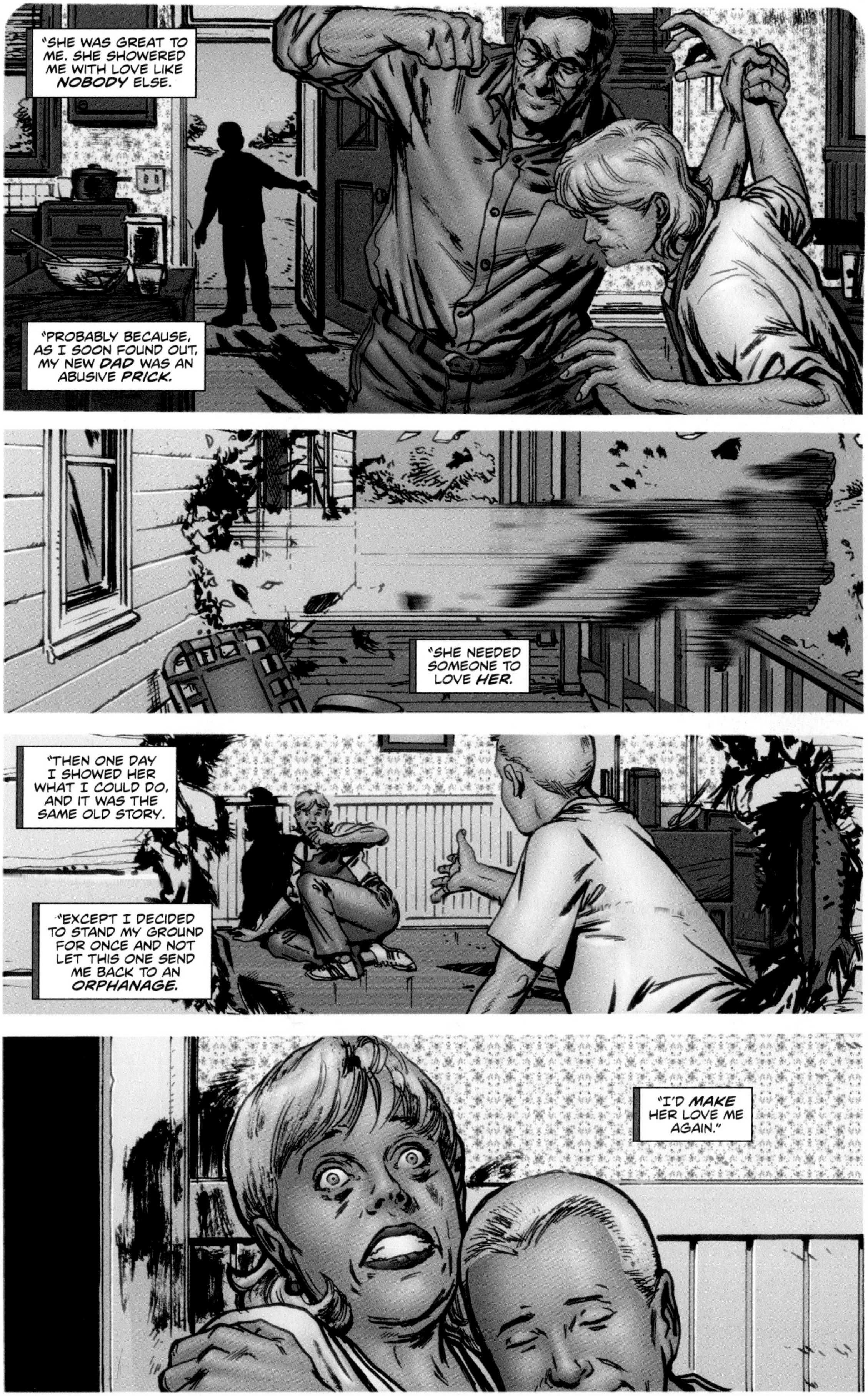
"SHE WAS GREAT TO ME. SHE SHOWERED ME WITH LOVE LIKE NOBODY ELSE.
"PROBABLY BECAUSE, AS I SOON FOUND OUT, MY NEW DAD WAS AN ABUSIVE PRICK.
"SHE NEEDED SOMEONE TO LOVE HER.
"THEN ONE DAY I SHOWED HER WHAT I COULD DO, AND IT WAS THE SAME OLD STORY.
"EXCEPT I DECIDED TO STAND MY GROUND FOR ONCE AND NOT LET THIS ONE SEND ME BACK TO AN ORPHANAGE.
"I'D MAKE HER LOVE ME AGAIN."

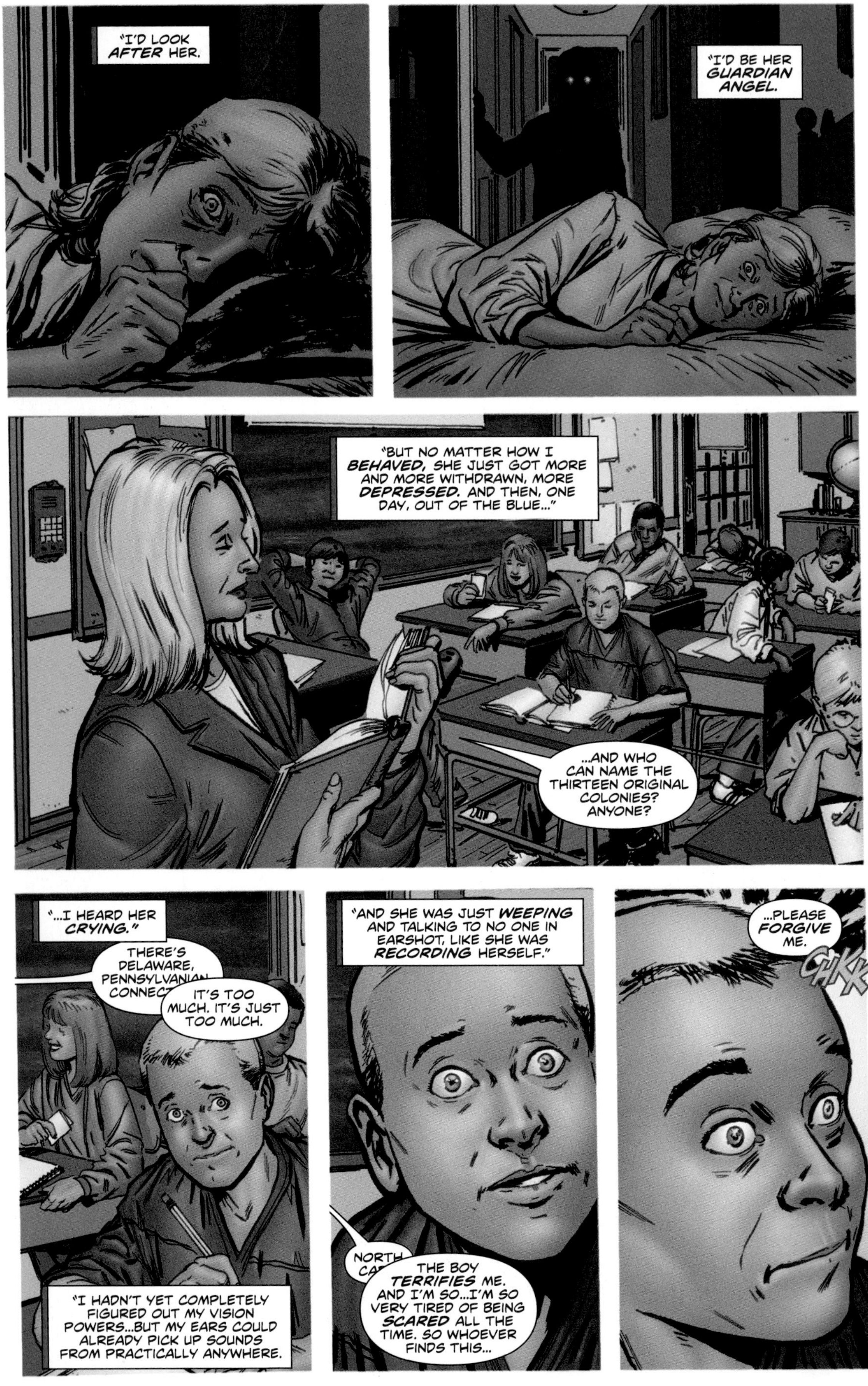

"I'D LOOK AFTER HER.
"I'D BE HER GUARDIAN ANGEL.
"BUT NO MATTER HOW I BEHAVED, SHE JUST GOT MORE AND MORE WITHDRAWN, MORE DEPRESSED. AND THEN, ONE DAY, OUT OF THE BLUE..."
...AND WHO CAN NAME THE THIRTEEN ORIGINAL COLONIES? ANYONE?
"...I HEARD HER CRYING."
THERE'S DELAWARE, PENNSYLVANIA, CONNECT
IT'S TOO MUCH. IT'S JUST TOO MUCH.
"I HADN'T YET COMPLETELY FIGURED OUT MY VISION POWERS...BUT MY EARS COULD ALREADY PICK UP SOUNDS FROM PRACTICALLY ANYWHERE.
"AND SHE WAS JUST WEEPING AND TALKING TO NO ONE IN EARSHOT, LIKE SHE WAS RECORDING HERSELF."
NORTH CA
THE BOY TERRIFIES ME. AND I'M SO...I'M SO VERY TIRED OF BEING SCARED ALL THE TIME. SO WHOEVER FINDS THIS...
...PLEASE FORGIVE ME.
CHKK

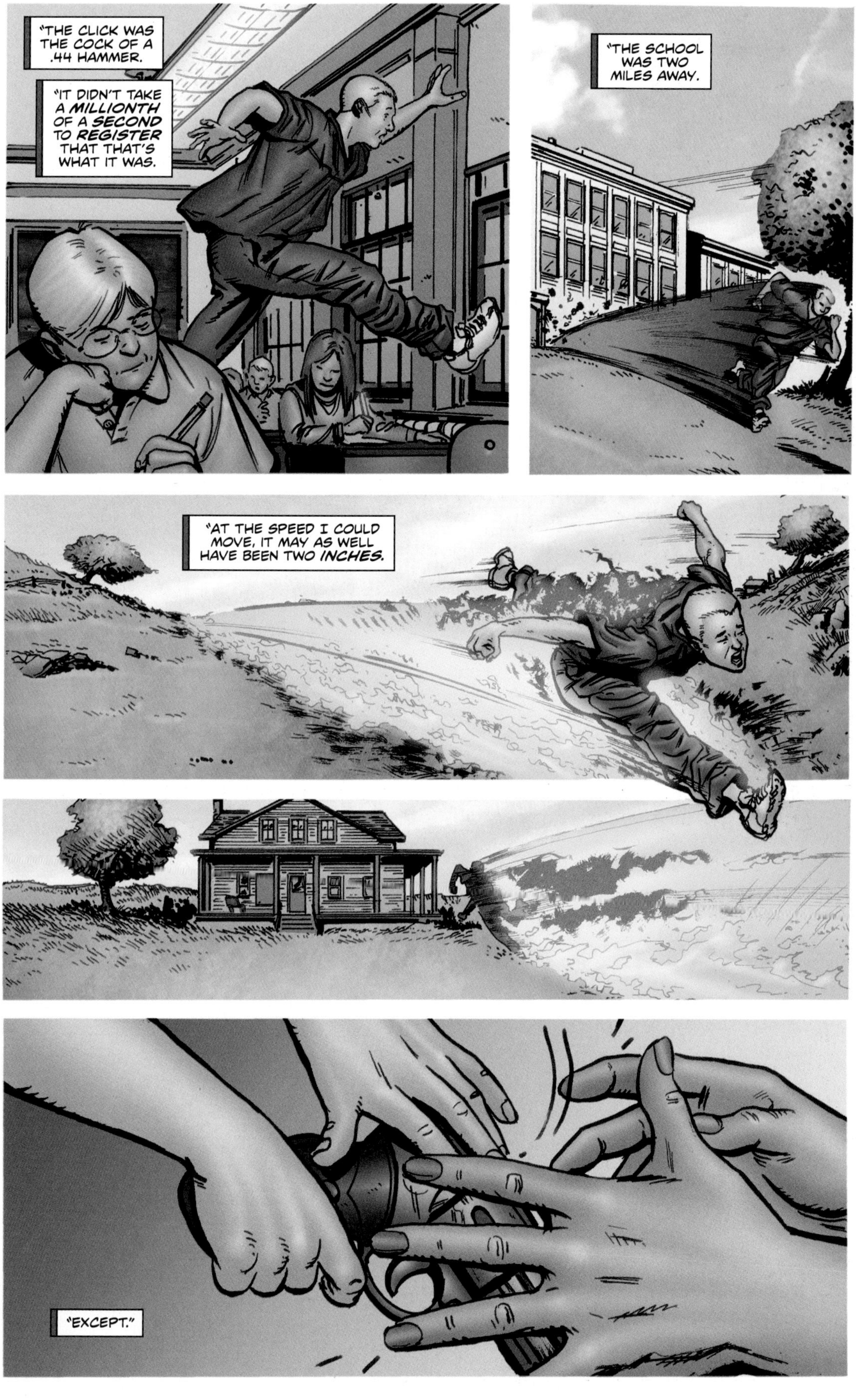
"THE CLICK WAS THE COCK OF A .44 HAMMER.
"IT DIDN'T TAKE A MILLIONTH OF A SECOND TO REGISTER THAT THAT'S WHAT IT WAS.
"THE SCHOOL WAS TWO MILES AWAY.
"AT THE SPEED I COULD MOVE, IT MAY AS WELL HAVE BEEN TWO INCHES.
"EXCEPT."

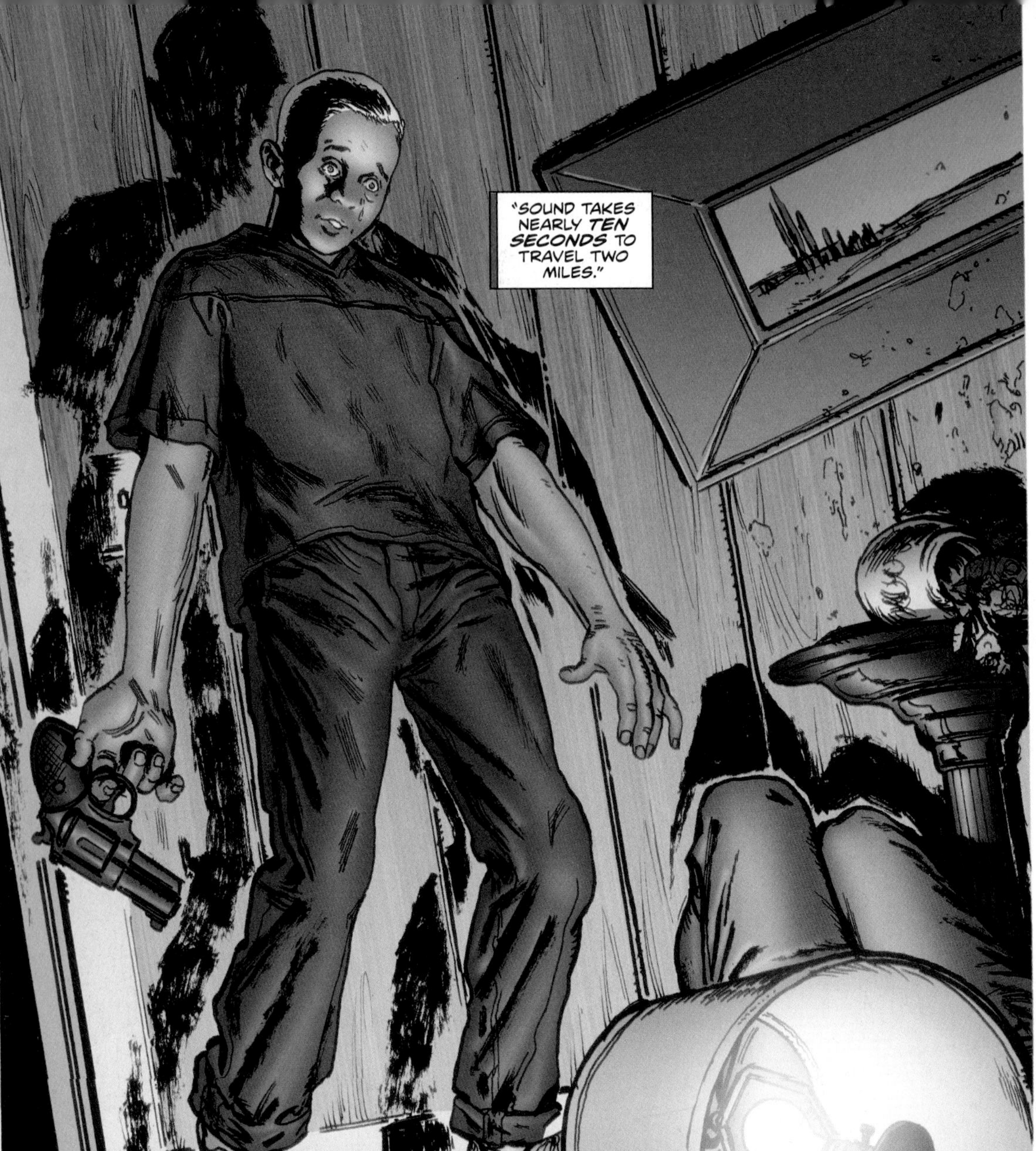
"SOUND TAKES NEARLY TEN SECONDS TO TRAVEL TWO MILES."

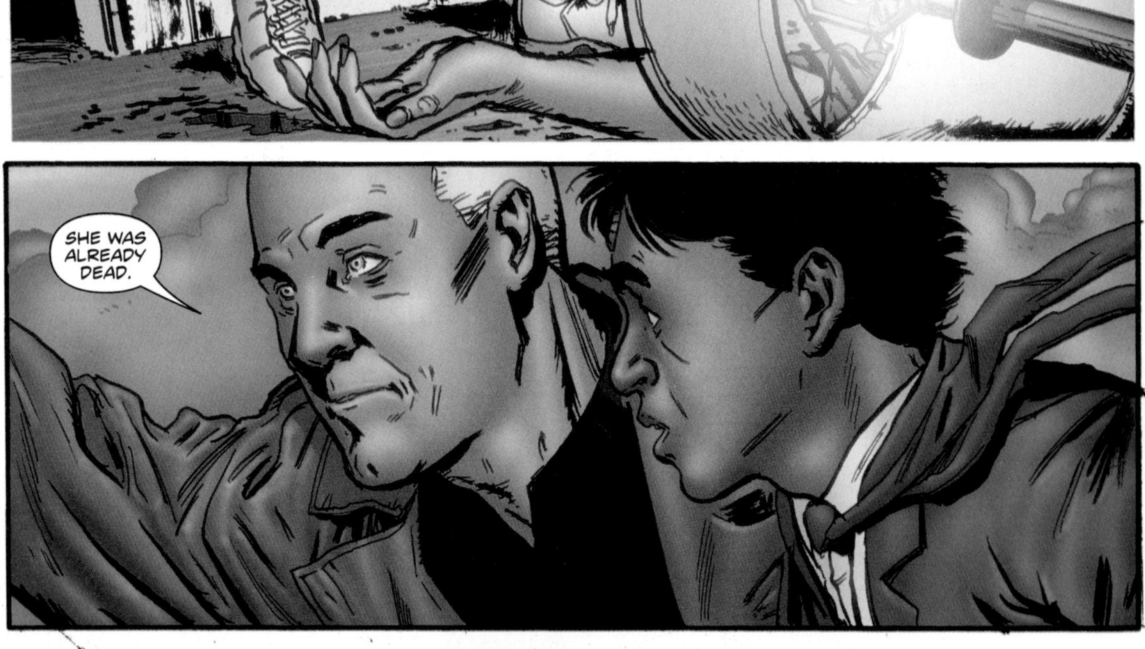
SHE WAS ALREADY DEAD.

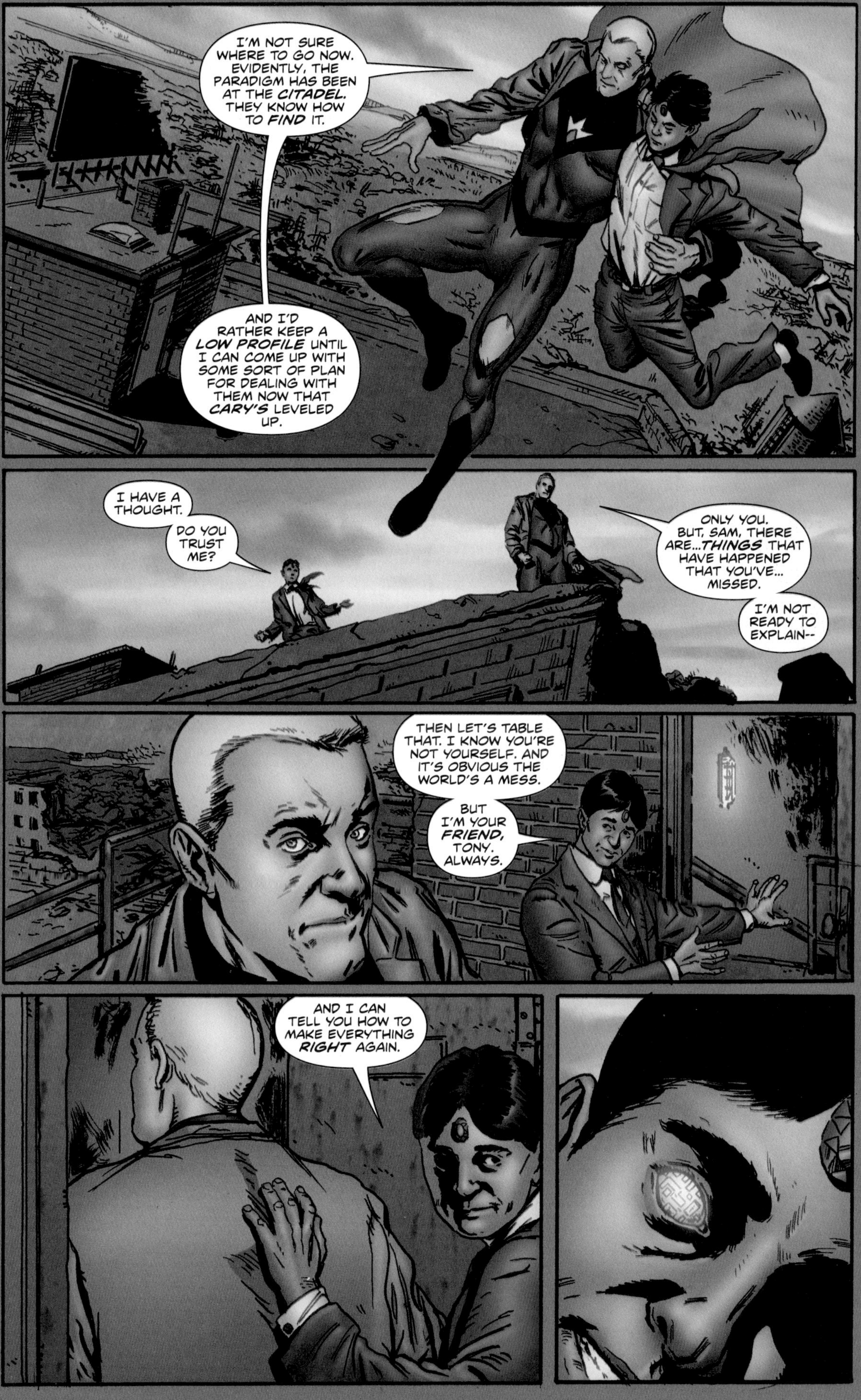
I'M NOT SURE WHERE TO GO NOW. EVIDENTLY, THE PARADIGM HAS BEEN AT THE CITADEL. THEY KNOW HOW TO FIND IT.
AND I'D RATHER KEEP A LOW PROFILE UNTIL I CAN COME UP WITH SOME SORT OF PLAN FOR DEALING WITH THEM NOW THAT CARY'S LEVELED UP.
I HAVE A THOUGHT.
DO YOU TRUST ME?
ONLY YOU. BUT, SAM, THERE ARE...THINGS THAT HAVE HAPPENED THAT YOU'VE... MISSED.
I'M NOT READY TO EXPLAIN--
THEN LET'S TABLE THAT. I KNOW YOU'RE NOT YOURSELF. AND IT'S OBVIOUS THE WORLD'S A MESS.
BUT I'M YOUR FRIEND, TONY. ALWAYS.
AND I CAN TELL YOU HOW TO MAKE EVERYTHING RIGHT AGAIN.

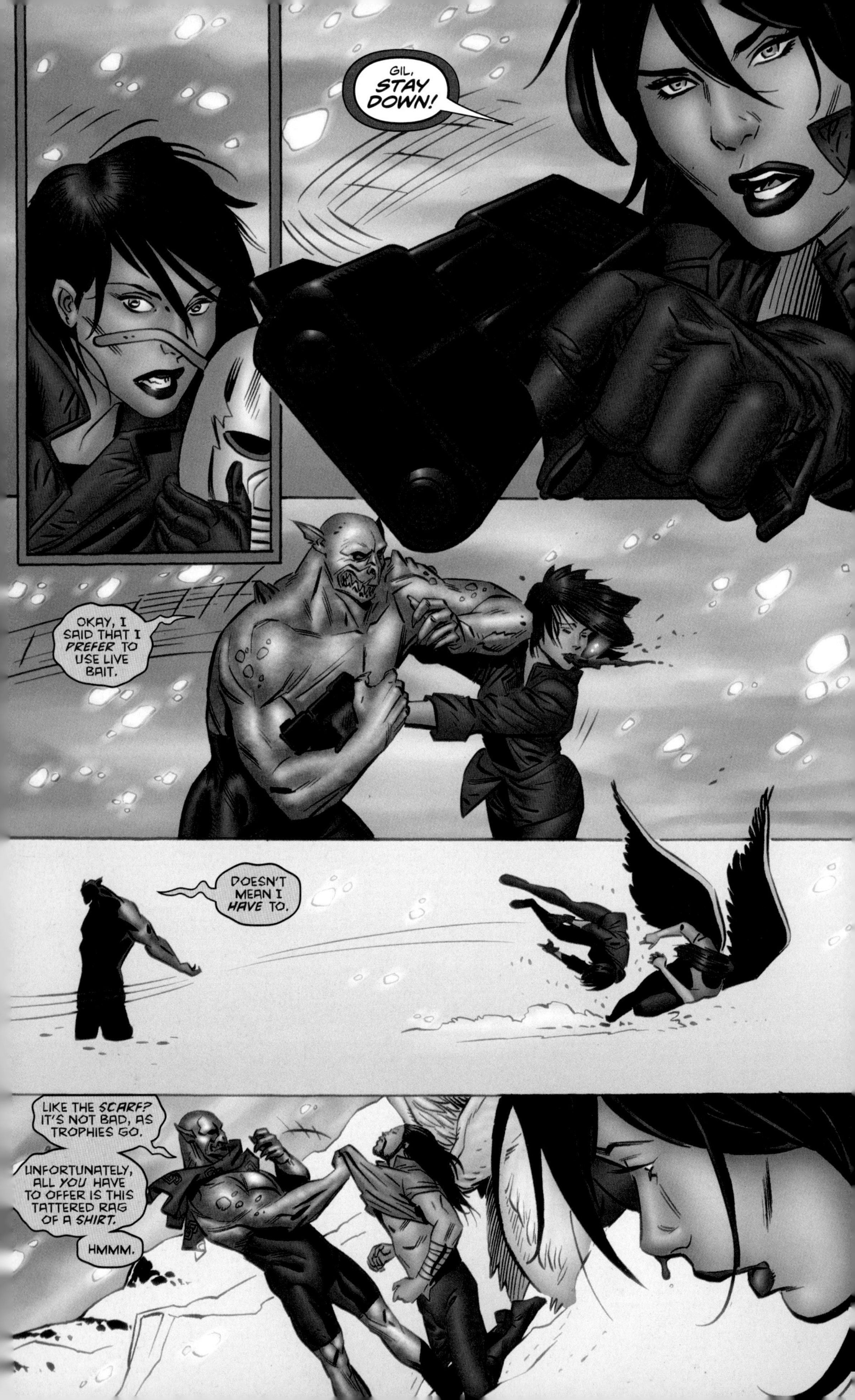
GIL, STAY DOWN!
OKAY, I SAID THAT I PREFER TO USE LIVE BAIT.
DOESN'T MEAN I HAVE TO.
LIKE THE SCARF? IT'S NOT BAD, AS TROPHIES GO.
UNFORTUNATELY, ALL YOU HAVE TO OFFER IS THIS TATTERED RAG OF A SHIRT.
HMMM.

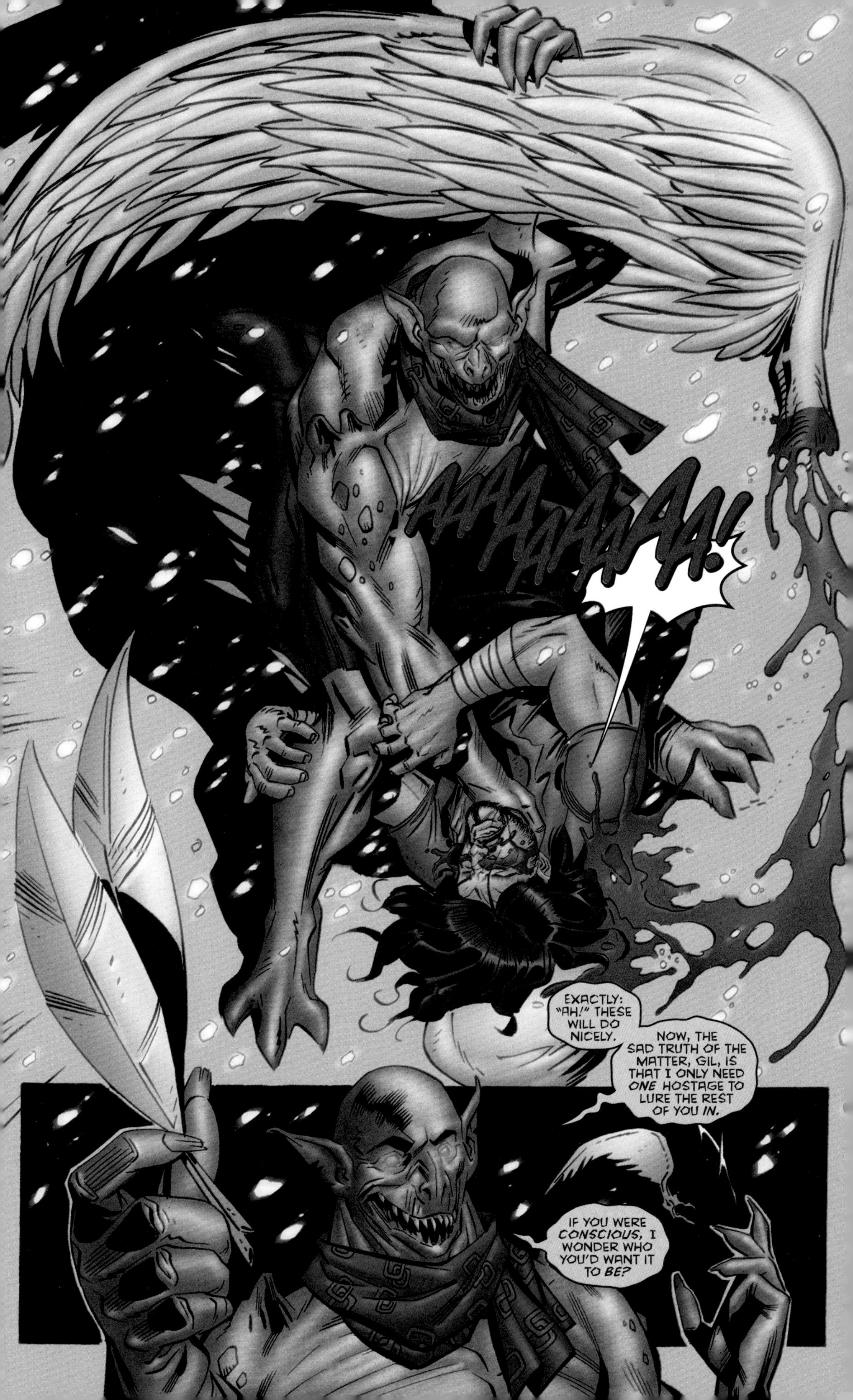
AAAAAAAAAAAA!
EXACTLY: "AH!" THESE WILL DO NICELY.
NOW, THE SAD TRUTH OF THE MATTER, GIL, IS THAT I ONLY NEED ONE HOSTAGE TO LURE THE REST OF YOU IN.
IF YOU WERE CONSCIOUS, I WONDER WHO YOU'D WANT IT TO BE?

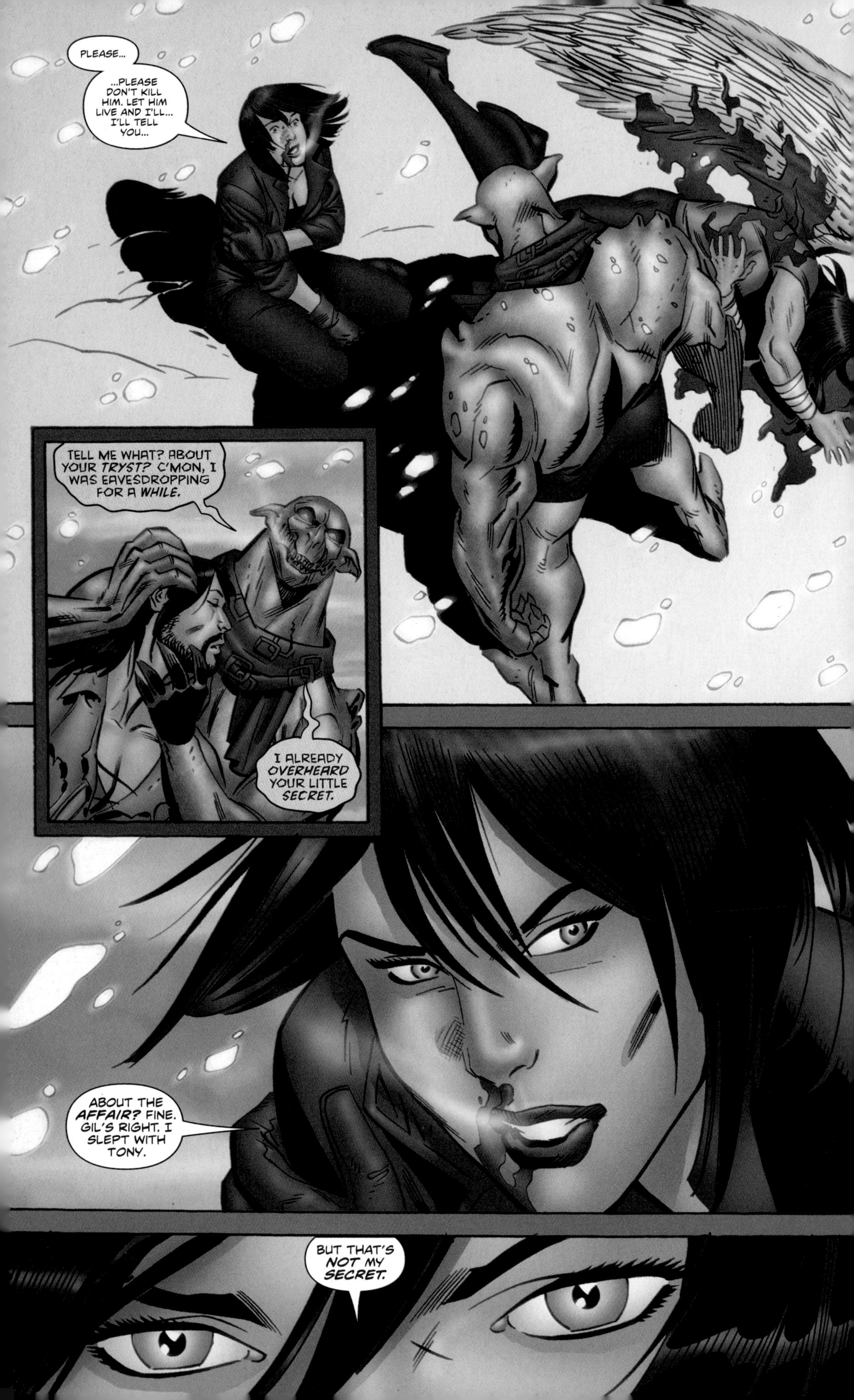
PLEASE...
...PLEASE DON'T KILL HIM. LET HIM LIVE AND I'LL... I'LL TELL YOU...
TELL ME WHAT? ABOUT YOUR TRYST? C'MON, I WAS EAVESDROPPING FOR A WHILE.
I ALREADY OVERHEARD YOUR LITTLE SECRET.
ABOUT THE AFFAIR? FINE. GIL'S RIGHT. I SLEPT WITH TONY.
BUT THAT'S NOT MY SECRET.

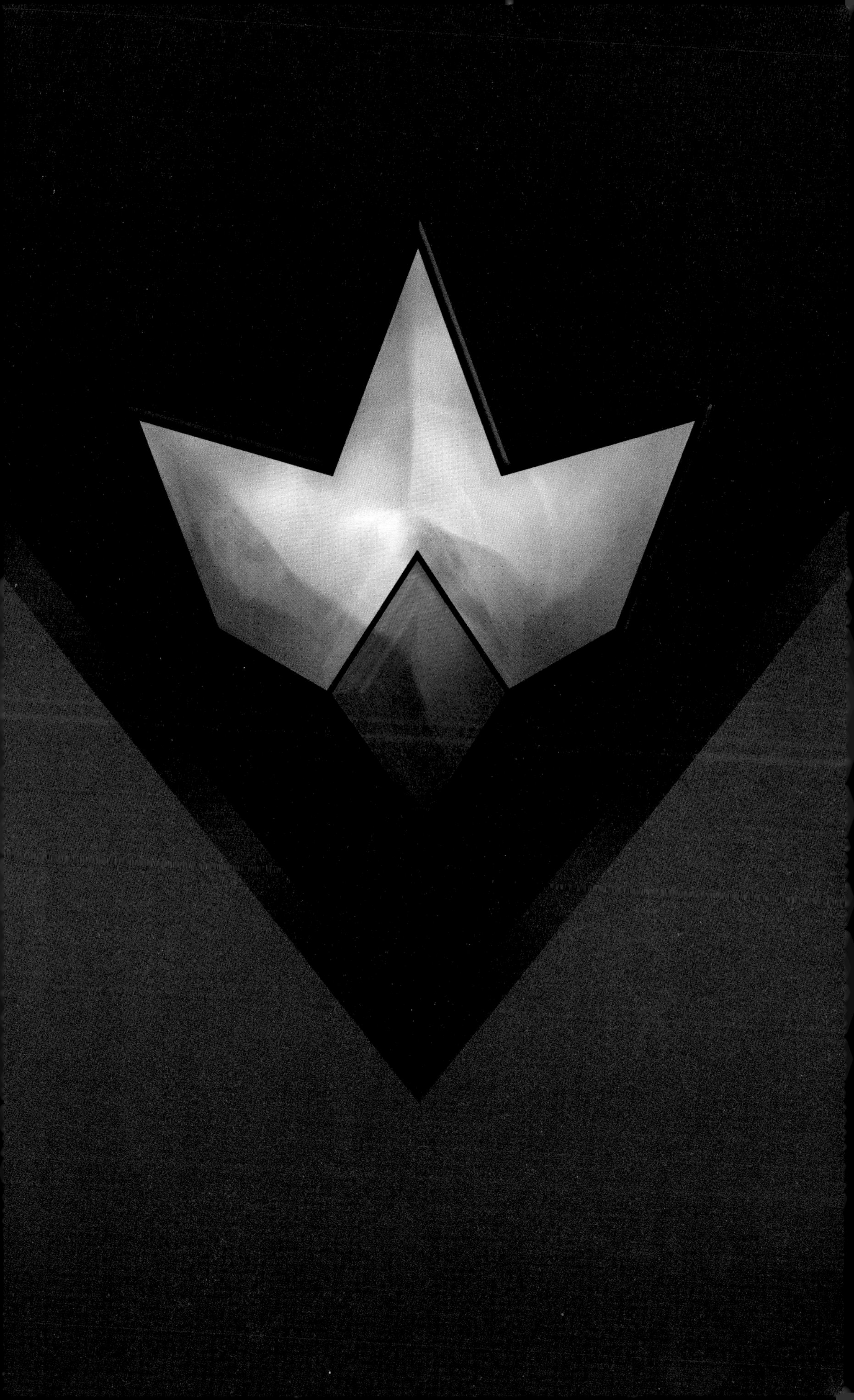

CHAPTER 11

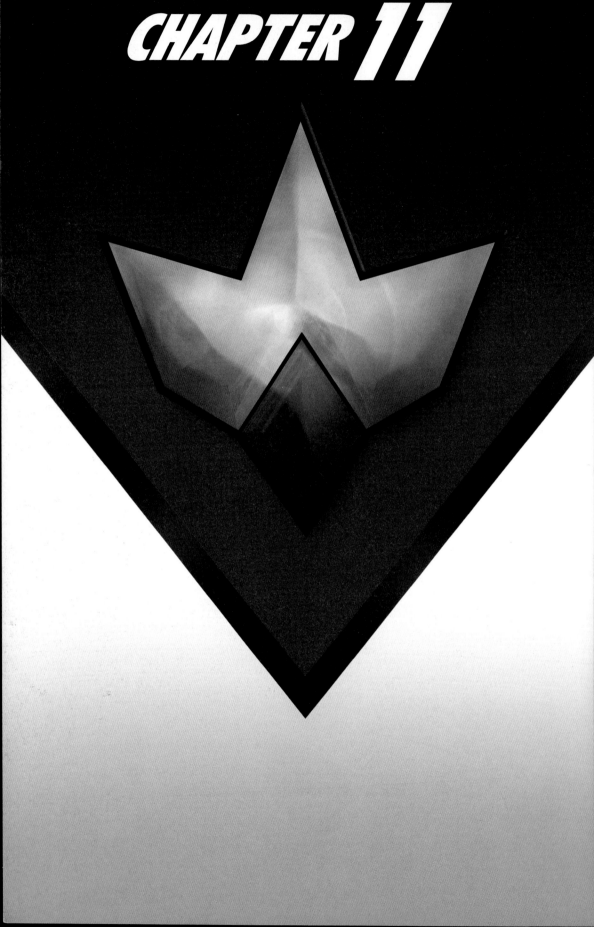

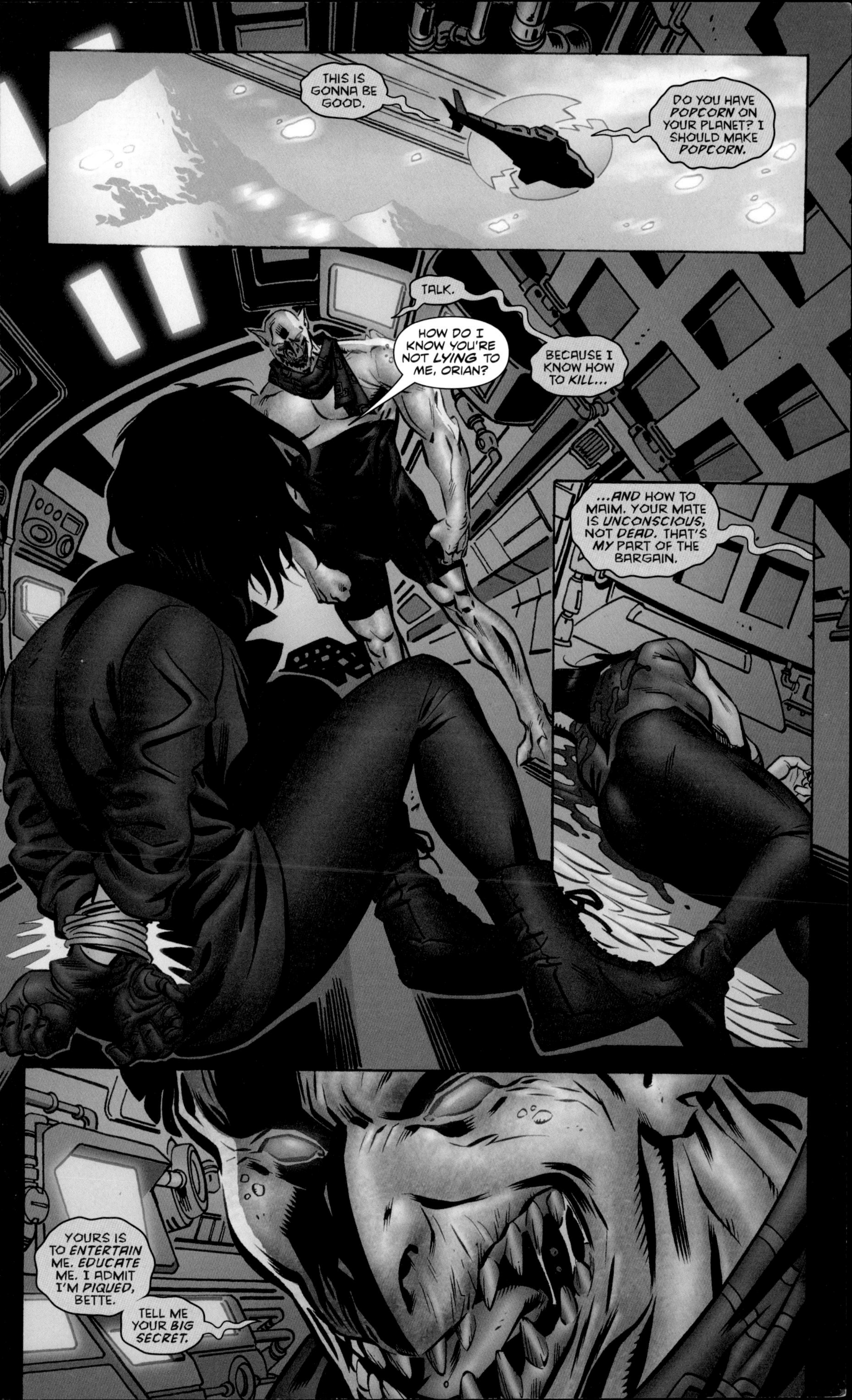

THIS IS GONNA BE GOOD.
DO YOU HAVE POPCORN ON YOUR PLANET? I SHOULD MAKE POPCORN.
TALK.
HOW DO I KNOW YOU'RE NOT LYING TO ME, ORIAN?
BECAUSE I KNOW HOW TO KILL...
...AND HOW TO MAIM. YOUR MATE IS UNCONSCIOUS, NOT DEAD. THAT'S MY PART OF THE BARGAIN.
YOURS IS TO ENTERTAIN ME. EDUCATE ME. I ADMIT I'M PIQUED, BETTE.
TELL ME YOUR BIG SECRET.

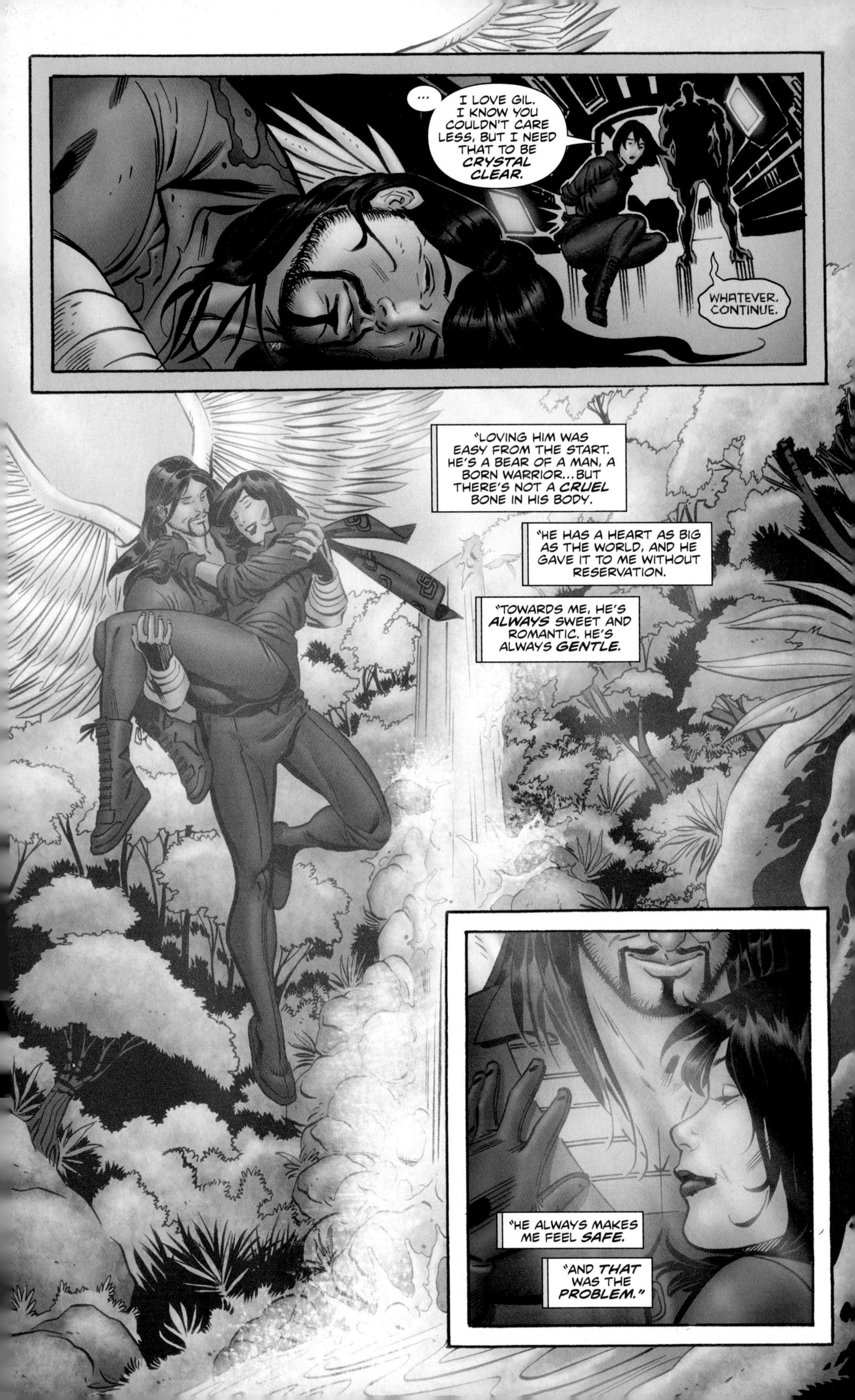
...
I LOVE GIL. I KNOW YOU COULDN'T CARE LESS, BUT I NEED THAT TO BE CRYSTAL CLEAR.
WHATEVER. CONTINUE.
"LOVING HIM WAS EASY FROM THE START. HE'S A BEAR OF A MAN, A BORN WARRIOR...BUT THERE'S NOT A CRUEL BONE IN HIS BODY.
"HE HAS A HEART AS BIG AS THE WORLD, AND HE GAVE IT TO ME WITHOUT RESERVATION.
"TOWARDS ME, HE'S ALWAYS SWEET AND ROMANTIC. HE'S ALWAYS GENTLE.
"HE ALWAYS MAKES ME FEEL SAFE.
"AND THAT WAS THE PROBLEM."

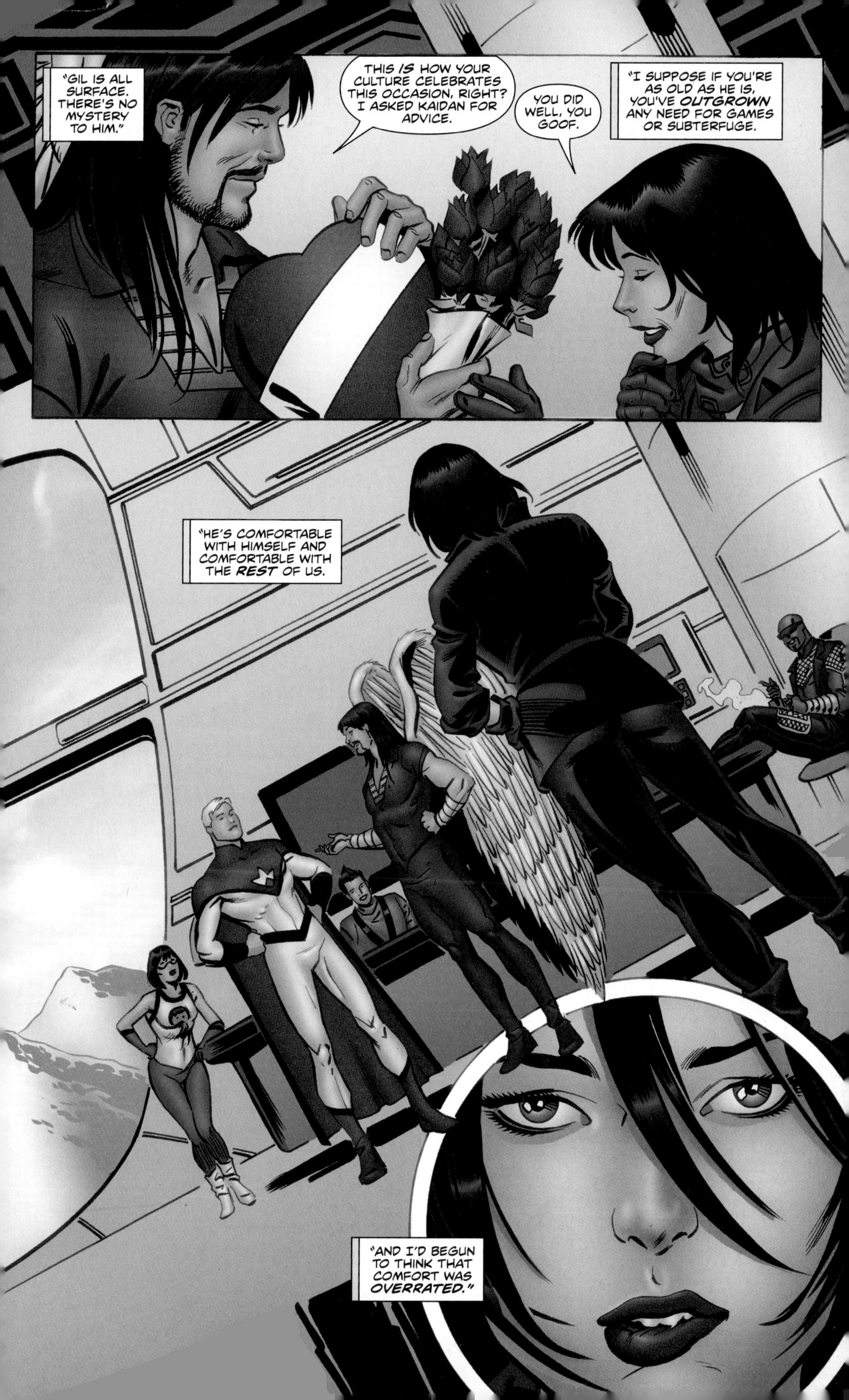
"GIL IS ALL SURFACE. THERE'S NO MYSTERY TO HIM."
THIS *IS* HOW YOUR CULTURE CELEBRATES THIS OCCASION, RIGHT? I ASKED KAIDAN FOR ADVICE.
YOU DID WELL, YOU GOOF.
"I SUPPOSE IF YOU'RE AS OLD AS HE IS, YOU'VE *OUTGROWN* ANY NEED FOR GAMES OR SUBTERFUGE.
"HE'S COMFORTABLE WITH HIMSELF AND COMFORTABLE WITH THE *REST* OF US.
"AND I'D BEGUN TO THINK THAT COMFORT WAS *OVERRATED.*"

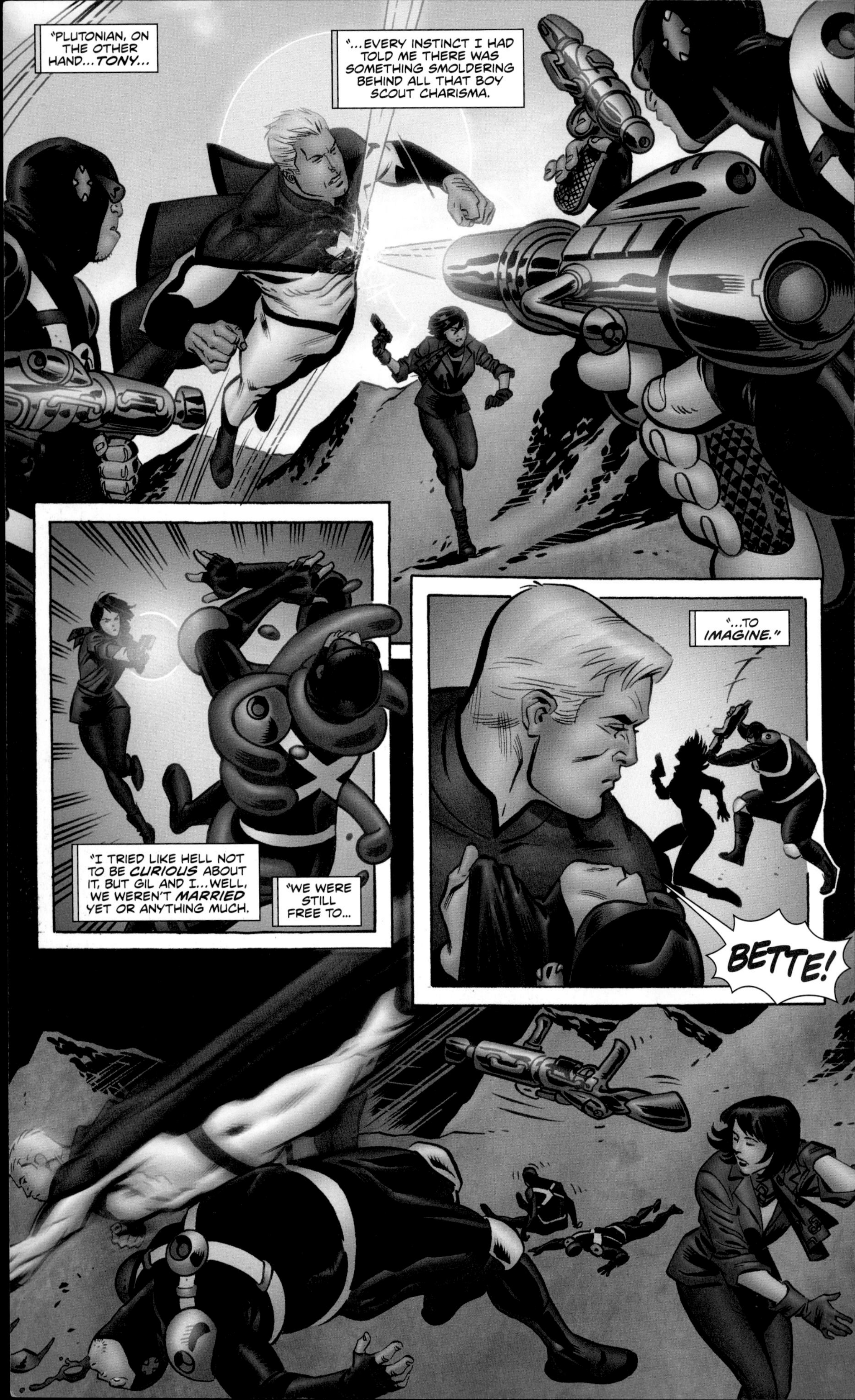
"PLUTONIAN, ON THE OTHER HAND...TONY...
"...EVERY INSTINCT I HAD TOLD ME THERE WAS SOMETHING SMOLDERING BEHIND ALL THAT BOY SCOUT CHARISMA.
"I TRIED LIKE HELL NOT TO BE CURIOUS ABOUT IT, BUT GIL AND I...WELL, WE WEREN'T MARRIED YET OR ANYTHING MUCH.
"WE WERE STILL FREE TO...
"...TO IMAGINE."
BETTE!

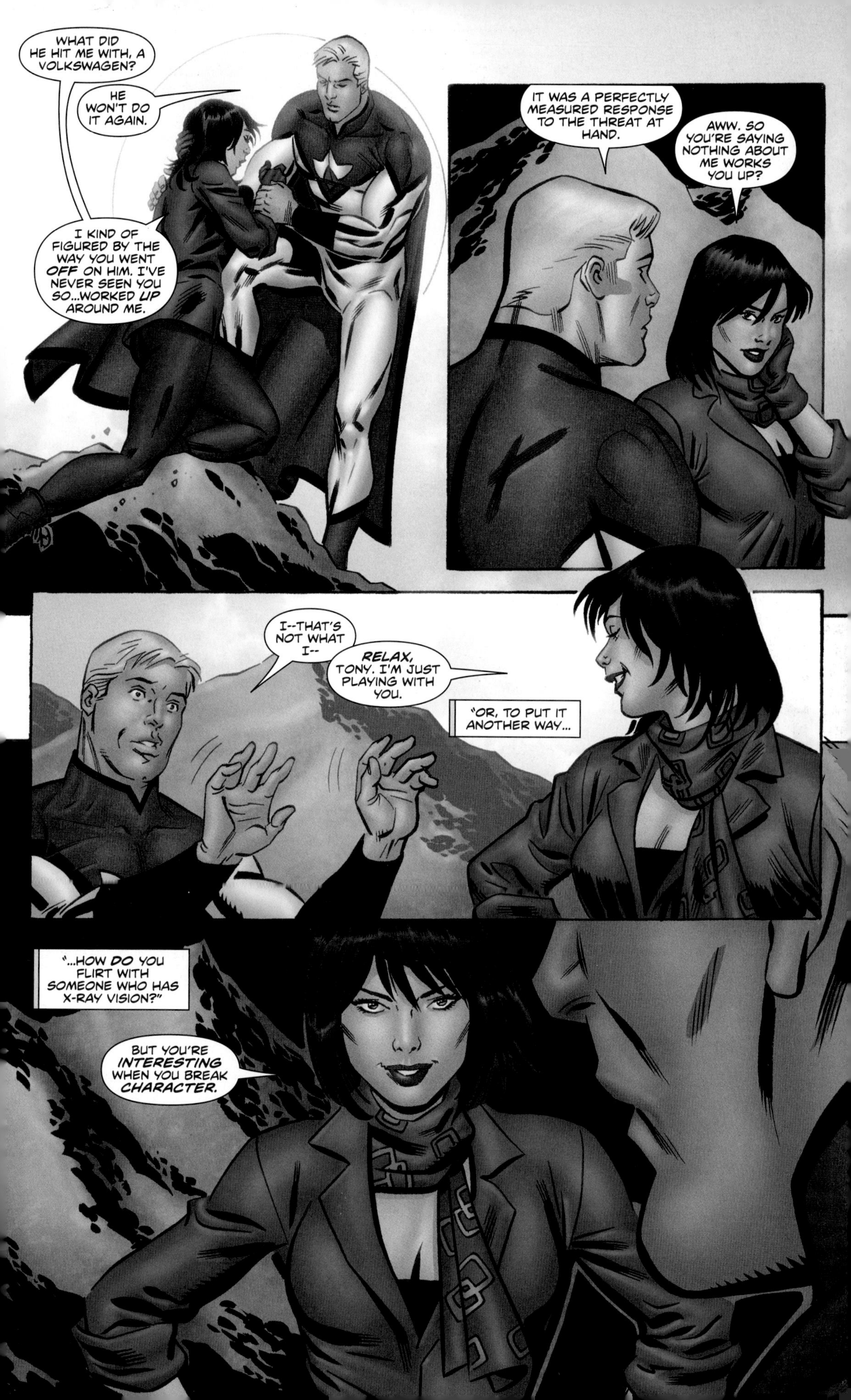
WHAT DID HE HIT ME WITH, A VOLKSWAGEN?
HE WON'T DO IT AGAIN.
I KIND OF FIGURED BY THE WAY YOU WENT OFF ON HIM. I'VE NEVER SEEN YOU SO...WORKED UP AROUND ME.
IT WAS A PERFECTLY MEASURED RESPONSE TO THE THREAT AT HAND.
AWW. SO YOU'RE SAYING NOTHING ABOUT ME WORKS YOU UP?
I--THAT'S NOT WHAT I--
RELAX, TONY. I'M JUST PLAYING WITH YOU.
"OR, TO PUT IT ANOTHER WAY...
"...HOW DO YOU FLIRT WITH SOMEONE WHO HAS X-RAY VISION?"
BUT YOU'RE INTERESTING WHEN YOU BREAK CHARACTER.

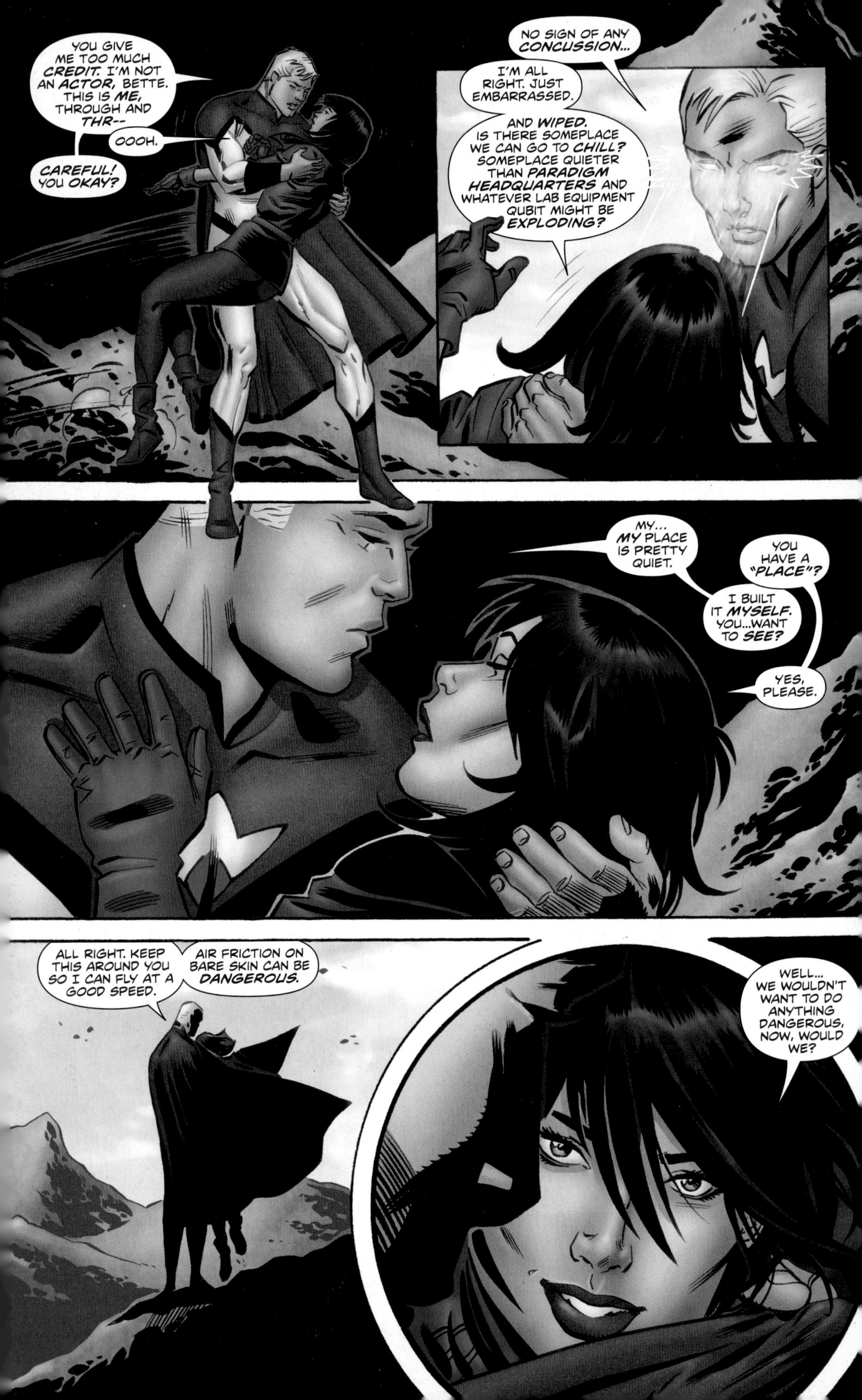
YOU GIVE ME TOO MUCH CREDIT. I'M NOT AN ACTOR, BETTE. THIS IS ME, THROUGH AND THR--
OOOH.
CAREFUL! YOU OKAY?
NO SIGN OF ANY CONCUSSION...
I'M ALL RIGHT. JUST EMBARRASSED.
AND WIPED. IS THERE SOMEPLACE WE CAN GO TO CHILL? SOMEPLACE QUIETER THAN PARADIGM HEADQUARTERS AND WHATEVER LAB EQUIPMENT QUBIT MIGHT BE EXPLODING?
MY... MY PLACE IS PRETTY QUIET.
YOU HAVE A "PLACE"?
I BUILT IT MYSELF. YOU...WANT TO SEE?
YES, PLEASE.
ALL RIGHT. KEEP THIS AROUND YOU SO I CAN FLY AT A GOOD SPEED.
AIR FRICTION ON BARE SKIN CAN BE DANGEROUS.
WELL... WE WOULDN'T WANT TO DO ANYTHING DANGEROUS, NOW, WOULD WE?

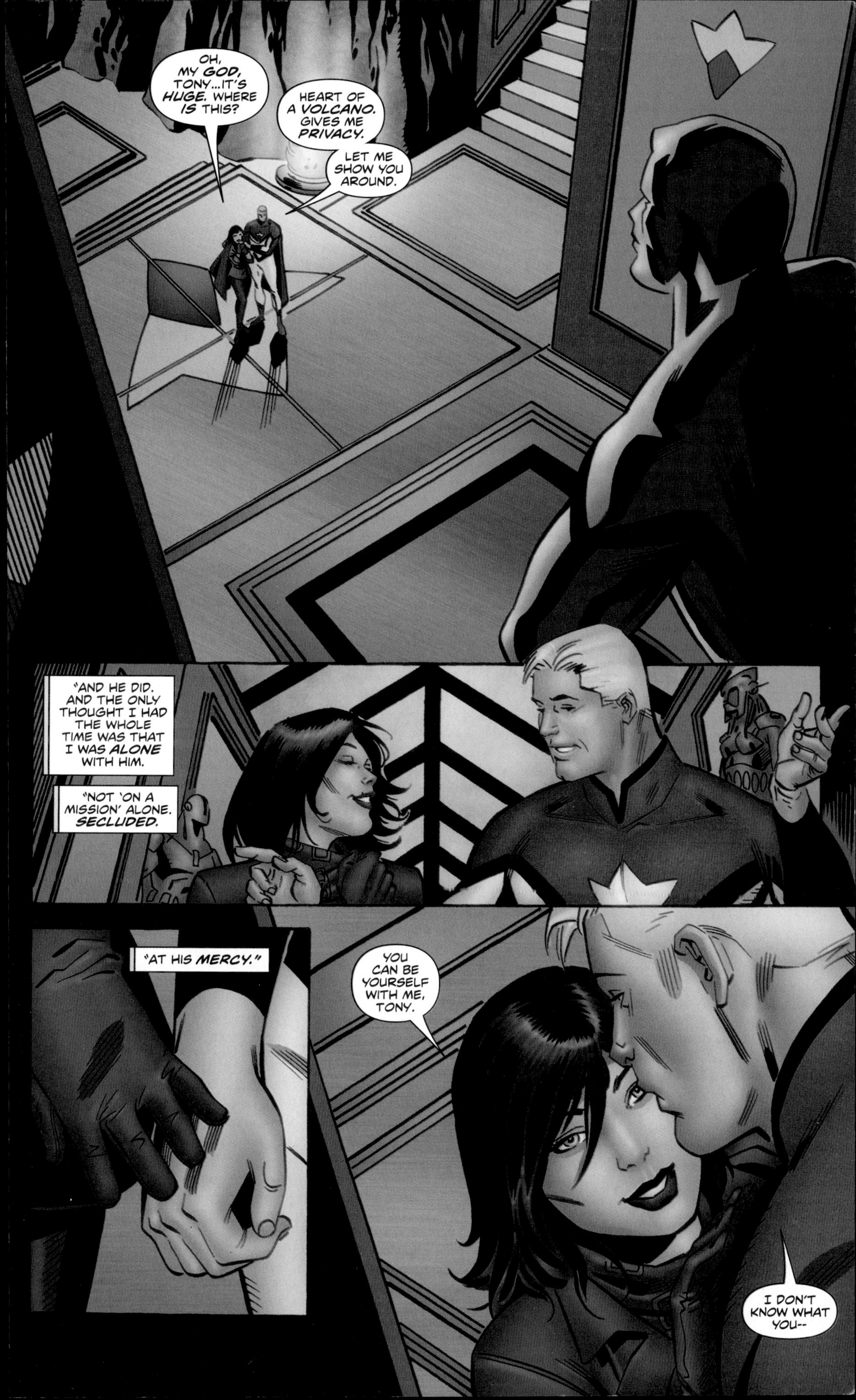
OH, MY GOD, TONY...IT'S HUGE. WHERE IS THIS?
HEART OF A VOLCANO. GIVES ME PRIVACY.
LET ME SHOW YOU AROUND.
"AND HE DID. AND THE ONLY THOUGHT I HAD THE WHOLE TIME WAS THAT I WAS ALONE WITH HIM.
"NOT 'ON A MISSION' ALONE. SECLUDED.
"AT HIS MERCY."
YOU CAN BE YOURSELF WITH ME, TONY.
I DON'T KNOW WHAT YOU--

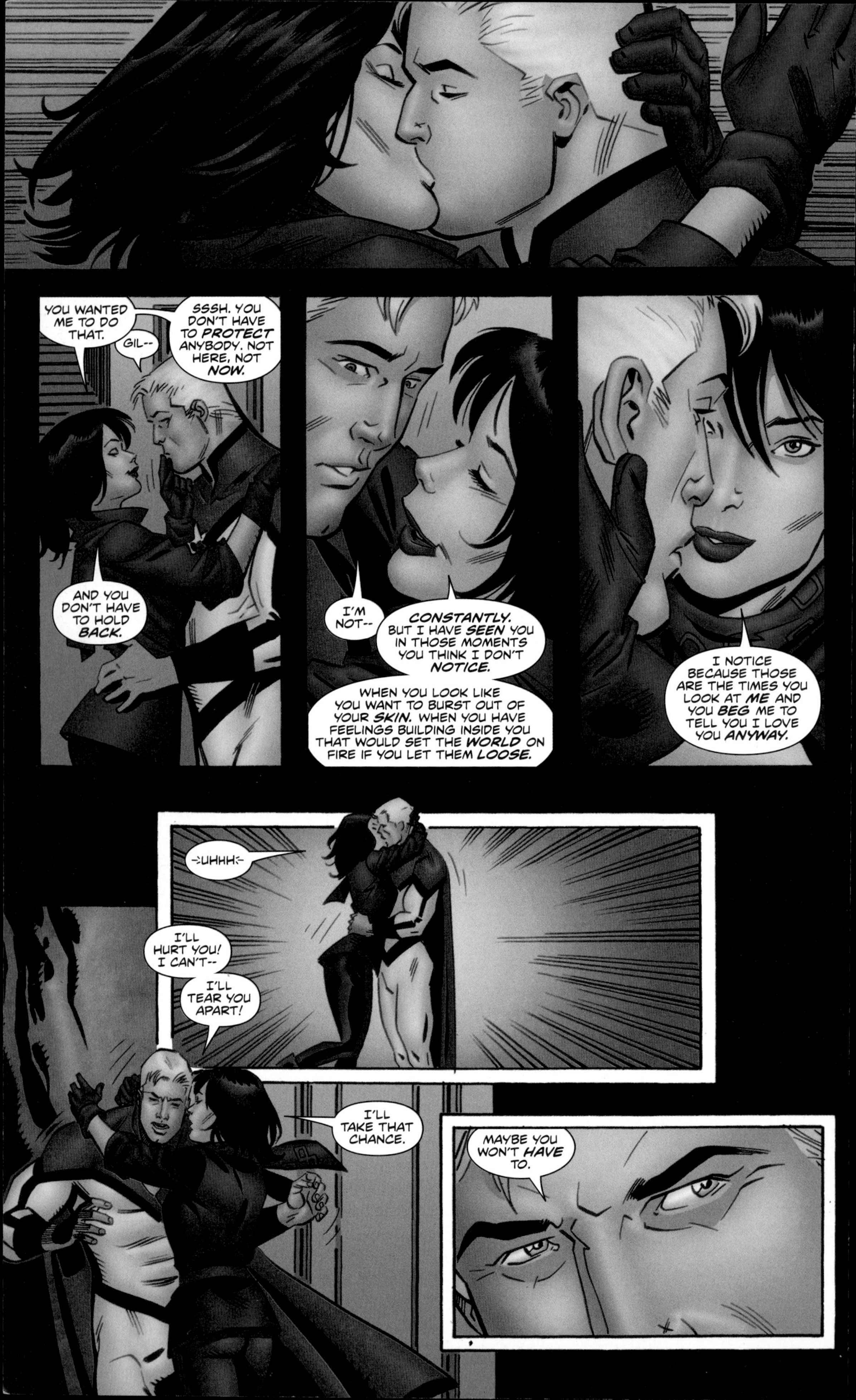
YOU WANTED ME TO DO THAT.
GIL--
SSSH. YOU DON'T HAVE TO PROTECT ANYBODY. NOT HERE, NOT NOW.
AND YOU DON'T HAVE TO HOLD BACK.
I'M NOT--
CONSTANTLY. BUT I HAVE SEEN YOU IN THOSE MOMENTS YOU THINK I DON'T NOTICE.
WHEN YOU LOOK LIKE YOU WANT TO BURST OUT OF YOUR SKIN. WHEN YOU HAVE FEELINGS BUILDING INSIDE YOU THAT WOULD SET THE WORLD ON FIRE IF YOU LET THEM LOOSE.
I NOTICE BECAUSE THOSE ARE THE TIMES YOU LOOK AT ME AND YOU BEG ME TO TELL YOU I LOVE YOU ANYWAY.
-UHHH-
I'LL HURT YOU! I CAN'T--
I'LL TEAR YOU APART!
I'LL TAKE THAT CHANCE.
MAYBE YOU WON'T HAVE TO.

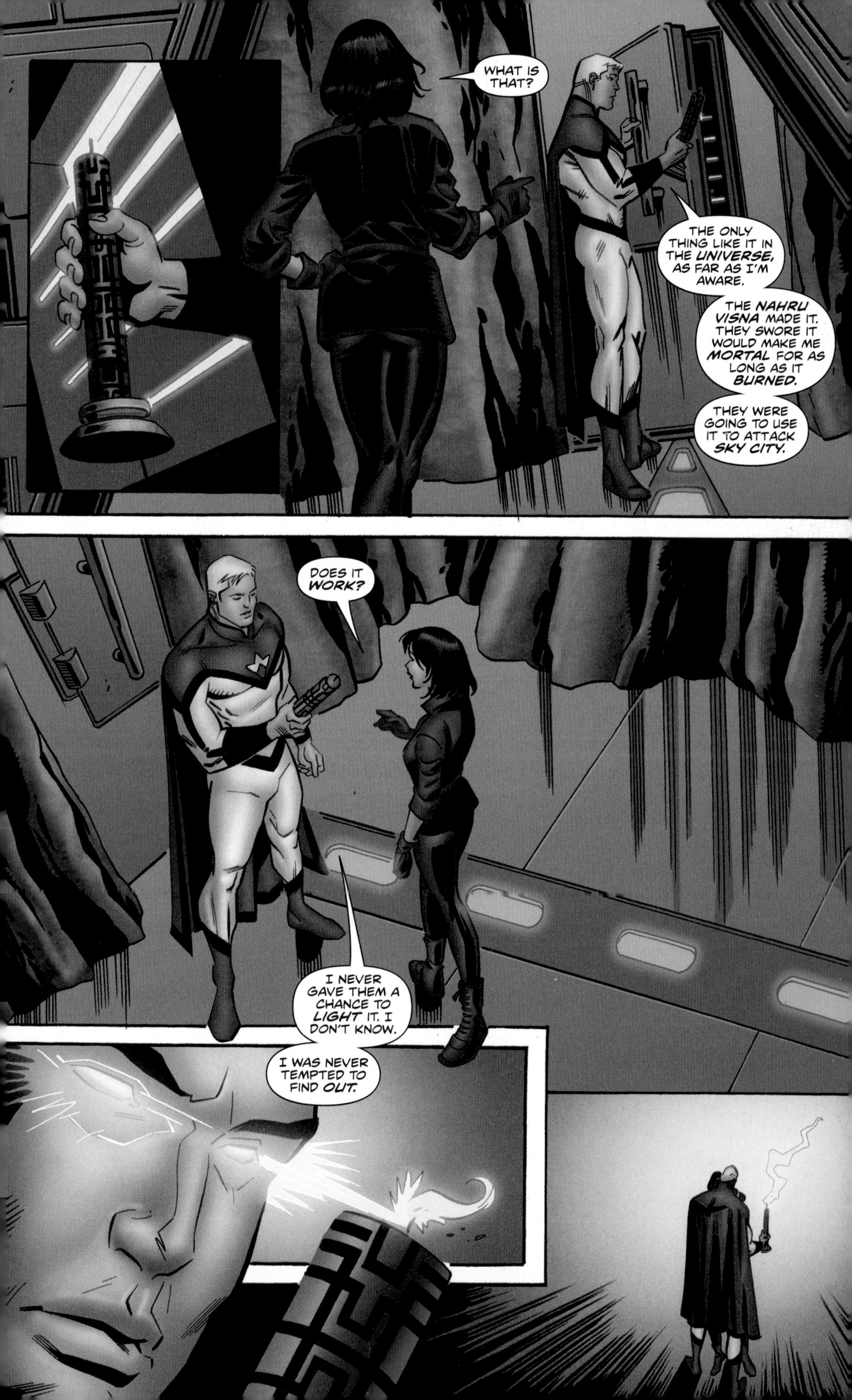
WHAT IS THAT?
THE ONLY THING LIKE IT IN THE UNIVERSE, AS FAR AS I'M AWARE.
THE NAHRU VISNA MADE IT. THEY SWORE IT WOULD MAKE ME MORTAL FOR AS LONG AS IT BURNED.
THEY WERE GOING TO USE IT TO ATTACK SKY CITY.
DOES IT WORK?
I NEVER GAVE THEM A CHANCE TO LIGHT IT. I DON'T KNOW.
I WAS NEVER TEMPTED TO FIND OUT.

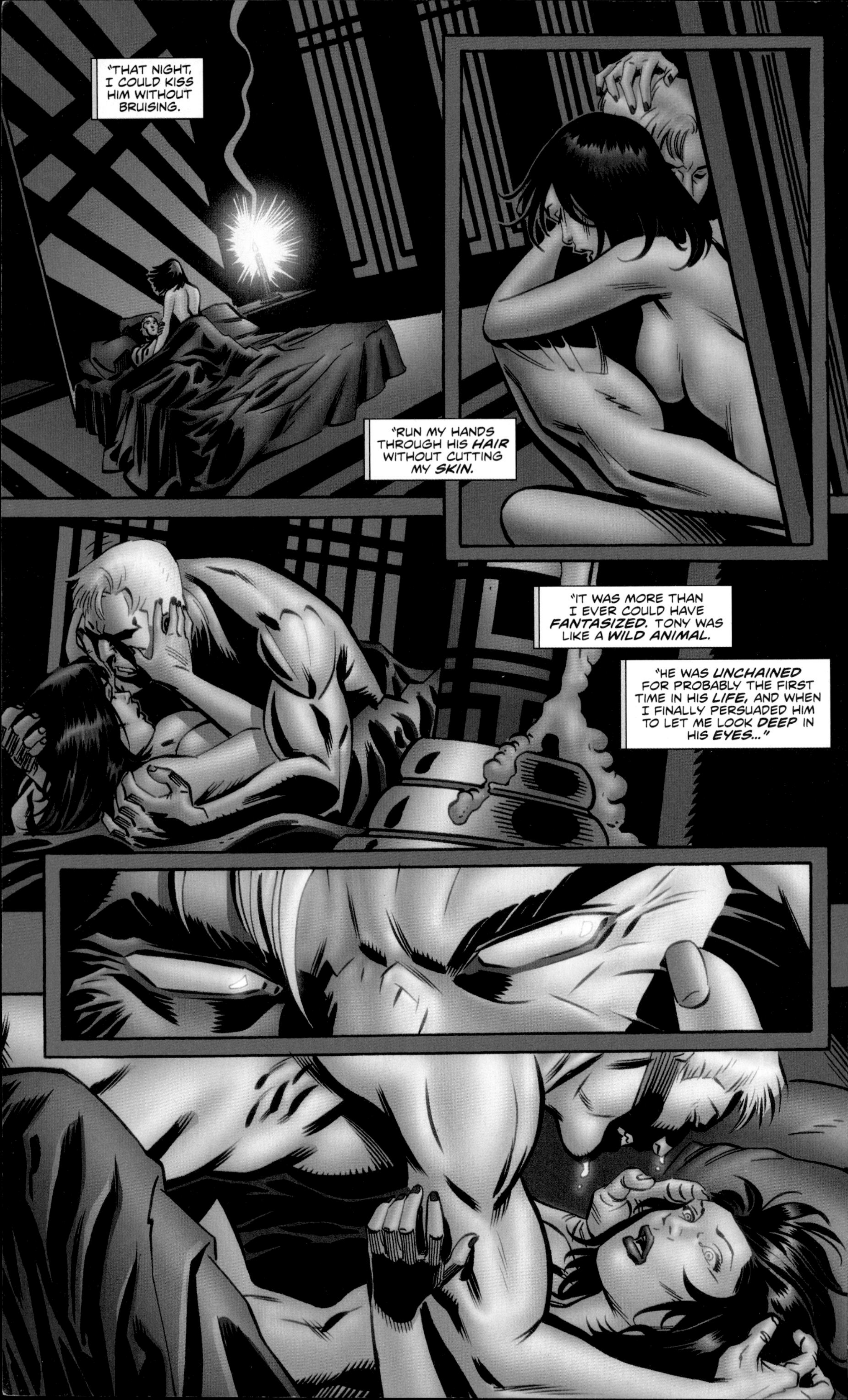
"THAT NIGHT, I COULD KISS HIM WITHOUT BRUISING.
"RUN MY HANDS THROUGH HIS HAIR WITHOUT CUTTING MY SKIN.
"IT WAS MORE THAN I EVER COULD HAVE FANTASIZED. TONY WAS LIKE A WILD ANIMAL.
"HE WAS UNCHAINED FOR PROBABLY THE FIRST TIME IN HIS LIFE, AND WHEN I FINALLY PERSUADED HIM TO LET ME LOOK DEEP IN HIS EYES..."

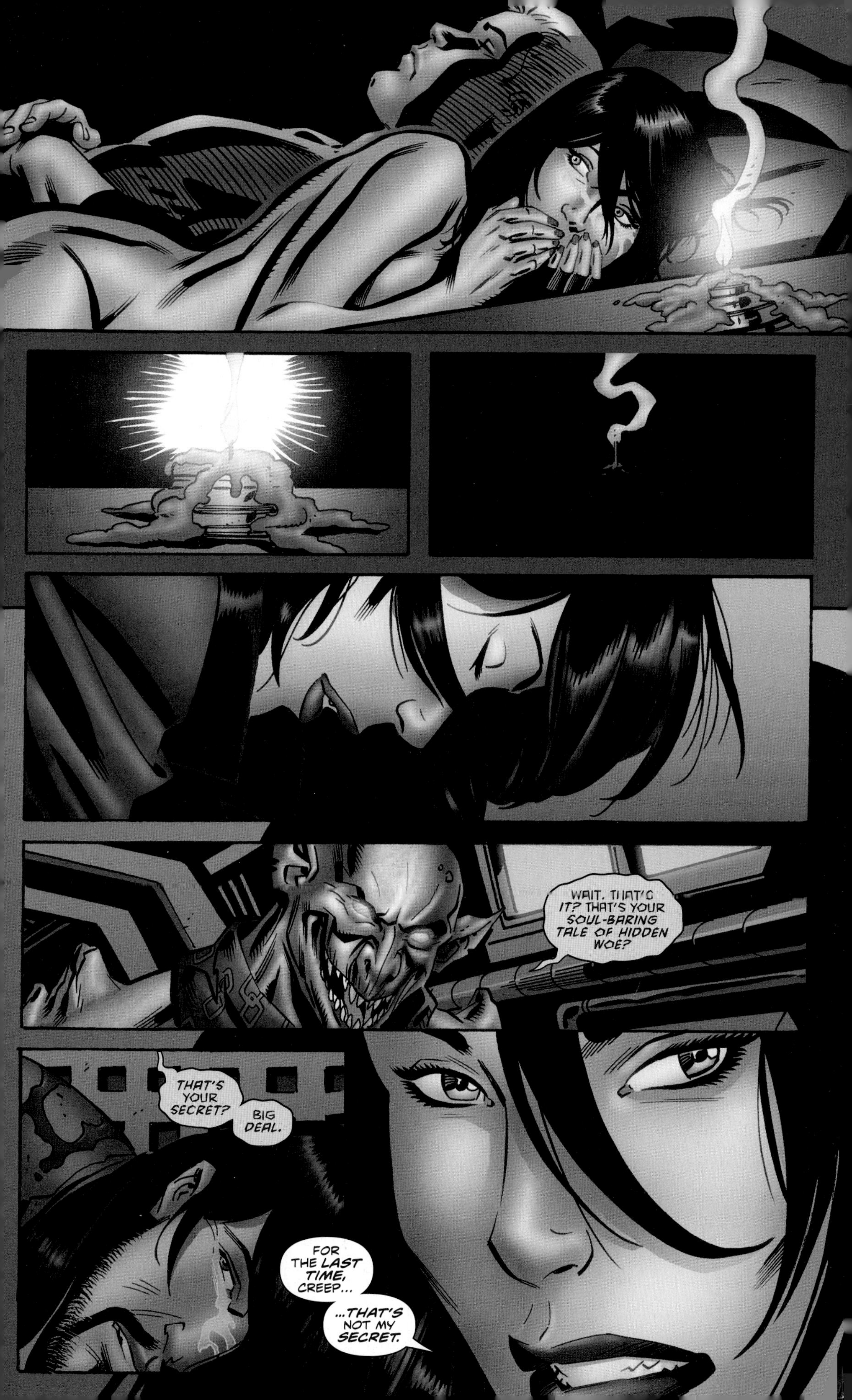
WAIT. THAT'S IT? THAT'S YOUR SOUL-BARING TALE OF HIDDEN WOE?
THAT'S YOUR SECRET?
BIG DEAL.
FOR THE LAST TIME, CREEP...
...THAT'S NOT MY SECRET.

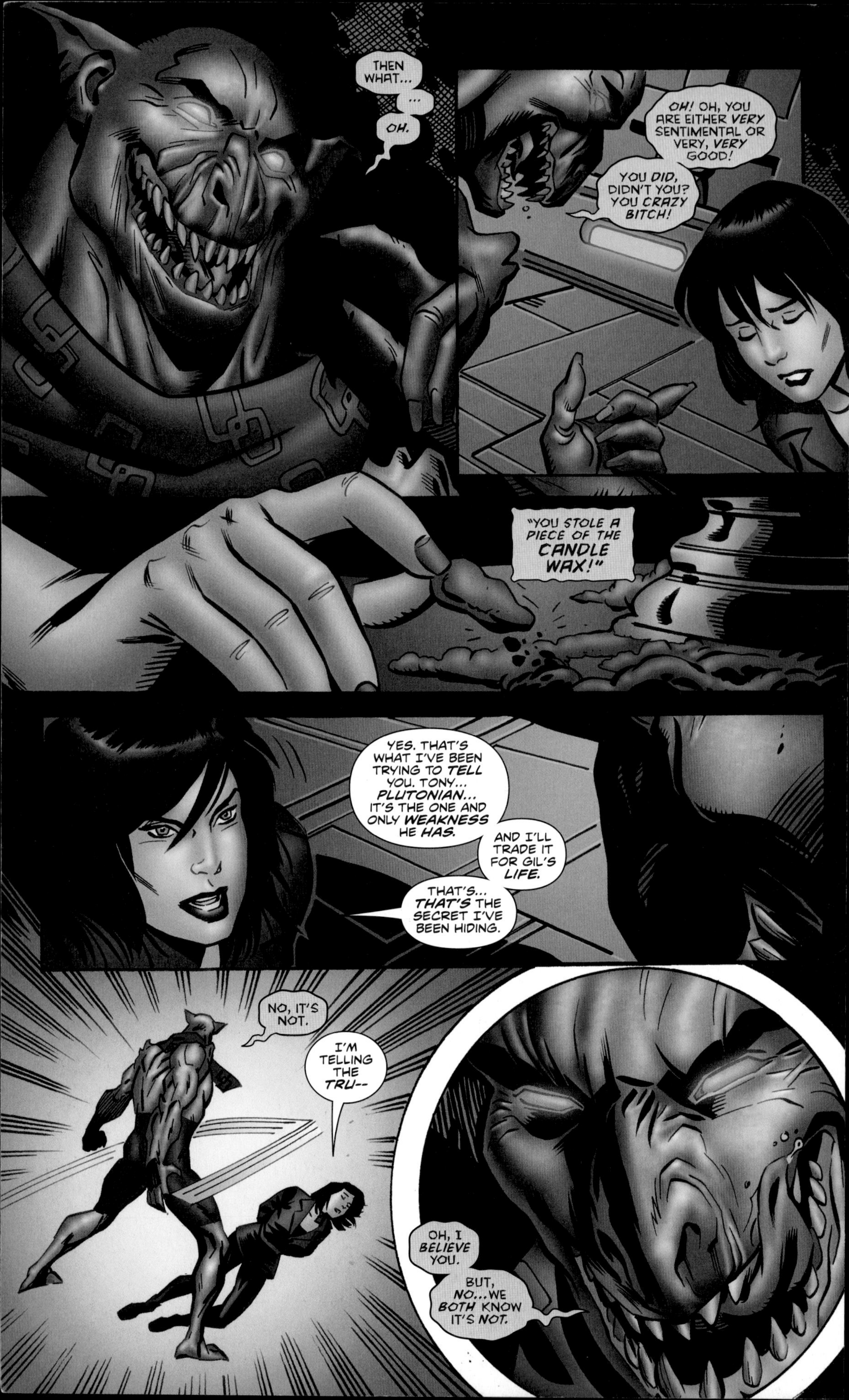
THEN WHAT...
...
OH.
OH! OH, YOU ARE EITHER VERY SENTIMENTAL OR VERY, VERY GOOD!
YOU DID, DIDN'T YOU? YOU CRAZY BITCH!
"YOU STOLE A PIECE OF THE CANDLE WAX!"
YES. THAT'S WHAT I'VE BEEN TRYING TO TELL YOU. TONY... PLUTONIAN... IT'S THE ONE AND ONLY WEAKNESS HE HAS.
AND I'LL TRADE IT FOR GIL'S LIFE.
THAT'S... THAT'S THE SECRET I'VE BEEN HIDING.
NO, IT'S NOT.
I'M TELLING THE TRU--
OH, I BELIEVE YOU.
BUT, NO... WE BOTH KNOW IT'S NOT.

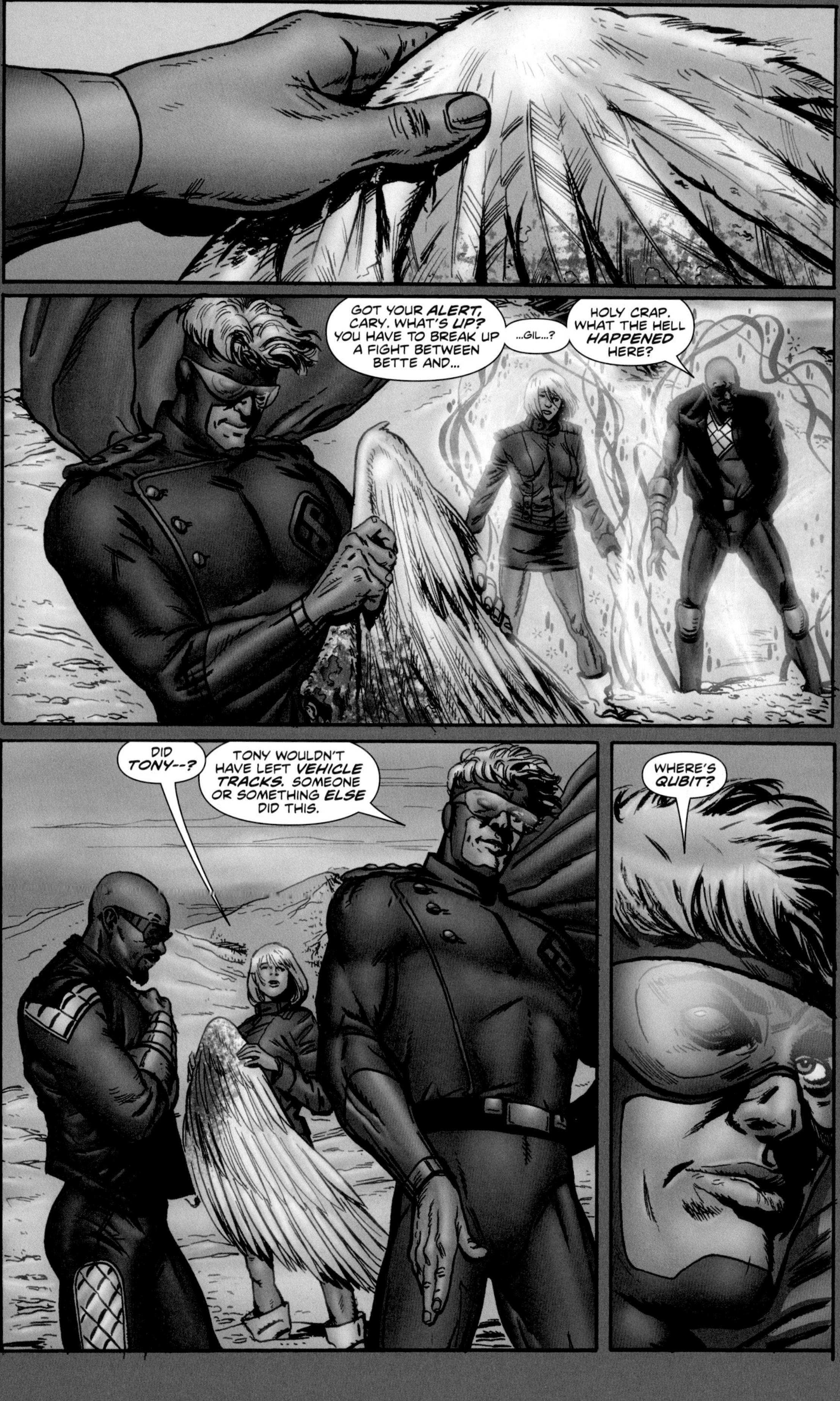
GOT YOUR ALERT, CARY. WHAT'S UP? YOU HAVE TO BREAK UP A FIGHT BETWEEN BETTE AND...
...GIL...?
HOLY CRAP. WHAT THE HELL HAPPENED HERE?
DID TONY--?
TONY WOULDN'T HAVE LEFT VEHICLE TRACKS. SOMEONE OR SOMETHING ELSE DID THIS.
WHERE'S QUBIT?

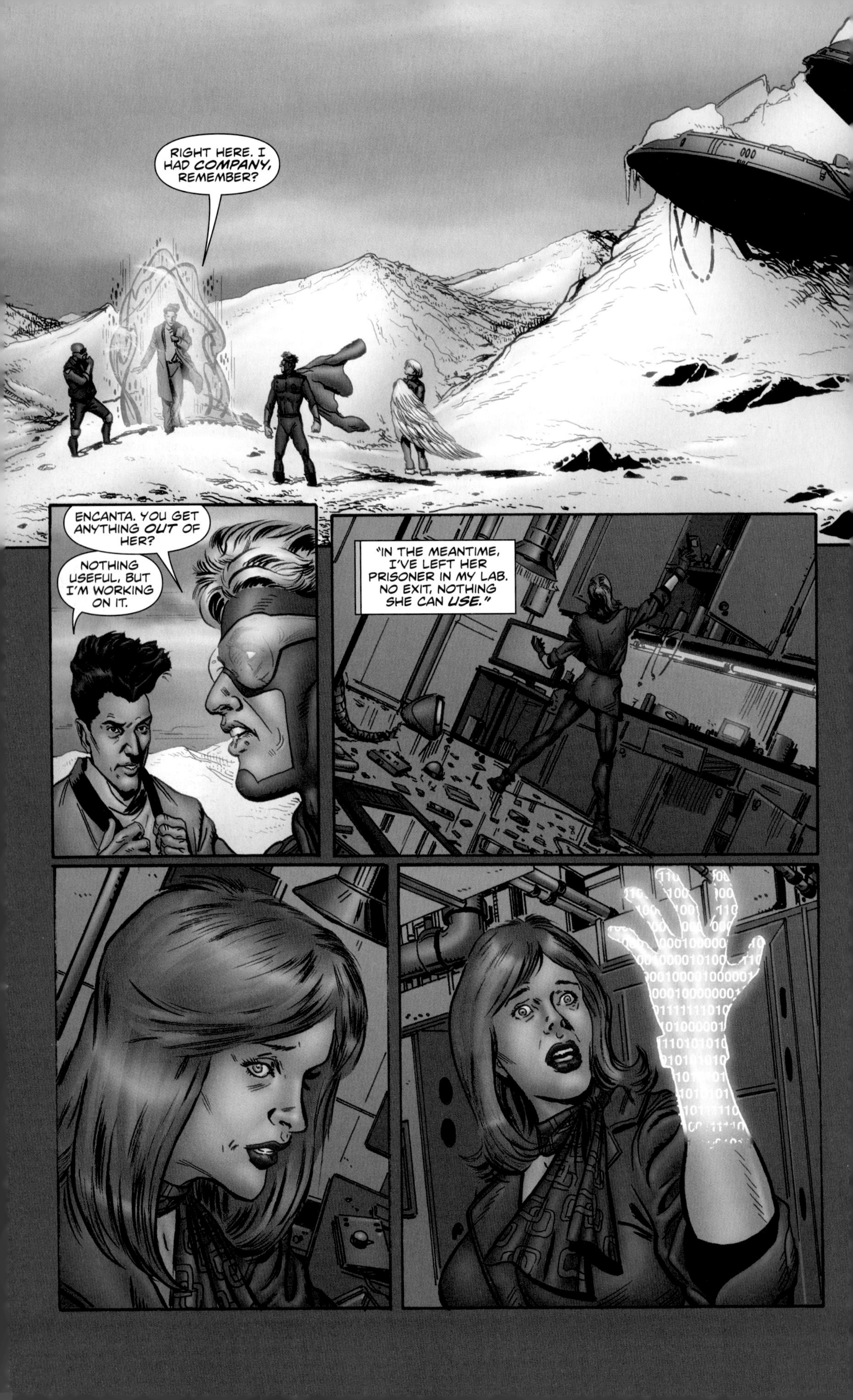
RIGHT HERE. I HAD COMPANY, REMEMBER?
ENCANTA. YOU GET ANYTHING OUT OF HER?
NOTHING USEFUL, BUT I'M WORKING ON IT.
"IN THE MEANTIME, I'VE LEFT HER PRISONER IN MY LAB. NO EXIT, NOTHING SHE CAN USE."

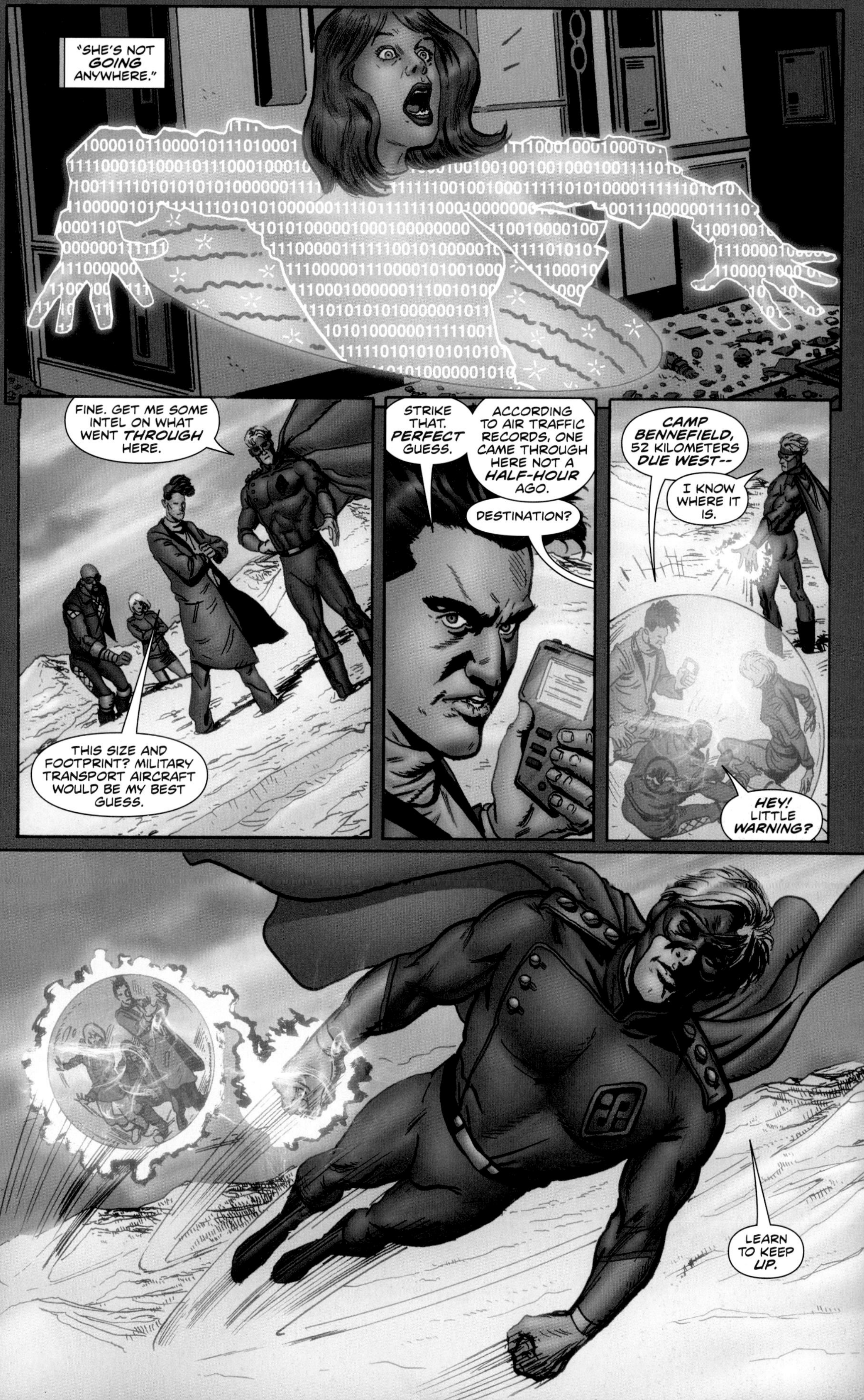
"SHE'S NOT GOING ANYWHERE."
FINE. GET ME SOME INTEL ON WHAT WENT THROUGH HERE.
THIS SIZE AND FOOTPRINT? MILITARY TRANSPORT AIRCRAFT WOULD BE MY BEST GUESS.
STRIKE THAT. PERFECT GUESS.
ACCORDING TO AIR TRAFFIC RECORDS, ONE CAME THROUGH HERE NOT A HALF-HOUR AGO.
DESTINATION?
CAMP BENNEFIELD, 52 KILOMETERS DUE WEST--
I KNOW WHERE IT IS.
HEY! LITTLE WARNING?
LEARN TO KEEP UP.

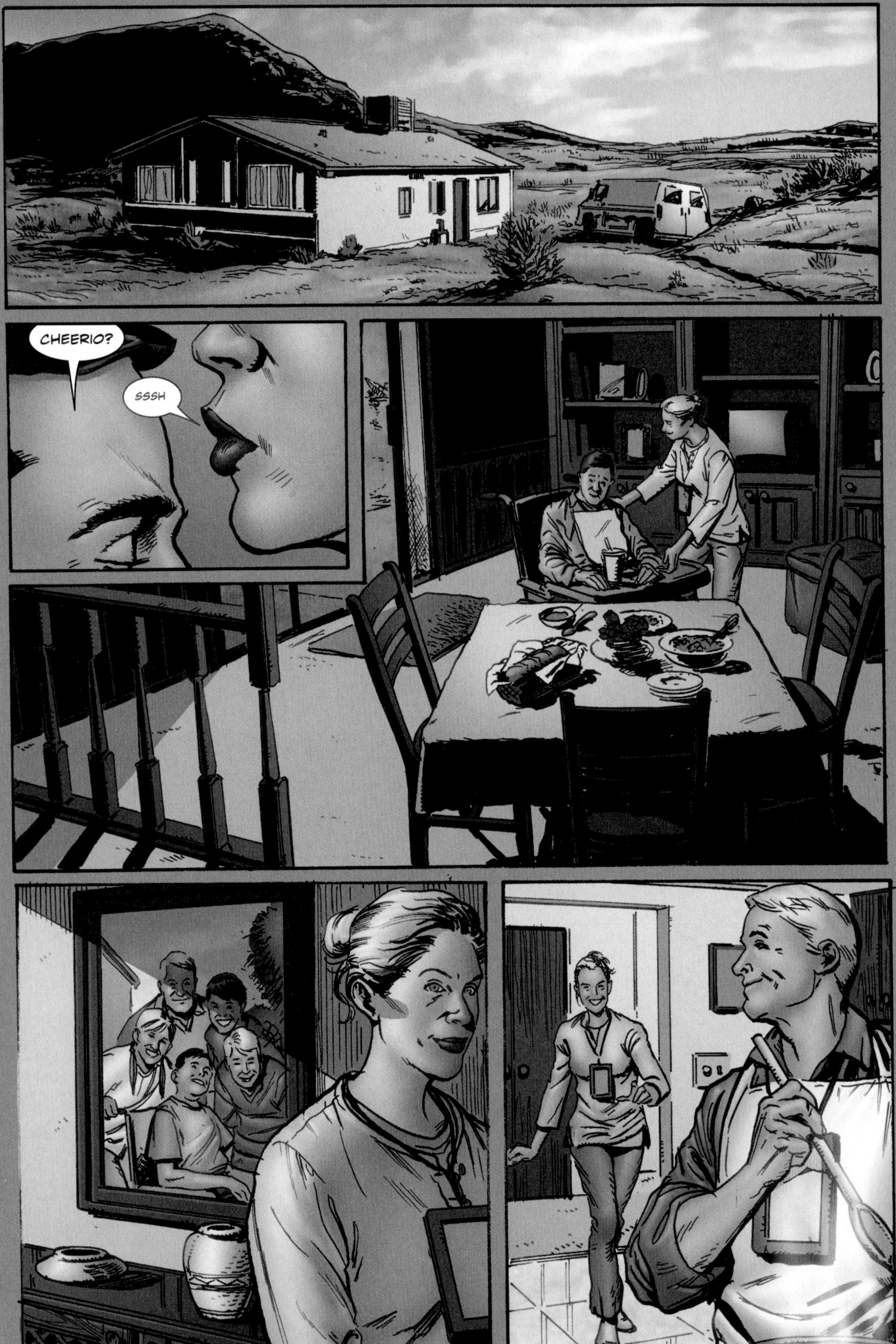
CHEERIO?
SSSH

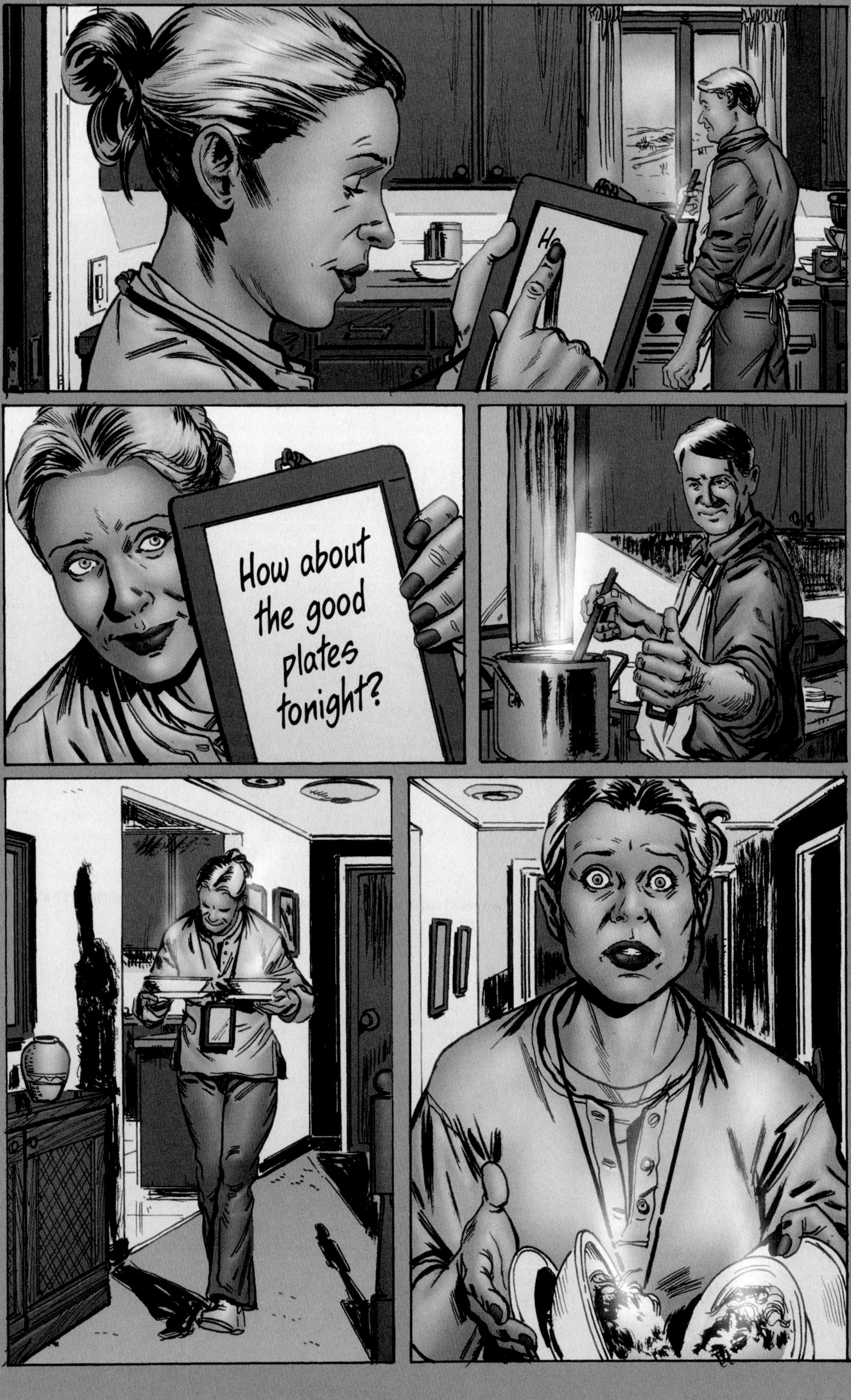
How about the good plates tonight?

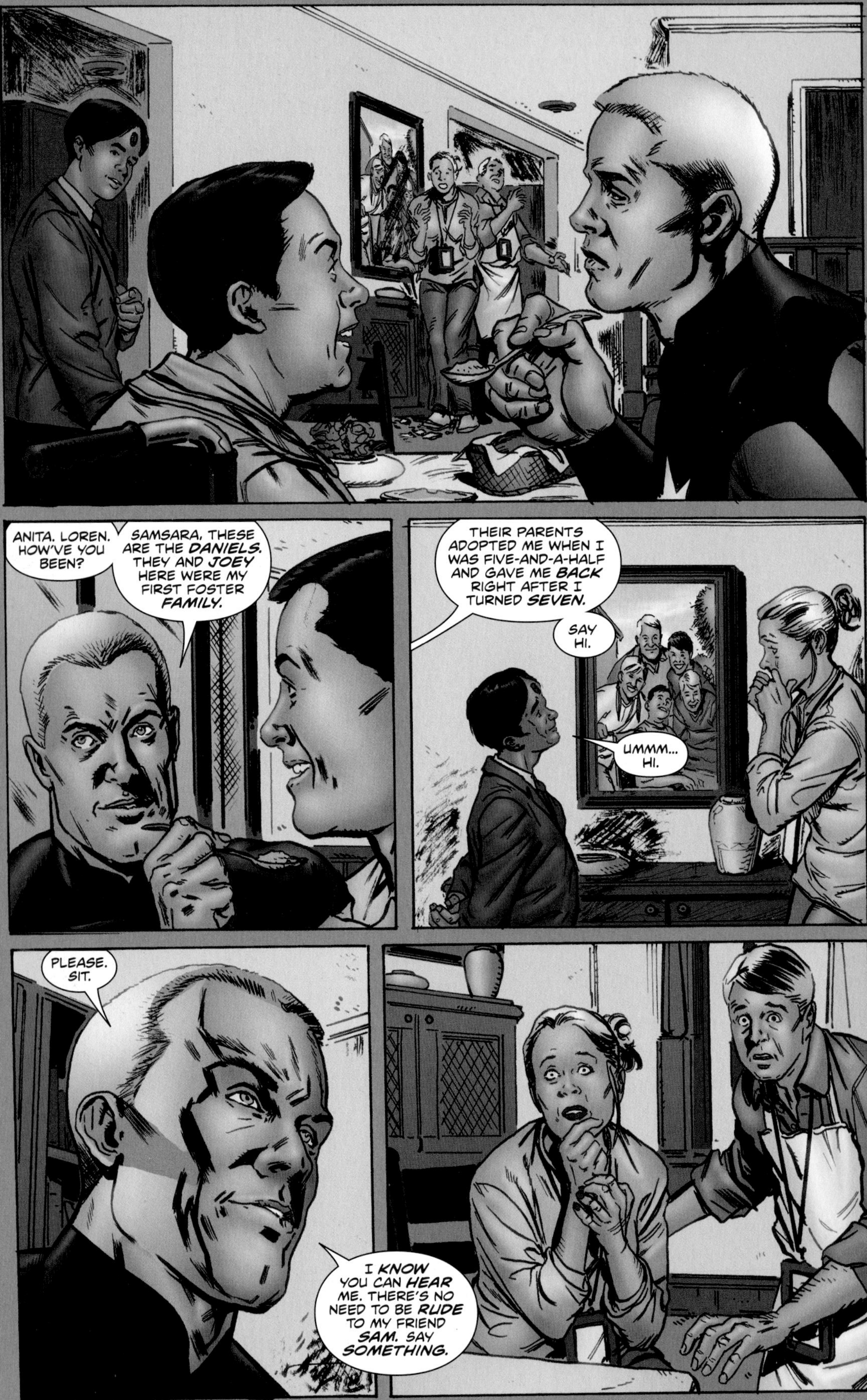

ANITA. LOREN. HOW'VE YOU BEEN?
SAMSARA, THESE ARE THE DANIELS. THEY AND JOEY HERE WERE MY FIRST FOSTER FAMILY.
THEIR PARENTS ADOPTED ME WHEN I WAS FIVE-AND-A-HALF AND GAVE ME BACK RIGHT AFTER I TURNED SEVEN.
SAY HI.
UMMM... HI.
PLEASE. SIT.
I KNOW YOU CAN HEAR ME. THERE'S NO NEED TO BE RUDE TO MY FRIEND SAM. SAY SOMETHING.

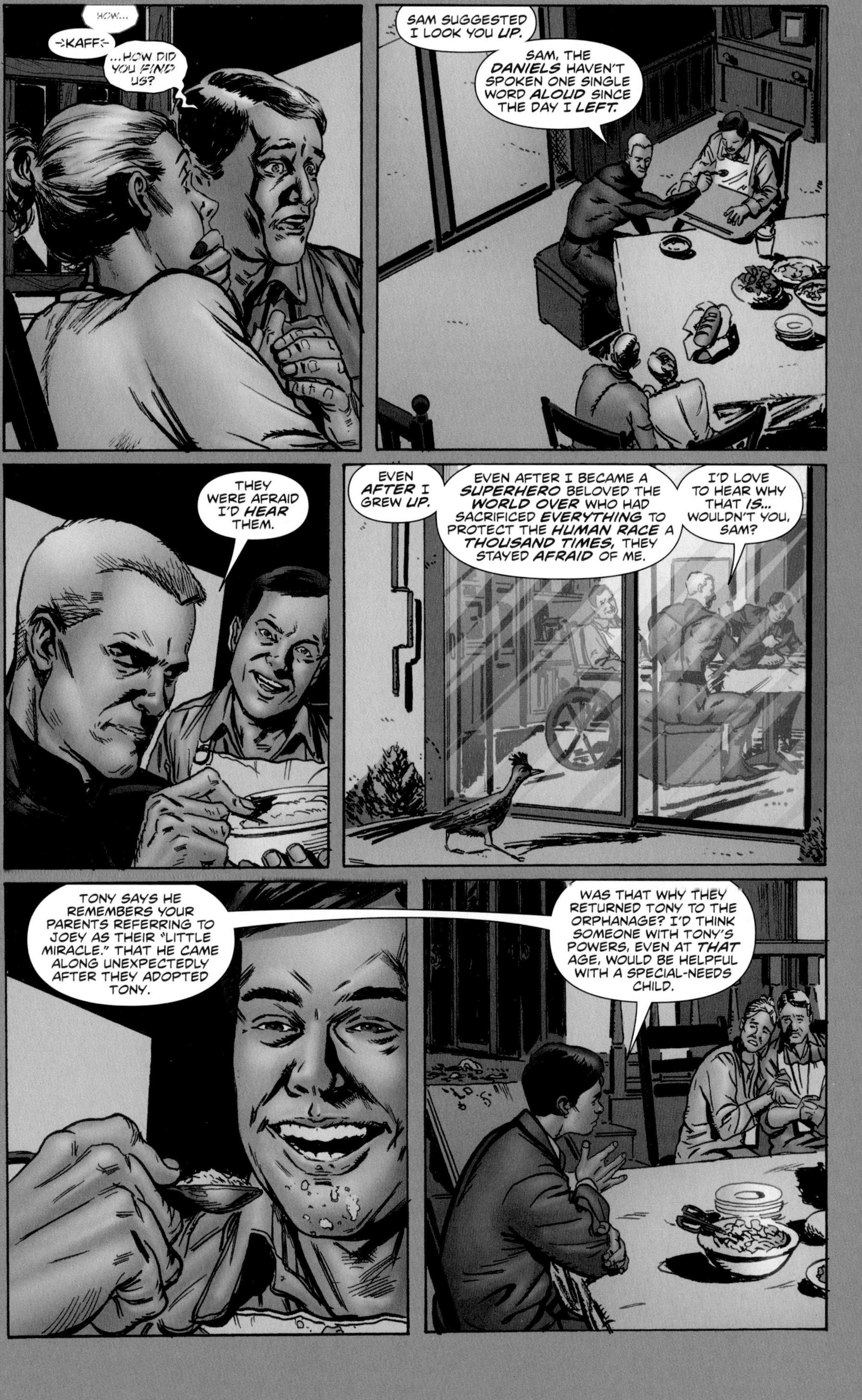
HOW...
-KAFF-
...HOW DID YOU FIND US?
SAM SUGGESTED I LOOK YOU UP.
SAM, THE DANIELS HAVEN'T SPOKEN ONE SINGLE WORD ALOUD SINCE THE DAY I LEFT.
THEY WERE AFRAID I'D HEAR THEM.
EVEN AFTER I GREW UP.
EVEN AFTER I BECAME A SUPERHERO BELOVED THE WORLD OVER WHO HAD SACRIFICED EVERYTHING TO PROTECT THE HUMAN RACE A THOUSAND TIMES, THEY STAYED AFRAID OF ME.
I'D LOVE TO HEAR WHY THAT IS... WOULDN'T YOU, SAM?
TONY SAYS HE REMEMBERS YOUR PARENTS REFERRING TO JOEY AS THEIR "LITTLE MIRACLE." THAT HE CAME ALONG UNEXPECTEDLY AFTER THEY ADOPTED TONY.
WAS THAT WHY THEY RETURNED TONY TO THE ORPHANAGE? I'D THINK SOMEONE WITH TONY'S POWERS, EVEN AT THAT AGE, WOULD BE HELPFUL WITH A SPECIAL-NEEDS CHILD.

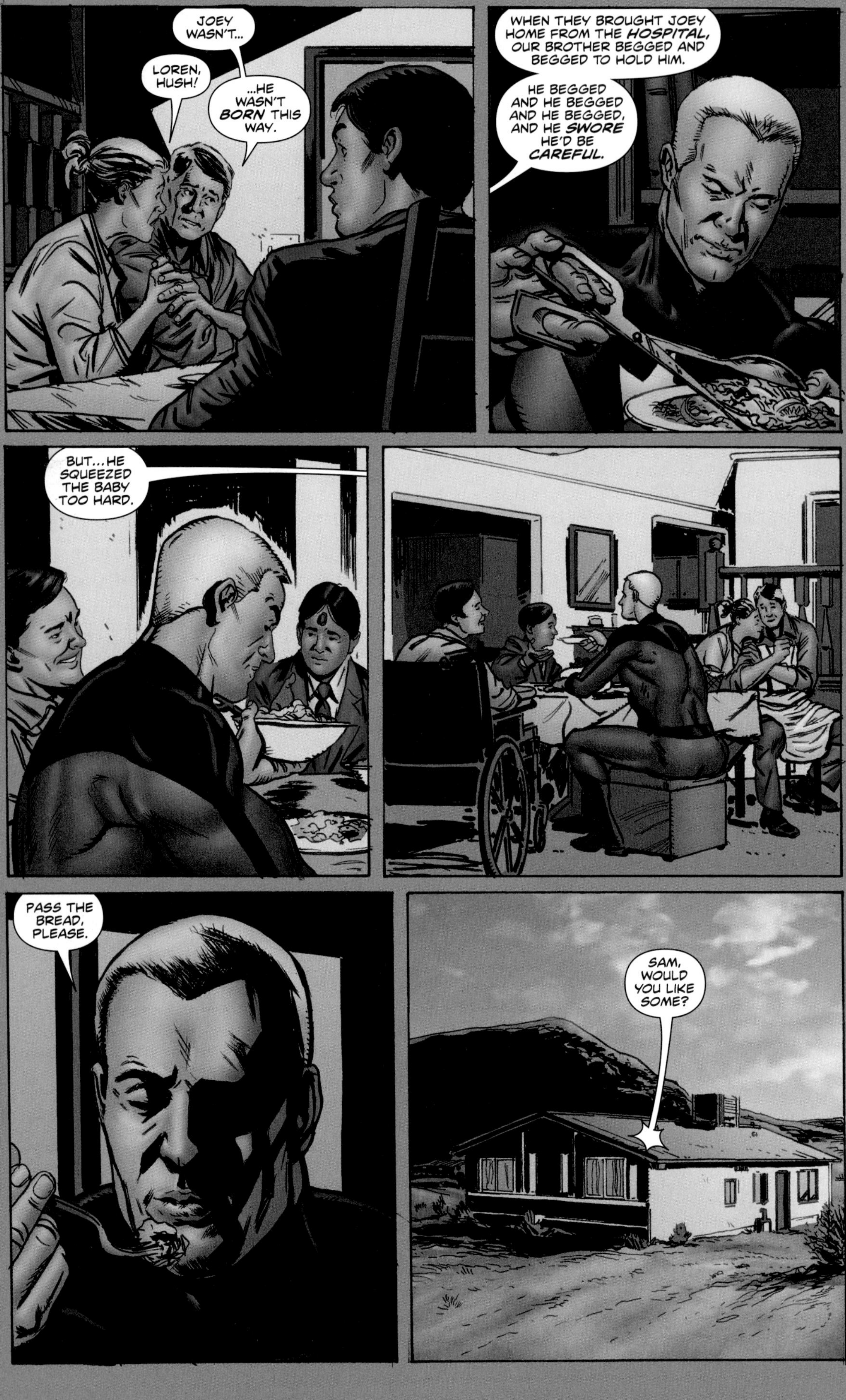
JOEY WASN'T...
LOREN, HUSH!
...HE WASN'T BORN THIS WAY.
WHEN THEY BROUGHT JOEY HOME FROM THE HOSPITAL, OUR BROTHER BEGGED AND BEGGED TO HOLD HIM.
HE BEGGED AND HE BEGGED AND HE BEGGED, AND HE SWORE HE'D BE CAREFUL.
BUT... HE SQUEEZED THE BABY TOO HARD.
PASS THE BREAD, PLEASE.
SAM, WOULD YOU LIKE SOME?

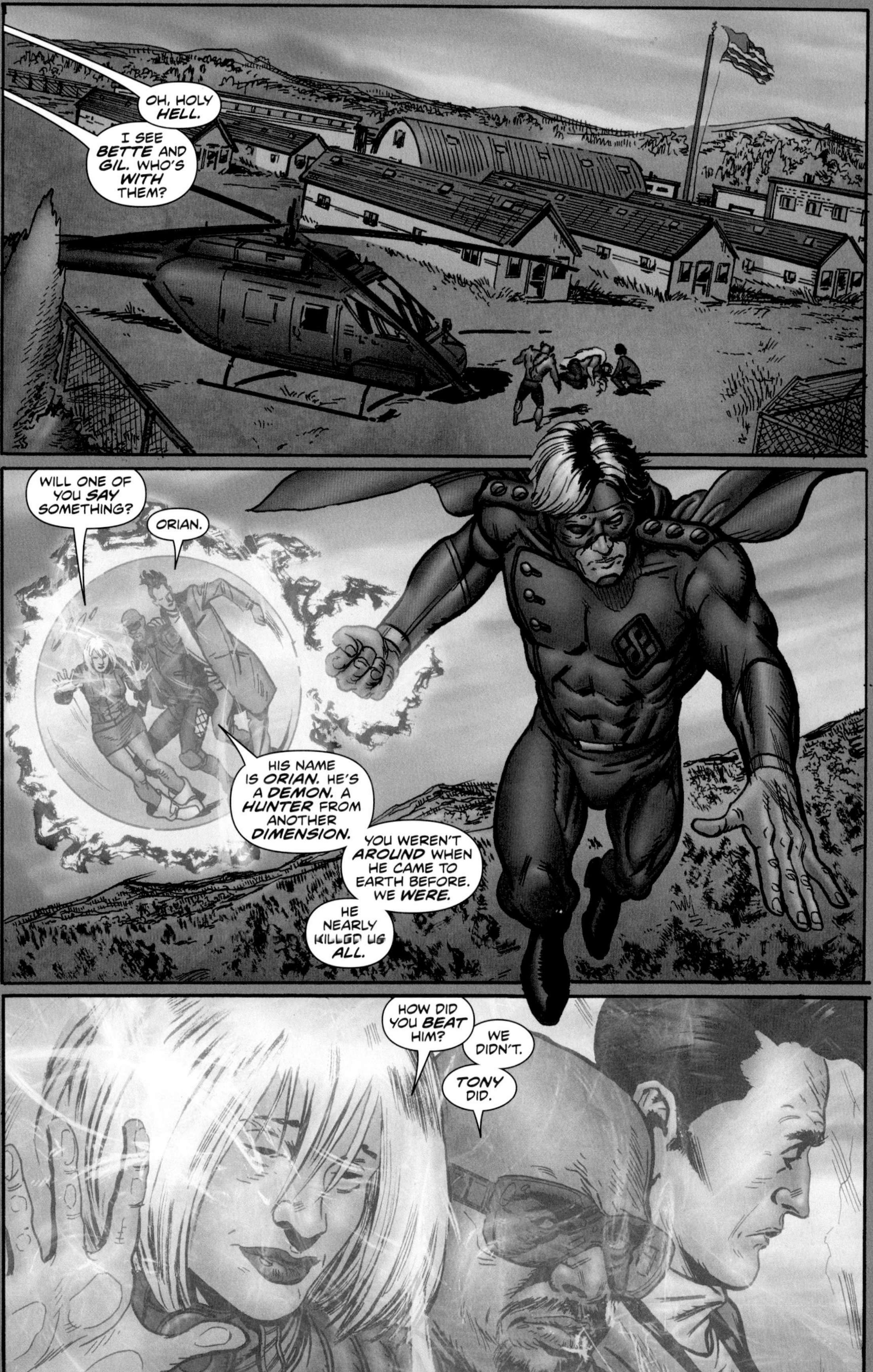
OH, HOLY HELL.
I SEE BETTE AND GIL. WHO'S WITH THEM?
WILL ONE OF YOU SAY SOMETHING?
ORIAN.
HIS NAME IS ORIAN. HE'S A DEMON. A HUNTER FROM ANOTHER DIMENSION.
YOU WEREN'T AROUND WHEN HE CAME TO EARTH BEFORE. WE WERE.
HE NEARLY KILLED US ALL.
HOW DID YOU BEAT HIM?
WE DIDN'T.
TONY DID.

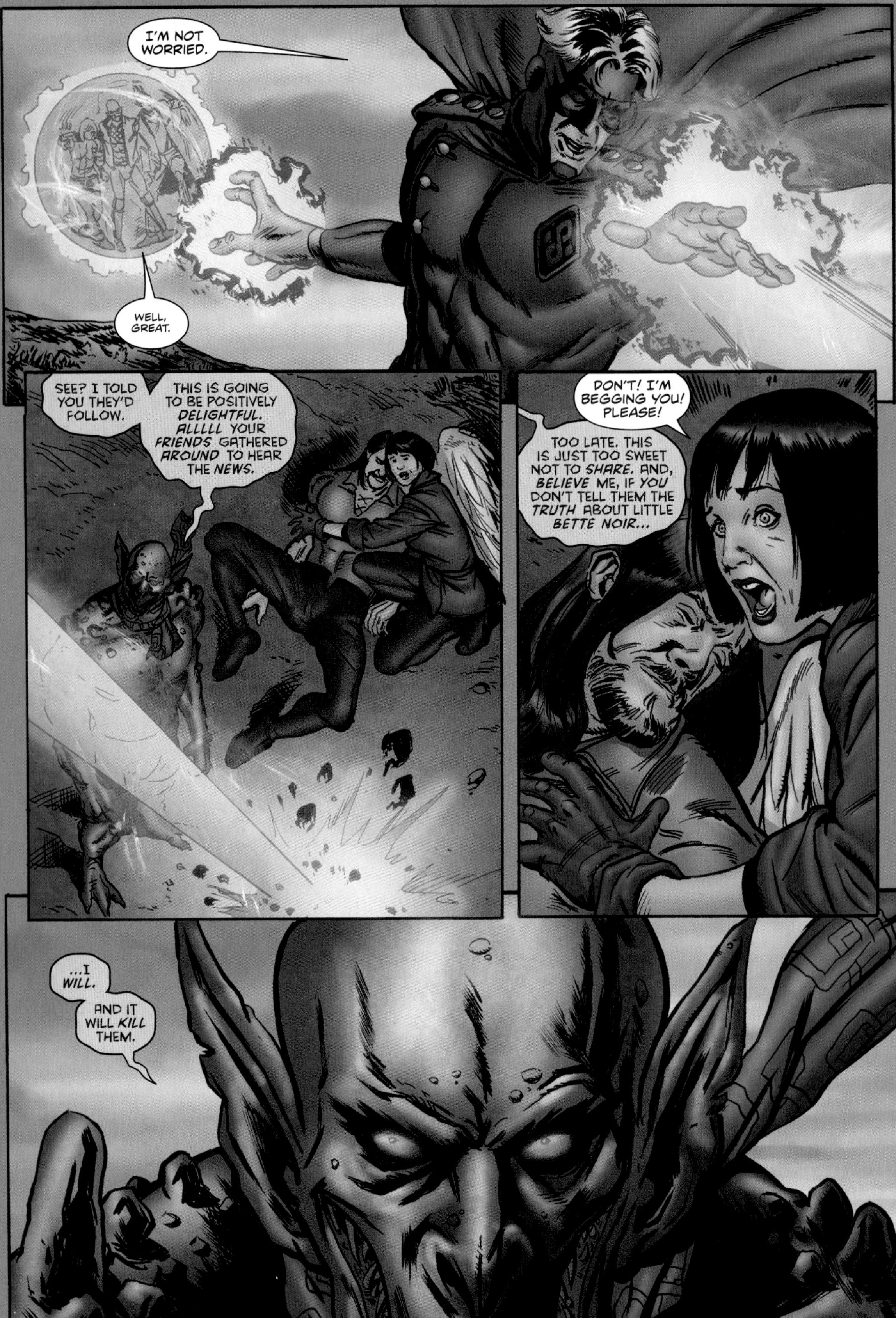
I'M NOT WORRIED.
WELL, GREAT.
SEE? I TOLD YOU THEY'D FOLLOW.
THIS IS GOING TO BE POSITIVELY DELIGHTFUL. ALLLLL YOUR FRIENDS GATHERED AROUND TO HEAR THE NEWS.
DON'T! I'M BEGGING YOU! PLEASE!
TOO LATE. THIS IS JUST TOO SWEET NOT TO SHARE. AND, BELIEVE ME, IF YOU DON'T TELL THEM THE TRUTH ABOUT LITTLE BETTE NOIR...
...I WILL.
AND IT WILL KILL THEM.

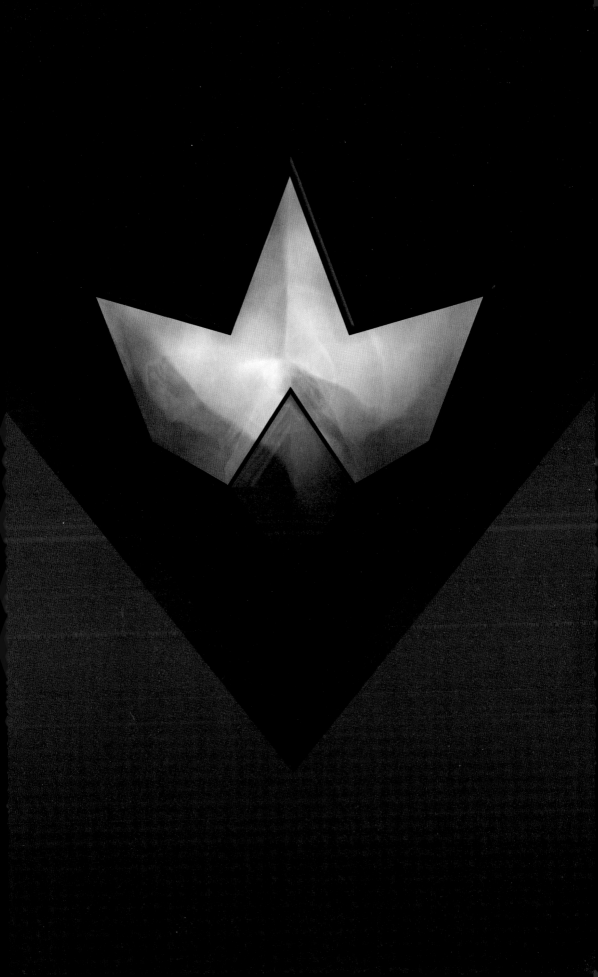

CHAPTER 12

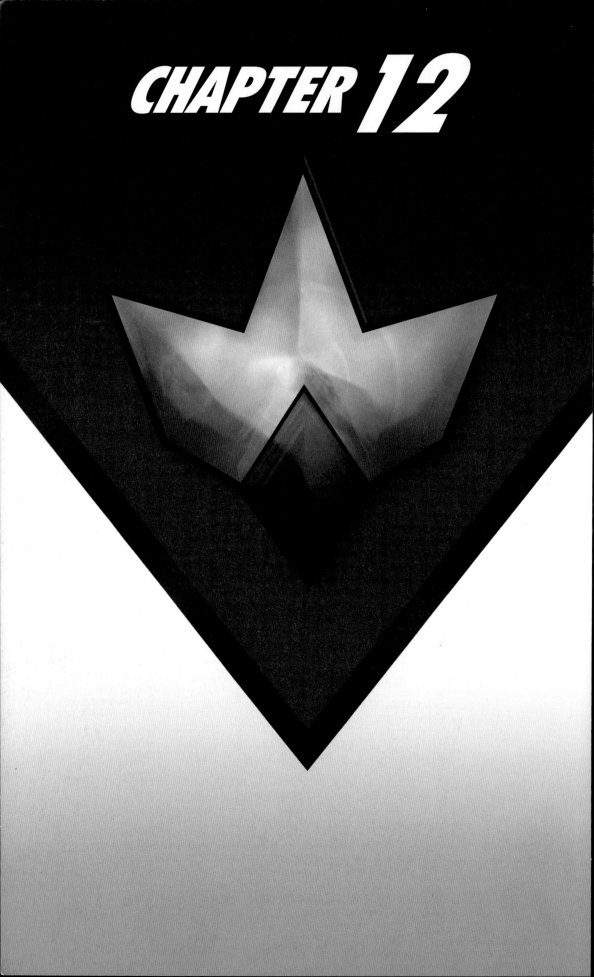

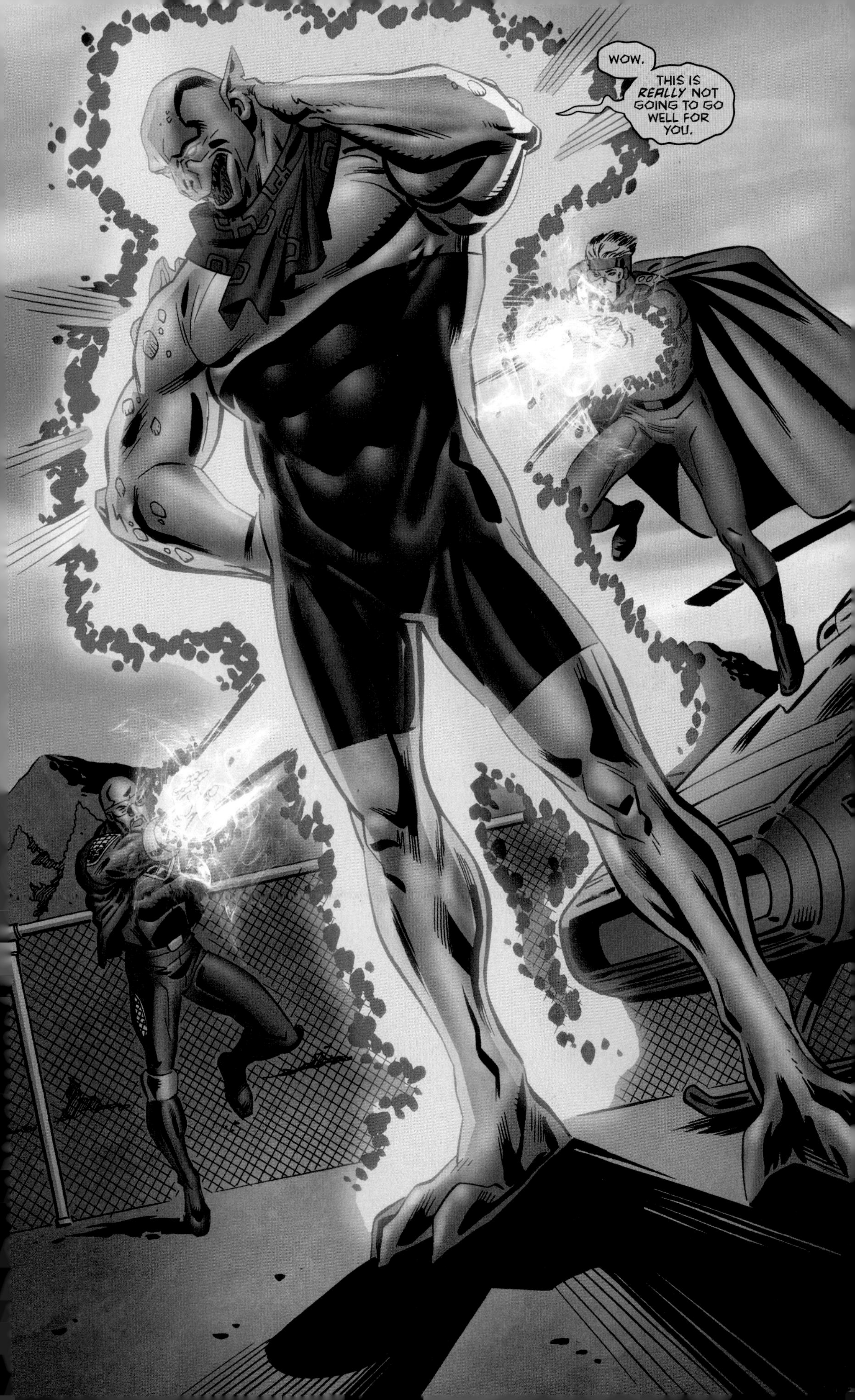
WOW.
THIS IS *REALLY* NOT GOING TO GO WELL FOR YOU.

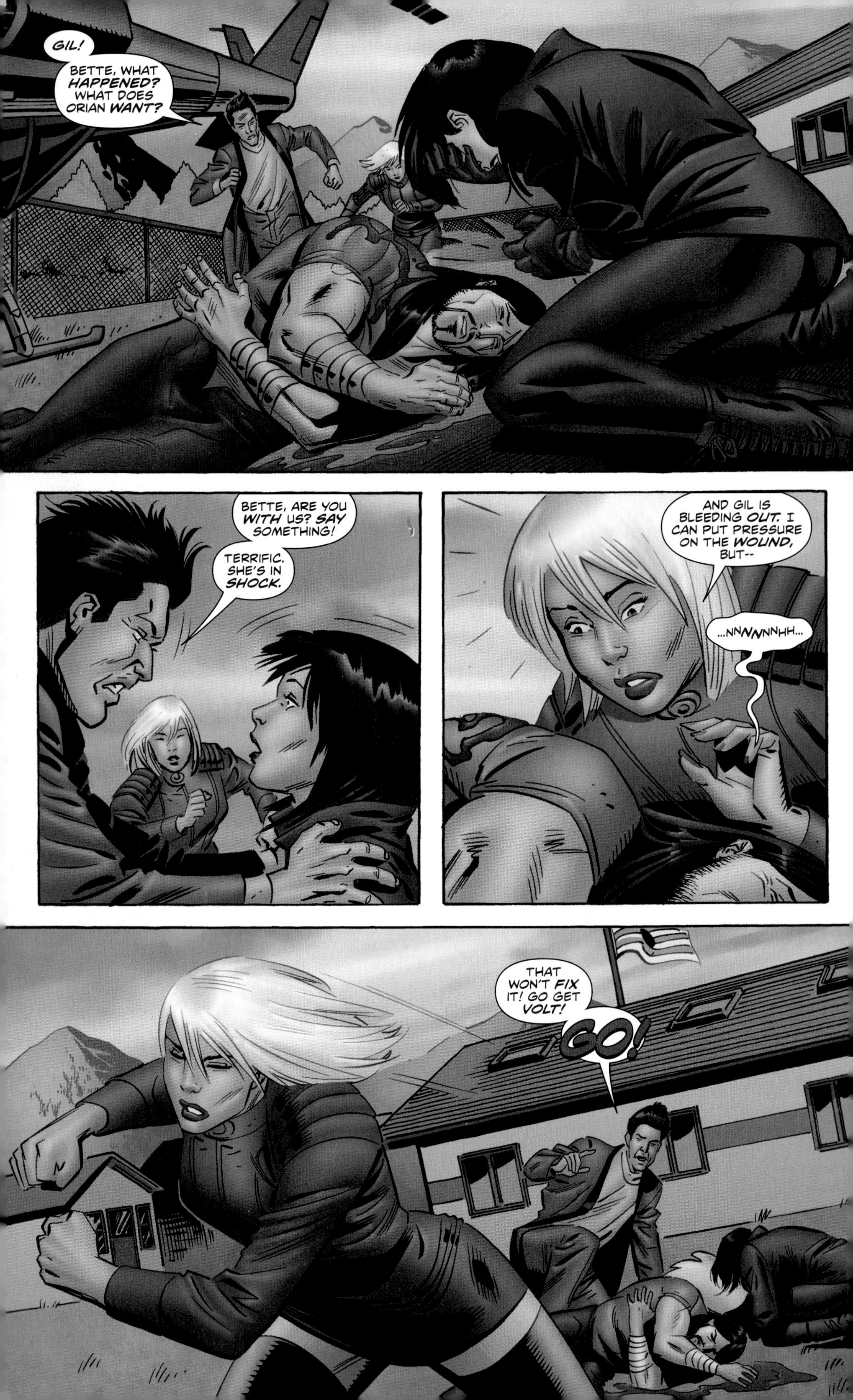
GIL!
BETTE, WHAT HAPPENED? WHAT DOES ORIAN WANT?
BETTE, ARE YOU WITH US? SAY SOMETHING!
TERRIFIC. SHE'S IN SHOCK.
AND GIL IS BLEEDING OUT. I CAN PUT PRESSURE ON THE WOUND, BUT--
...NNNNNNHH...
THAT WON'T FIX IT! GO GET VOLT!
GO!

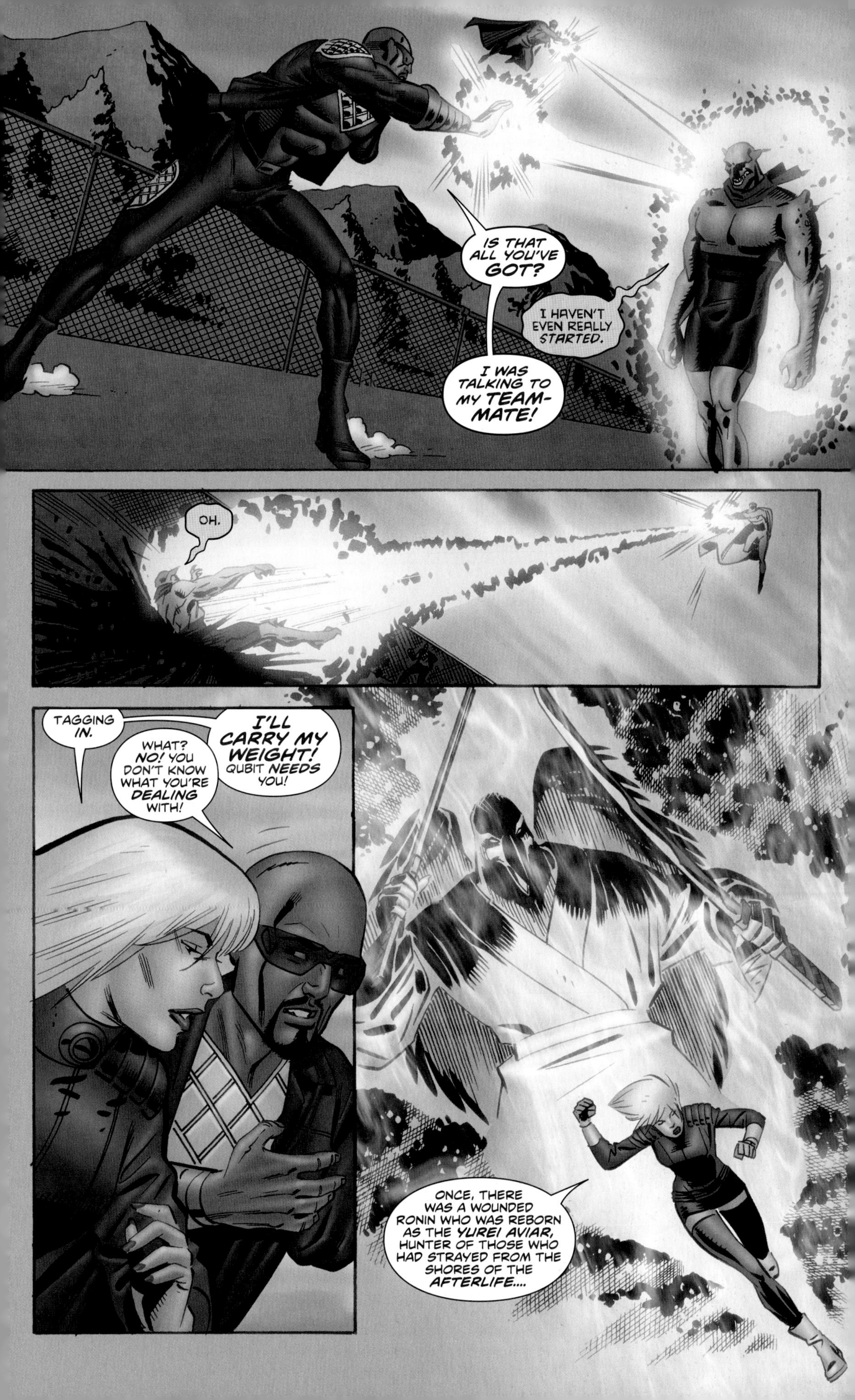
IS THAT ALL YOU'VE GOT?
I HAVEN'T EVEN REALLY STARTED.
I WAS TALKING TO MY TEAM-MATE!
OH.
TAGGING IN.
I'LL CARRY MY WEIGHT! QUBIT NEEDS YOU!
WHAT? NO! YOU DON'T KNOW WHAT YOU'RE DEALING WITH!
ONCE, THERE WAS A WOUNDED RONIN WHO WAS REBORN AS THE YUREI AVIAR, HUNTER OF THOSE WHO HAD STRAYED FROM THE SHORES OF THE AFTERLIFE....

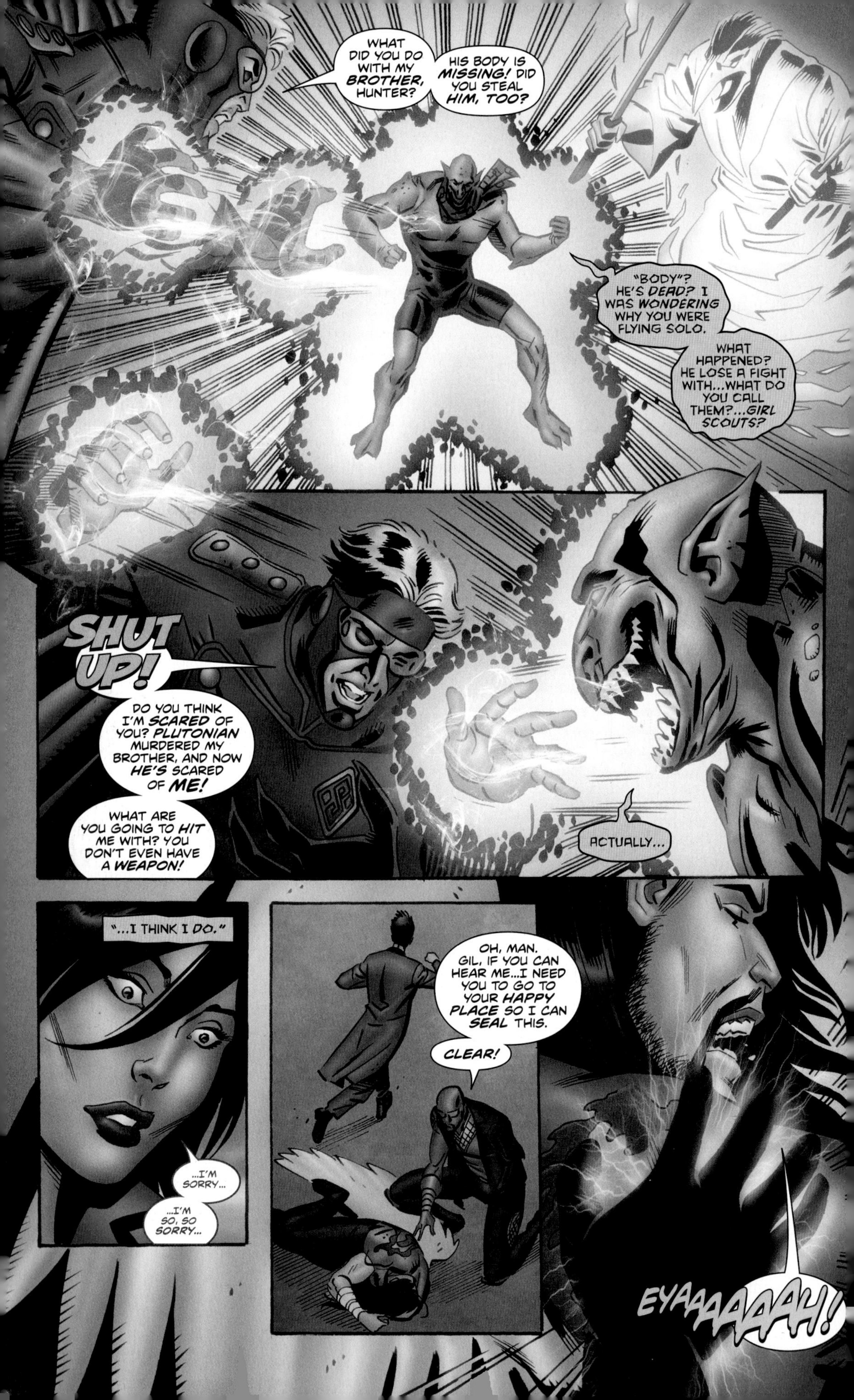
WHAT DID YOU DO WITH MY BROTHER, HUNTER?
HIS BODY IS MISSING! DID YOU STEAL HIM, TOO?
"BODY"? HE'S DEAD? I WAS WONDERING WHY YOU WERE FLYING SOLO.
WHAT HAPPENED? HE LOSE A FIGHT WITH...WHAT DO YOU CALL THEM?...GIRL SCOUTS?
SHUT UP!
DO YOU THINK I'M SCARED OF YOU? PLUTONIAN MURDERED MY BROTHER, AND NOW HE'S SCARED OF ME!
WHAT ARE YOU GOING TO HIT ME WITH? YOU DON'T EVEN HAVE A WEAPON!
ACTUALLY...
"...I THINK I DO."
...I'M SORRY...
...I'M SO, SO SORRY...
OH, MAN. GIL, IF YOU CAN HEAR ME...I NEED YOU TO GO TO YOUR HAPPY PLACE SO I CAN SEAL THIS.
CLEAR!
EYAAAAAAH!

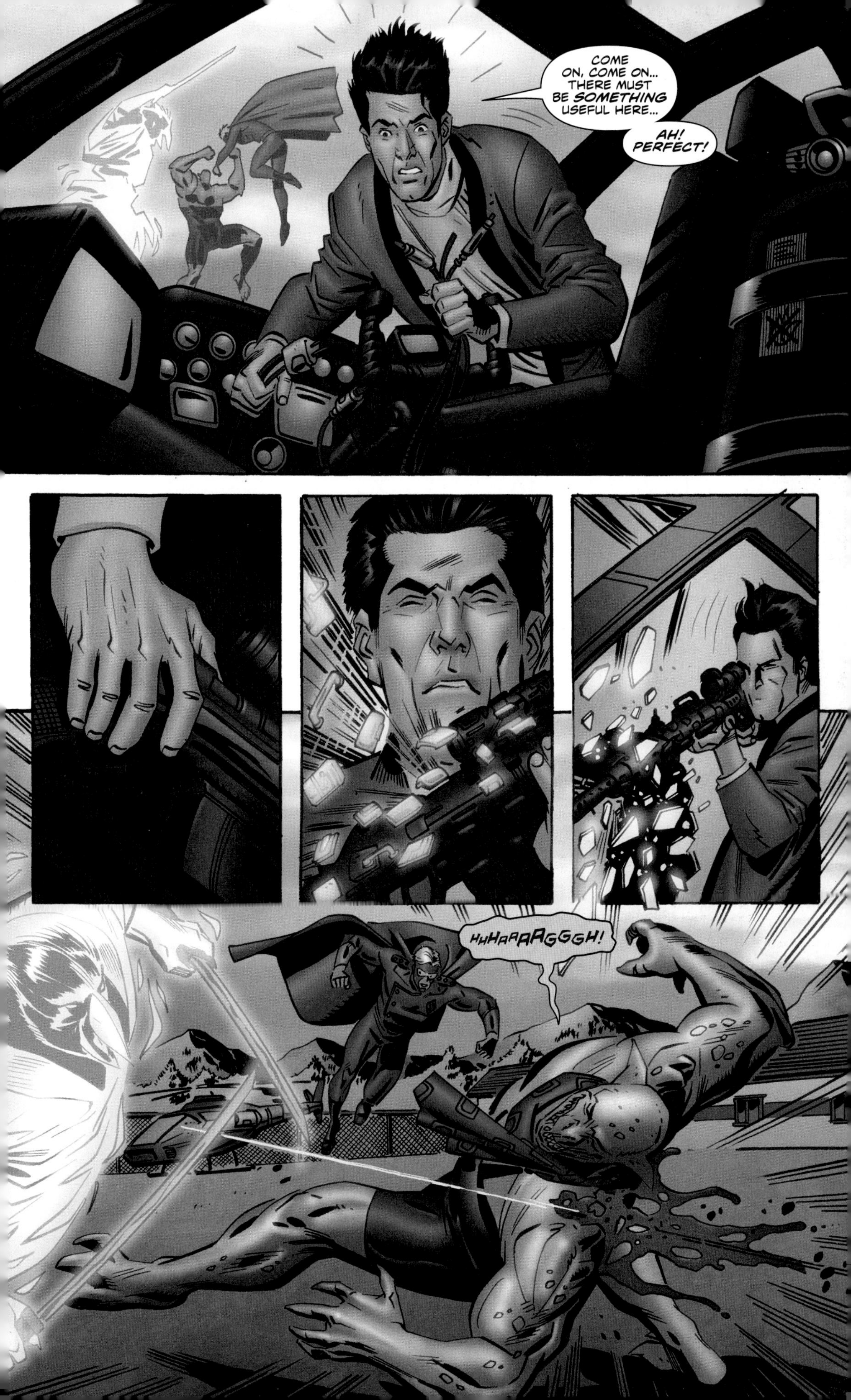
COME ON, COME ON... THERE MUST BE SOMETHING USEFUL HERE...
AH! PERFECT!
HHHAAAAAGGGH!

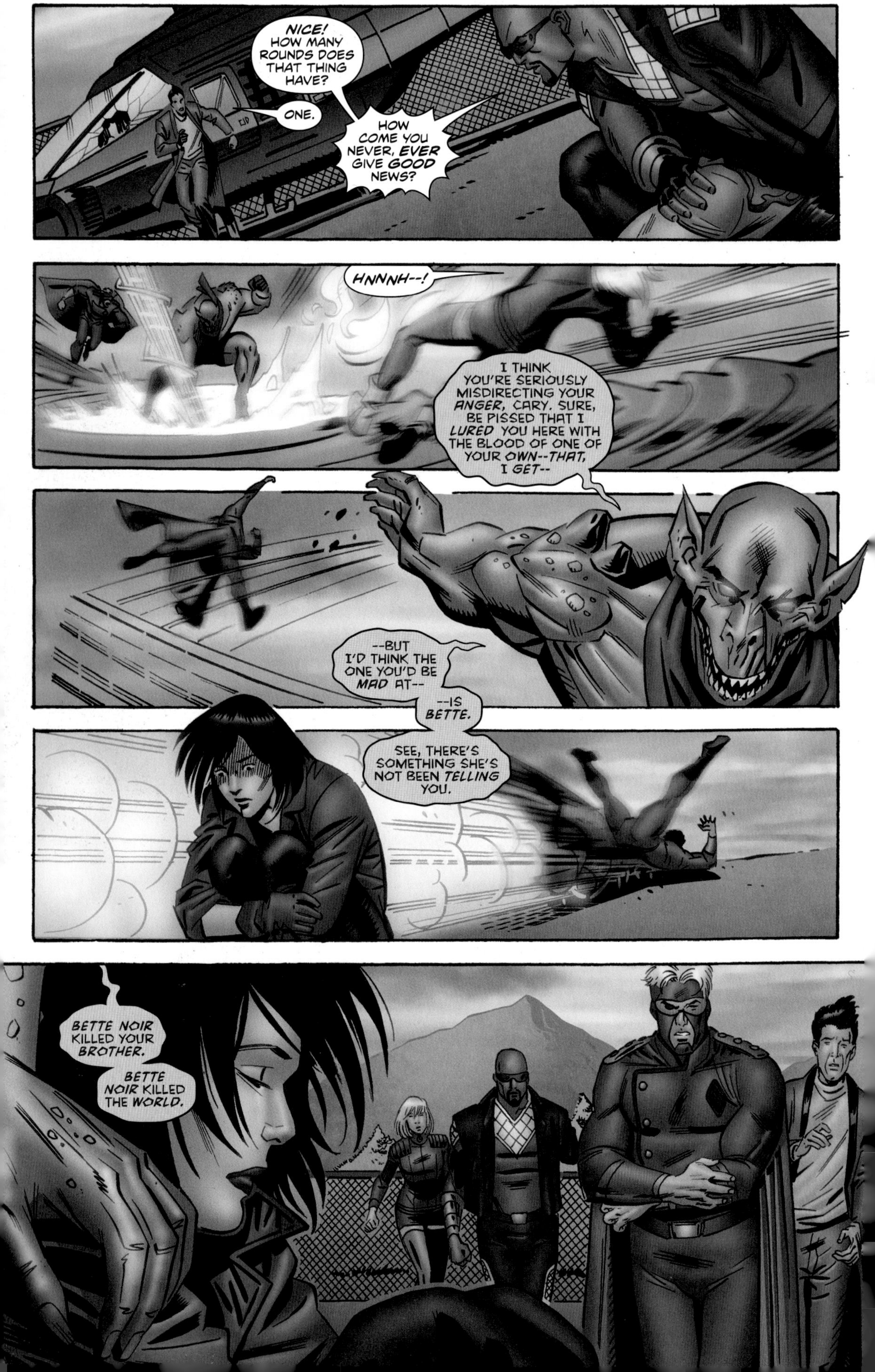
NICE! HOW MANY ROUNDS DOES THAT THING HAVE?
ONE.
HOW COME YOU NEVER, EVER GIVE GOOD NEWS?
HNNNH--!
I THINK YOU'RE SERIOUSLY MISDIRECTING YOUR ANGER, CARY. SURE, BE PISSED THAT I LURED YOU HERE WITH THE BLOOD OF ONE OF YOUR OWN--THAT, I GET--
--BUT I'D THINK THE ONE YOU'D BE MAD AT--
--IS BETTE.
SEE, THERE'S SOMETHING SHE'S NOT BEEN TELLING YOU.
BETTE NOIR KILLED YOUR BROTHER.
BETTE NOIR KILLED THE WORLD.

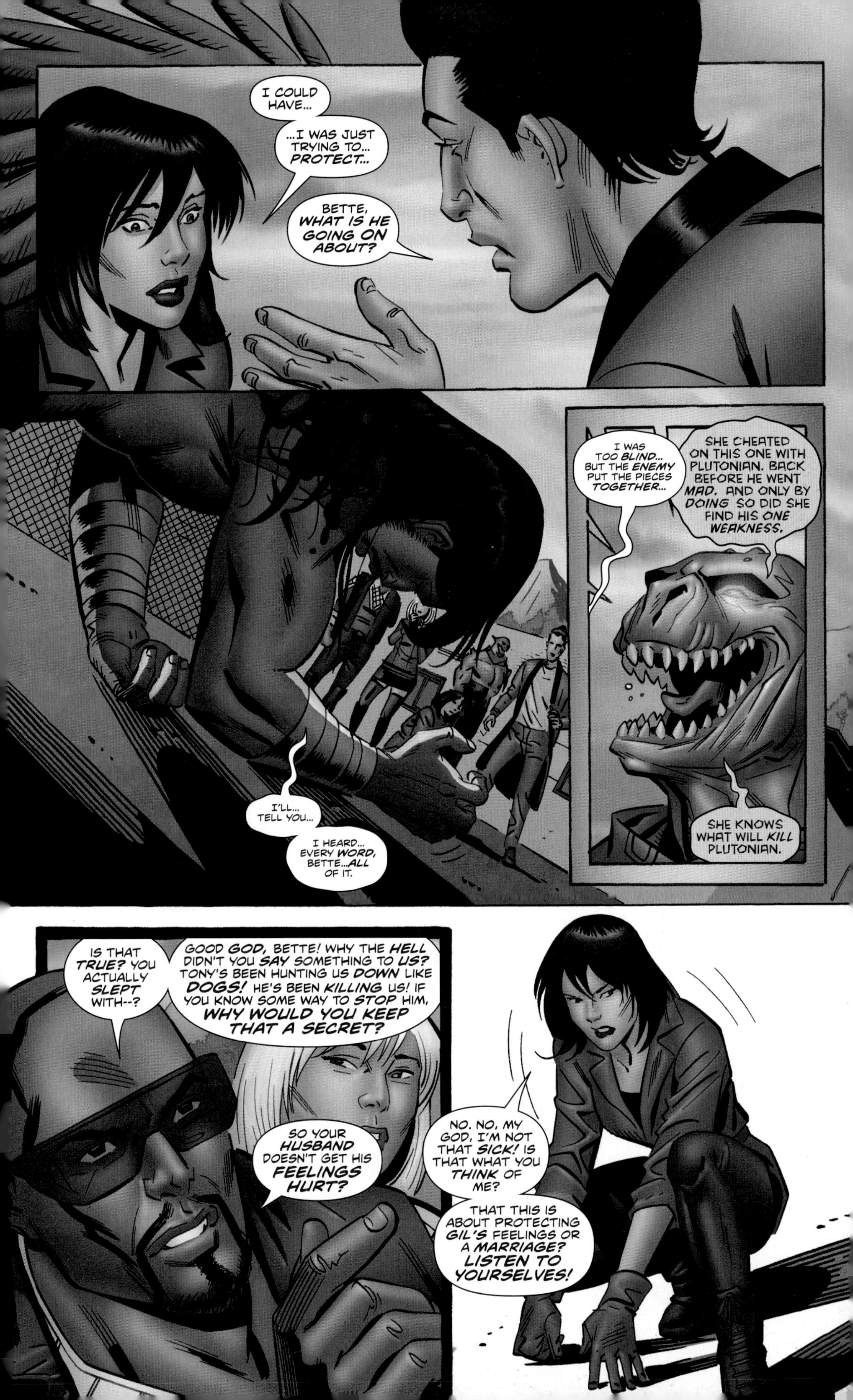
I COULD HAVE...
...I WAS JUST TRYING TO... PROTECT...
BETTE, WHAT IS HE GOING ON ABOUT?
I'LL... TELL YOU...
I HEARD... EVERY WORD, BETTE...ALL OF IT.
I WAS TOO BLIND... BUT THE ENEMY PUT THE PIECES TOGETHER...
SHE CHEATED ON THIS ONE WITH PLUTONIAN. BACK BEFORE HE WENT MAD. AND ONLY BY DOING SO DID SHE FIND HIS ONE WEAKNESS.
SHE KNOWS WHAT WILL KILL PLUTONIAN.
IS THAT TRUE? YOU ACTUALLY SLEPT WITH--?
GOOD GOD, BETTE! WHY THE HELL DIDN'T YOU SAY SOMETHING TO US? TONY'S BEEN HUNTING US DOWN LIKE DOGS! HE'S BEEN KILLING US! IF YOU KNOW SOME WAY TO STOP HIM, WHY WOULD YOU KEEP THAT A SECRET?
SO YOUR HUSBAND DOESN'T GET HIS FEELINGS HURT?
NO. NO, MY GOD, I'M NOT THAT SICK! IS THAT WHAT YOU THINK OF ME?
THAT THIS IS ABOUT PROTECTING GIL'S FEELINGS OR A MARRIAGE? LISTEN TO YOURSELVES!

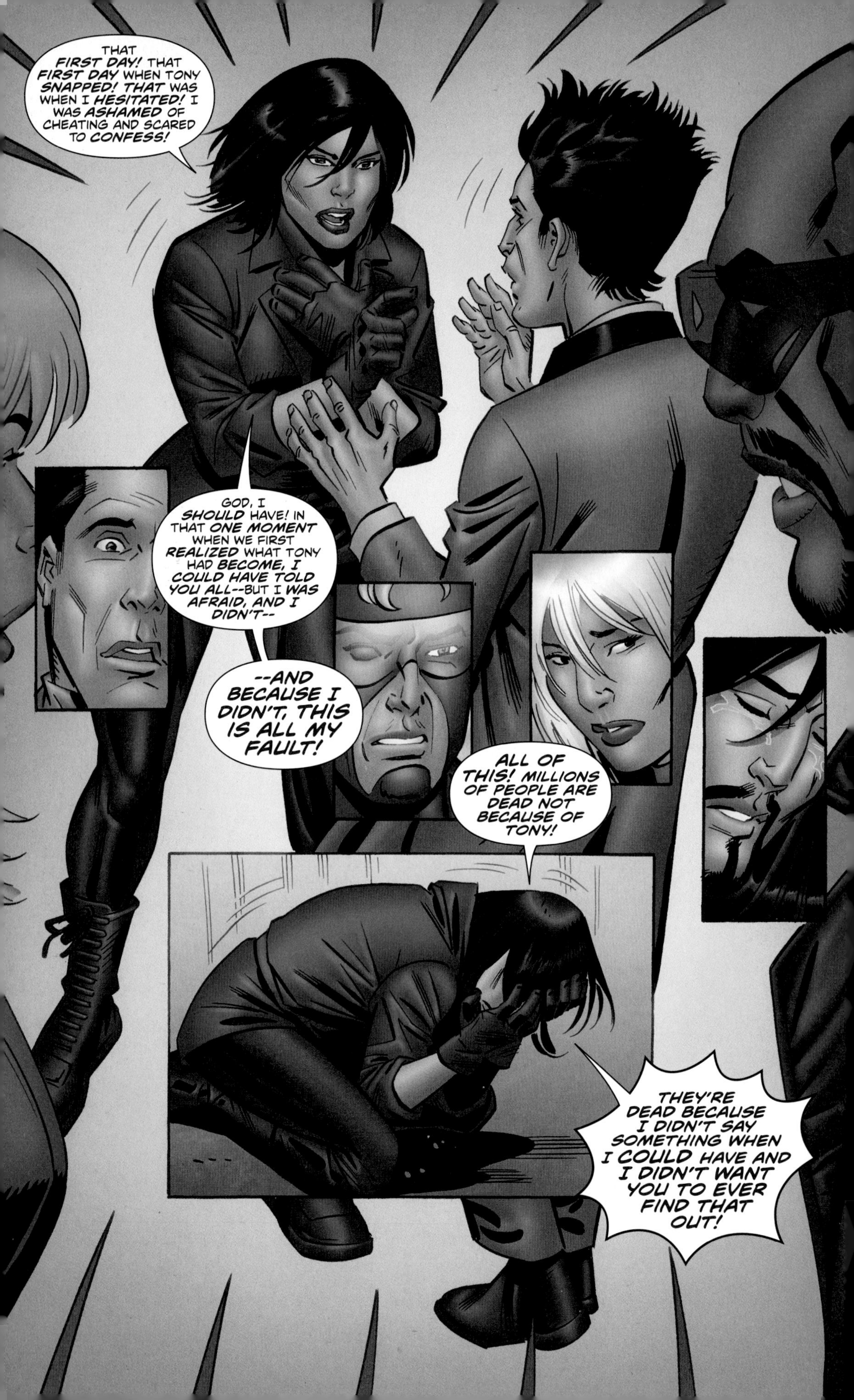
THAT FIRST DAY! THAT FIRST DAY WHEN TONY SNAPPED! THAT WAS WHEN I HESITATED! I WAS ASHAMED OF CHEATING AND SCARED TO CONFESS!
GOD, I SHOULD HAVE! IN THAT ONE MOMENT WHEN WE FIRST REALIZED WHAT TONY HAD BECOME, I COULD HAVE TOLD YOU ALL--BUT I WAS AFRAID, AND I DIDN'T--
--AND BECAUSE I DIDN'T, THIS IS ALL MY FAULT!
ALL OF THIS! MILLIONS OF PEOPLE ARE DEAD NOT BECAUSE OF TONY!
THEY'RE DEAD BECAUSE I DIDN'T SAY SOMETHING WHEN I COULD HAVE AND I DIDN'T WANT YOU TO EVER FIND THAT OUT!

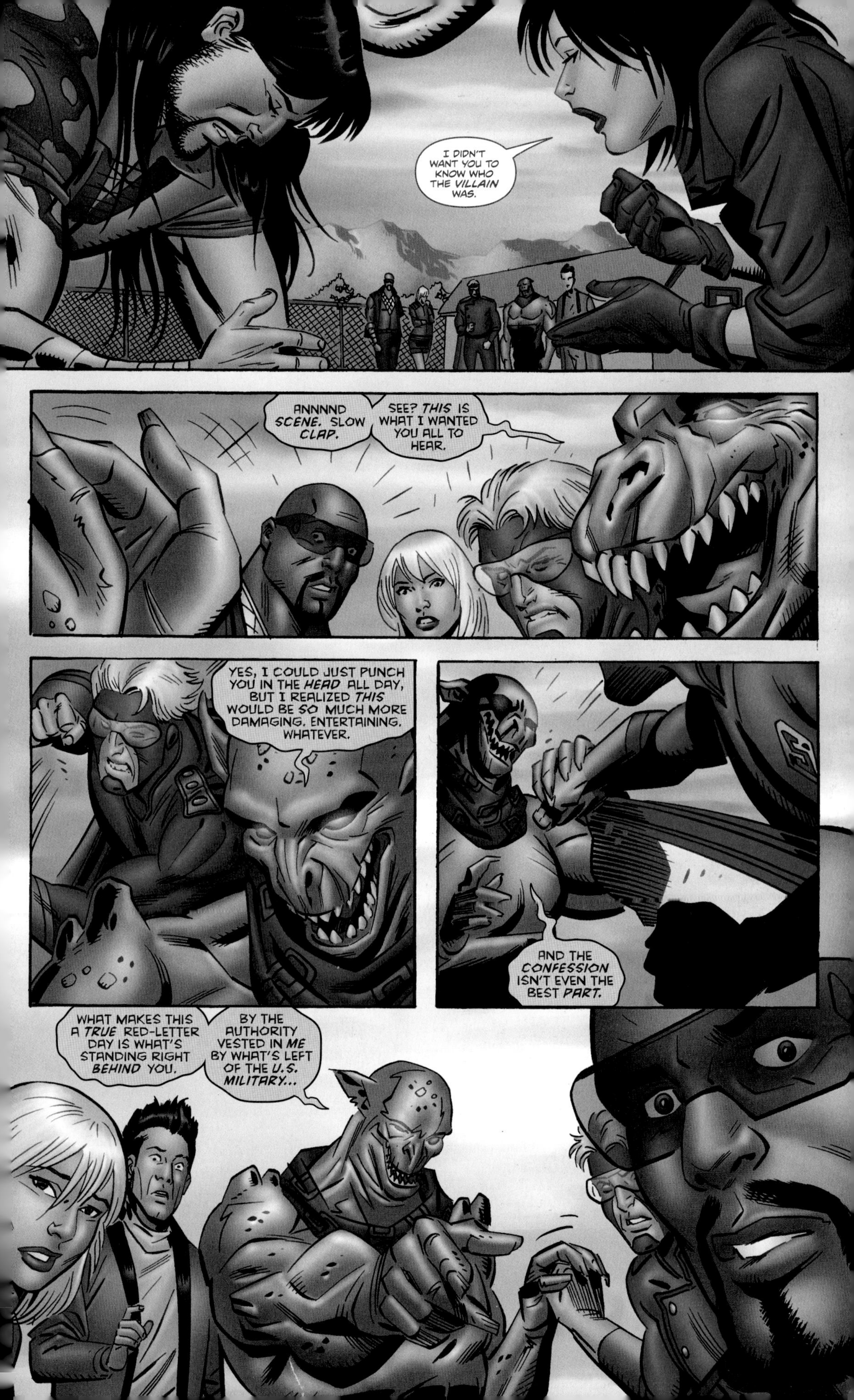
I DIDN'T WANT YOU TO KNOW WHO THE *VILLAIN* WAS.
ANNNND *SCENE.* SLOW *CLAP.*
SEE? *THIS* IS WHAT I WANTED YOU ALL TO HEAR.
YES, I COULD JUST PUNCH YOU IN THE *HEAD* ALL DAY, BUT I REALIZED *THIS* WOULD BE *SO* MUCH MORE DAMAGING. ENTERTAINING. WHATEVER.
AND THE *CONFESSION* ISN'T EVEN THE BEST *PART.*
WHAT MAKES THIS A *TRUE* RED-LETTER DAY IS WHAT'S STANDING RIGHT *BEHIND* YOU.
BY THE AUTHORITY VESTED IN *ME* BY WHAT'S LEFT OF THE *U.S. MILITARY...*

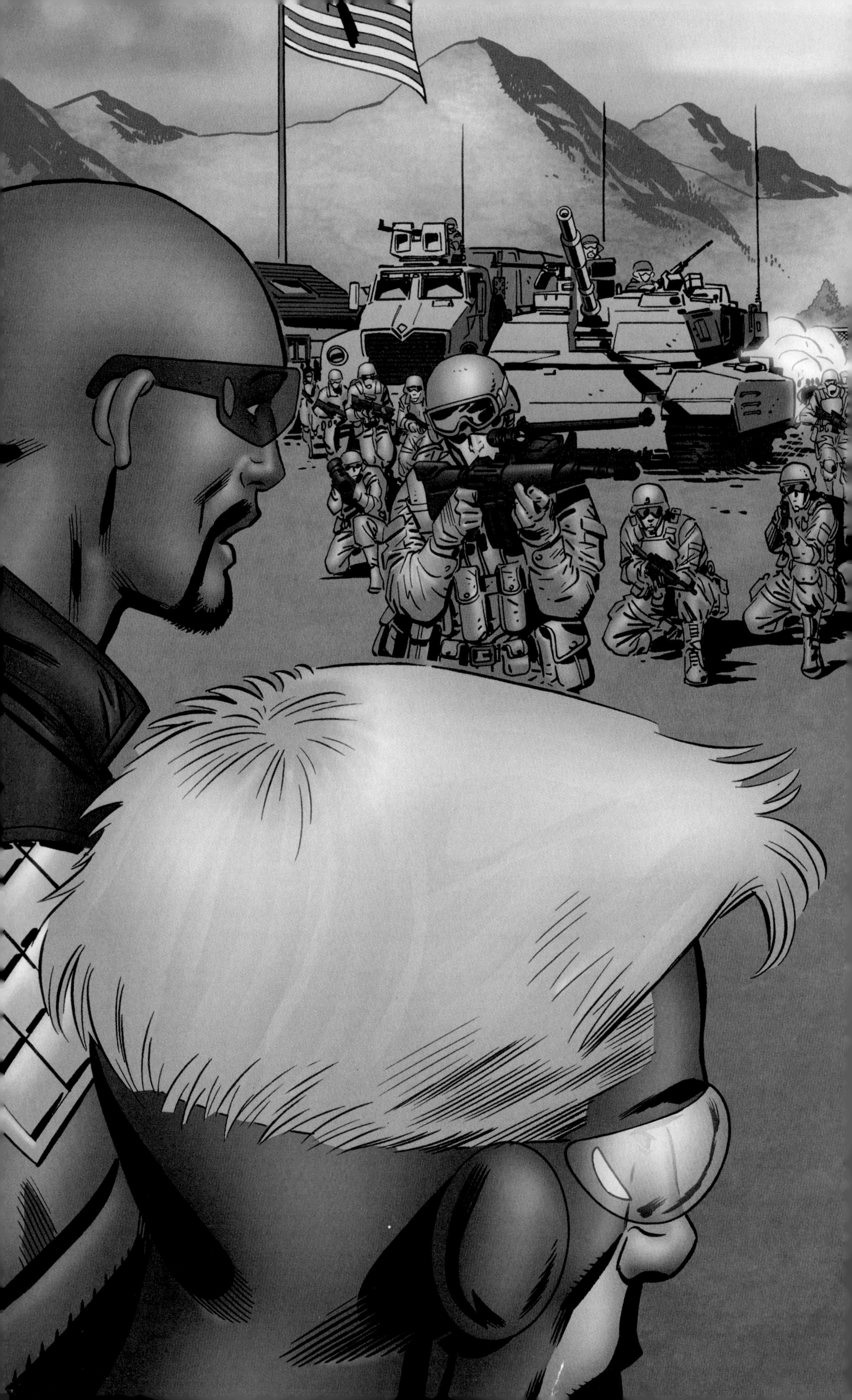

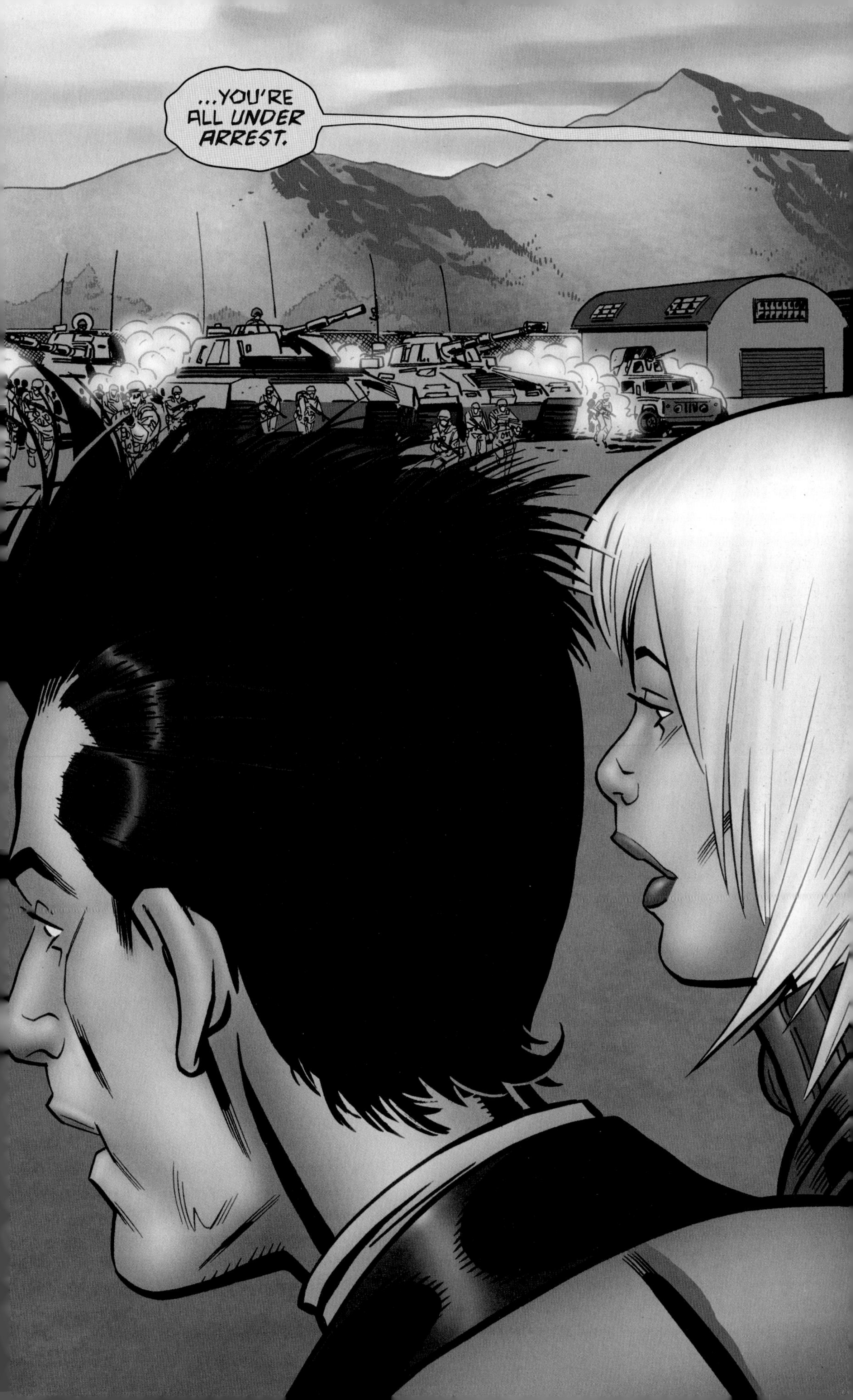
...YOU'RE ALL UNDER ARREST.

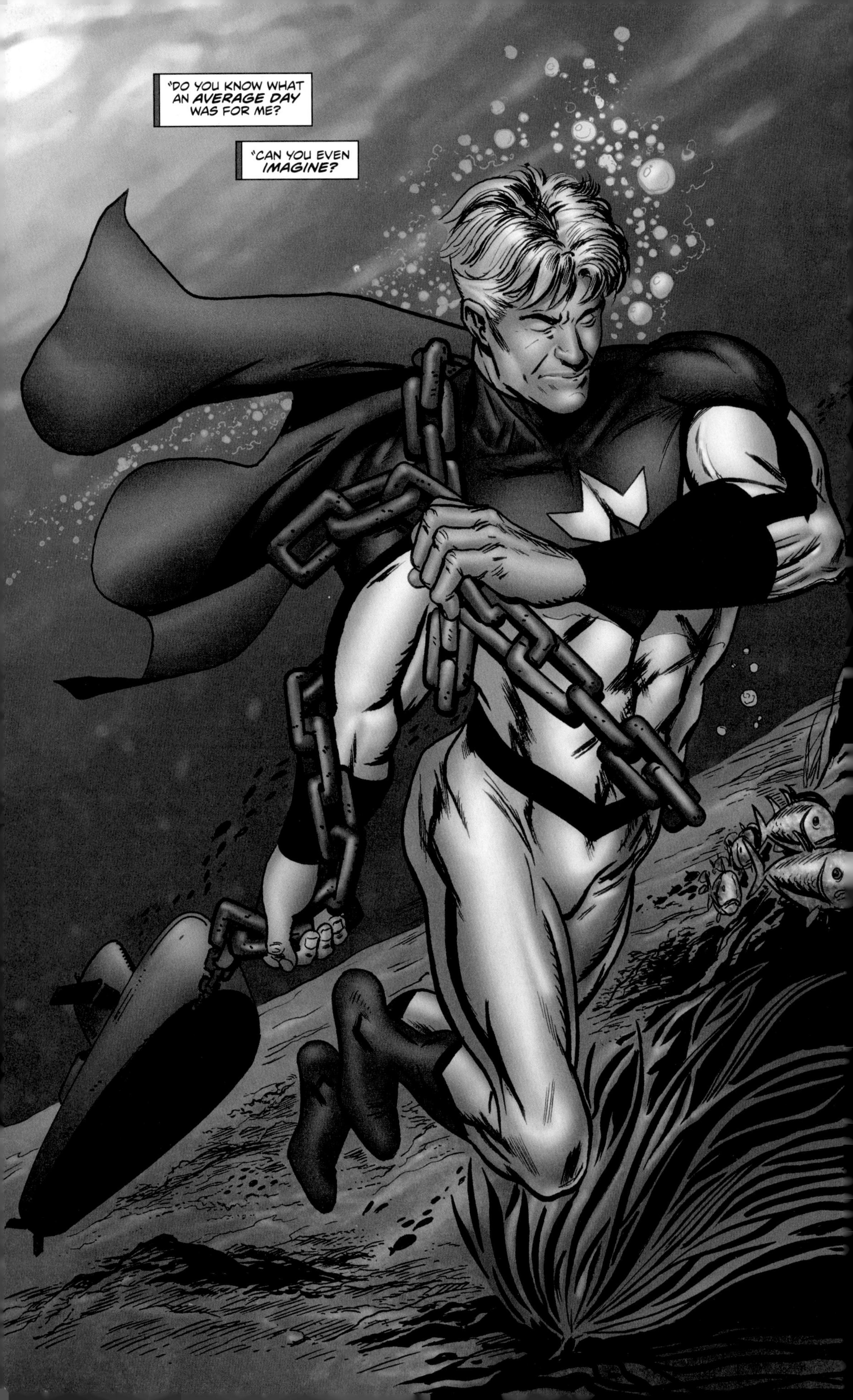
"DO YOU KNOW WHAT AN *AVERAGE DAY* WAS FOR ME?
"CAN YOU EVEN *IMAGINE?*

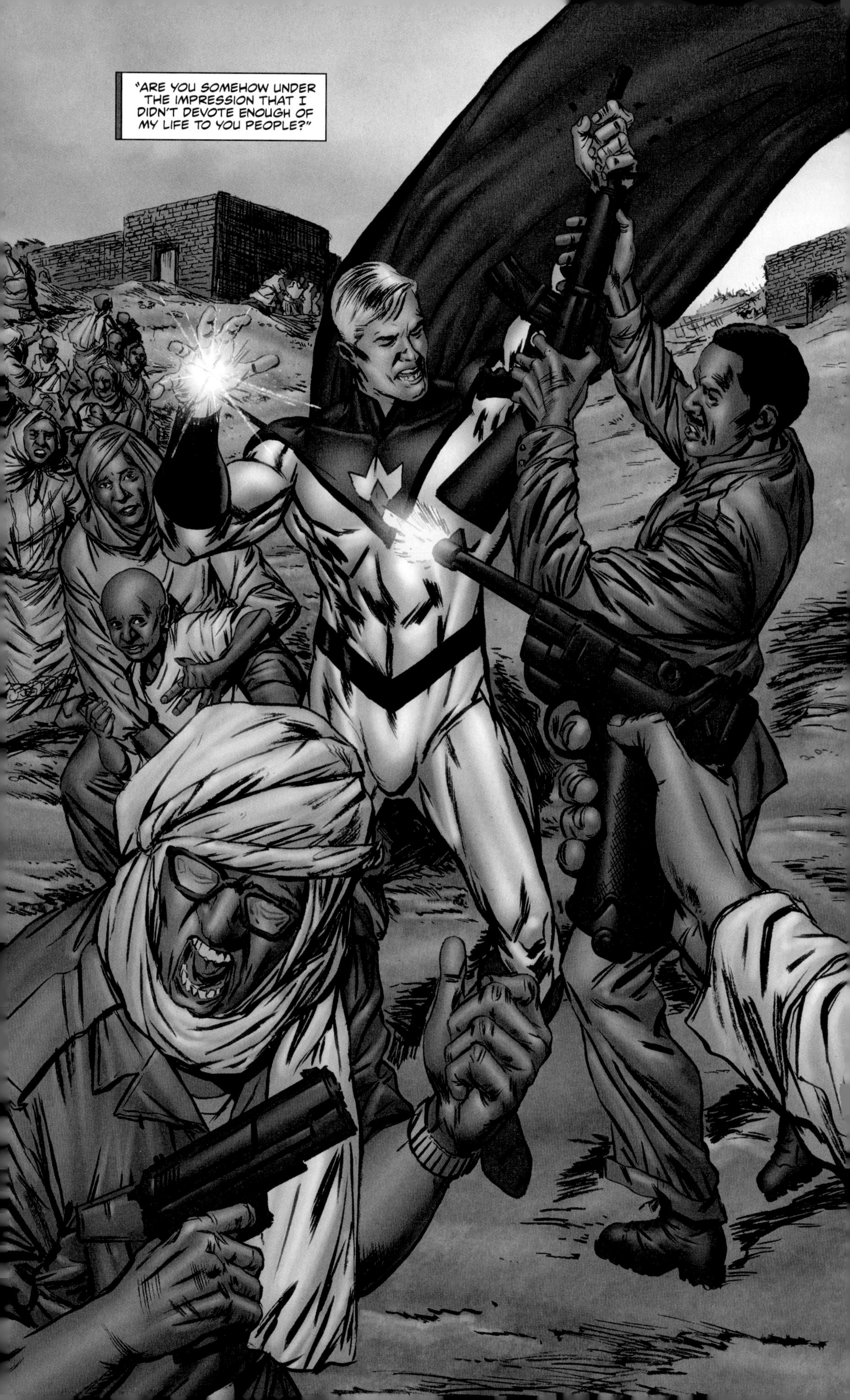
"ARE YOU SOMEHOW UNDER THE IMPRESSION THAT I DIDN'T DEVOTE ENOUGH OF MY LIFE TO YOU PEOPLE?"

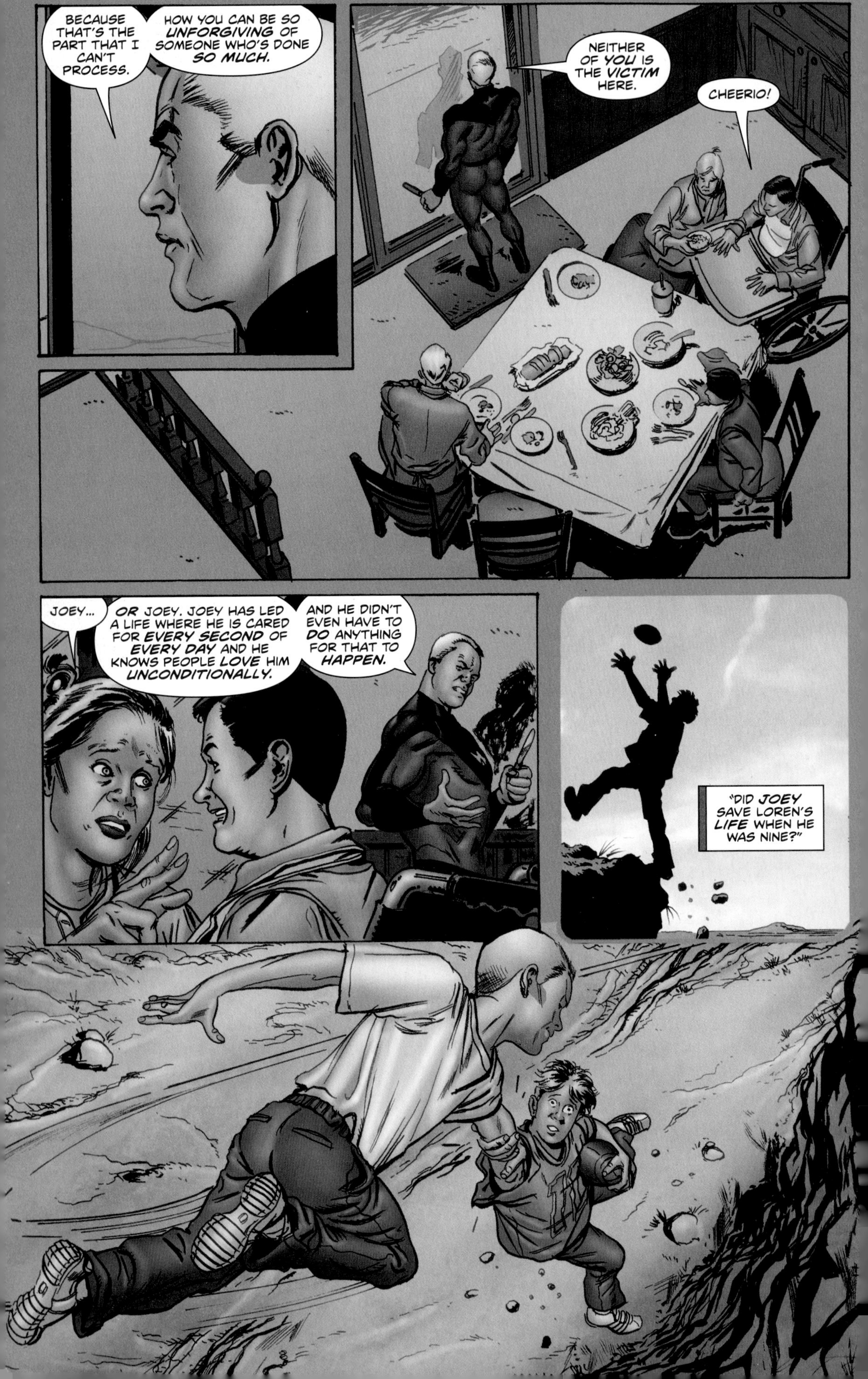

BECAUSE THAT'S THE PART THAT I CAN'T PROCESS.
HOW YOU CAN BE SO UNFORGIVING OF SOMEONE WHO'S DONE SO MUCH.
NEITHER OF YOU IS THE VICTIM HERE.
CHEERIO!
JOEY...
OR JOEY. JOEY HAS LED A LIFE WHERE HE IS CARED FOR EVERY SECOND OF EVERY DAY AND HE KNOWS PEOPLE LOVE HIM UNCONDITIONALLY.
AND HE DIDN'T EVEN HAVE TO DO ANYTHING FOR THAT TO HAPPEN.
"DID JOEY SAVE LOREN'S LIFE WHEN HE WAS NINE?"

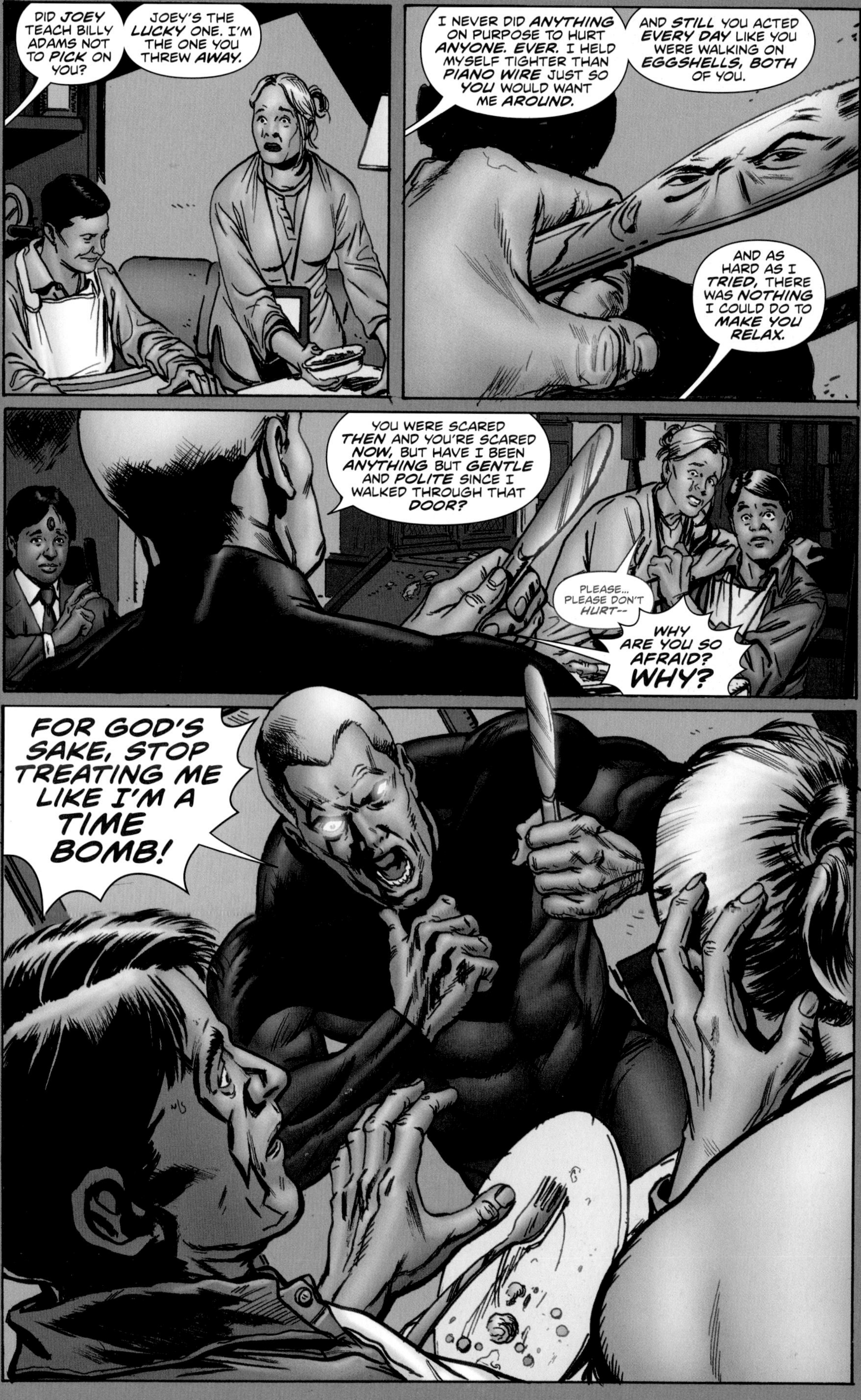

DID JOEY TEACH BILLY ADAMS NOT TO PICK ON YOU?
JOEY'S THE LUCKY ONE. I'M THE ONE YOU THREW AWAY.
I NEVER DID ANYTHING ON PURPOSE TO HURT ANYONE. EVER. I HELD MYSELF TIGHTER THAN PIANO WIRE JUST SO YOU WOULD WANT ME AROUND.
AND STILL YOU ACTED EVERY DAY LIKE YOU WERE WALKING ON EGGSHELLS, BOTH OF YOU.
AND AS HARD AS I TRIED, THERE WAS NOTHING I COULD DO TO MAKE YOU RELAX.
YOU WERE SCARED THEN AND YOU'RE SCARED NOW, BUT HAVE I BEEN ANYTHING BUT GENTLE AND POLITE SINCE I WALKED THROUGH THAT DOOR?
PLEASE... PLEASE DON'T HURT--
WHY ARE YOU SO AFRAID? WHY?
FOR GOD'S SAKE, STOP TREATING ME LIKE I'M A TIME BOMB!

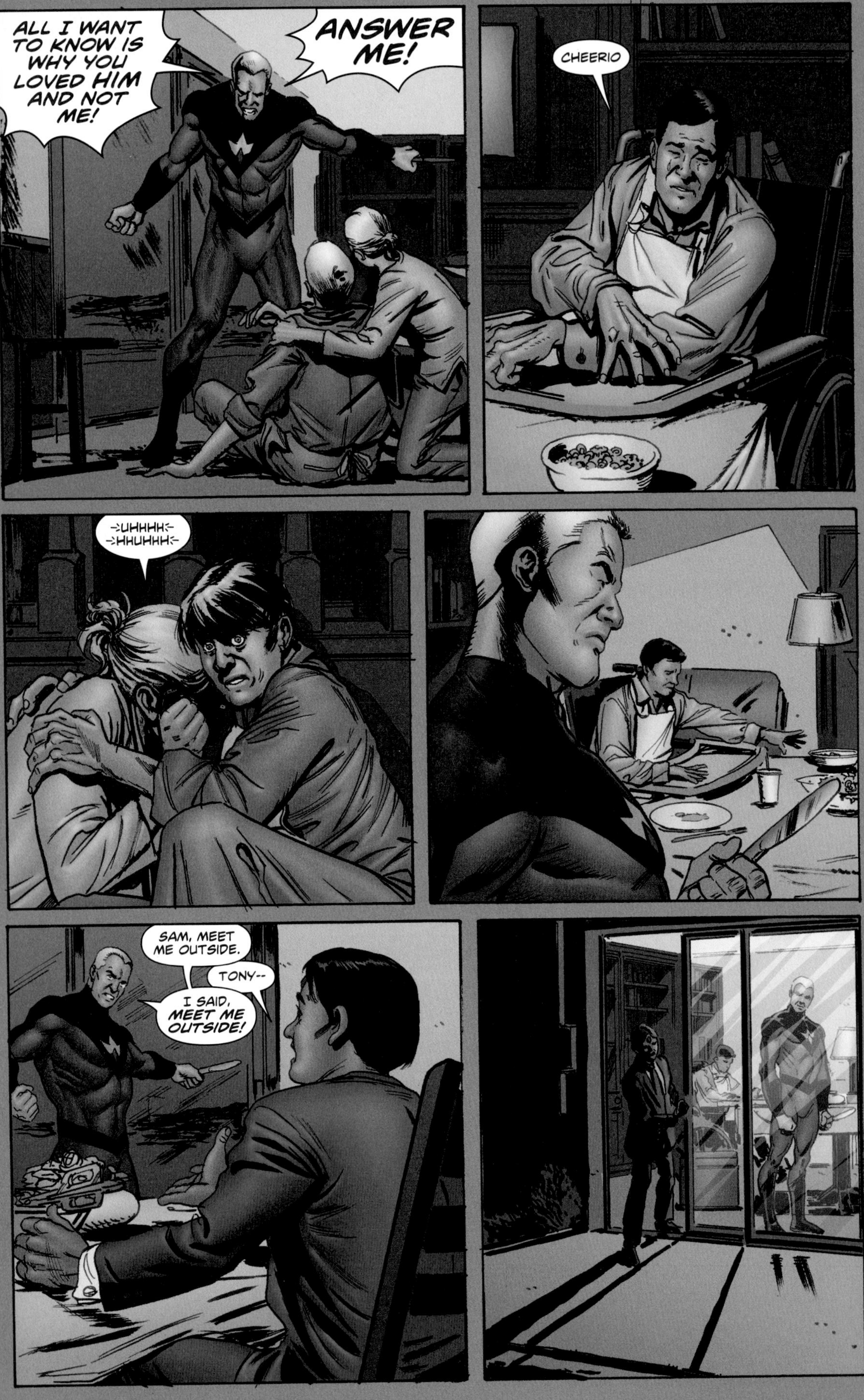
ALL I WANT TO KNOW IS WHY YOU LOVED HIM AND NOT ME!
ANSWER ME!
CHEERIO
-UHHHH- -HHUHHH-
SAM, MEET ME OUTSIDE.
TONY--
I SAID, MEET ME OUTSIDE!

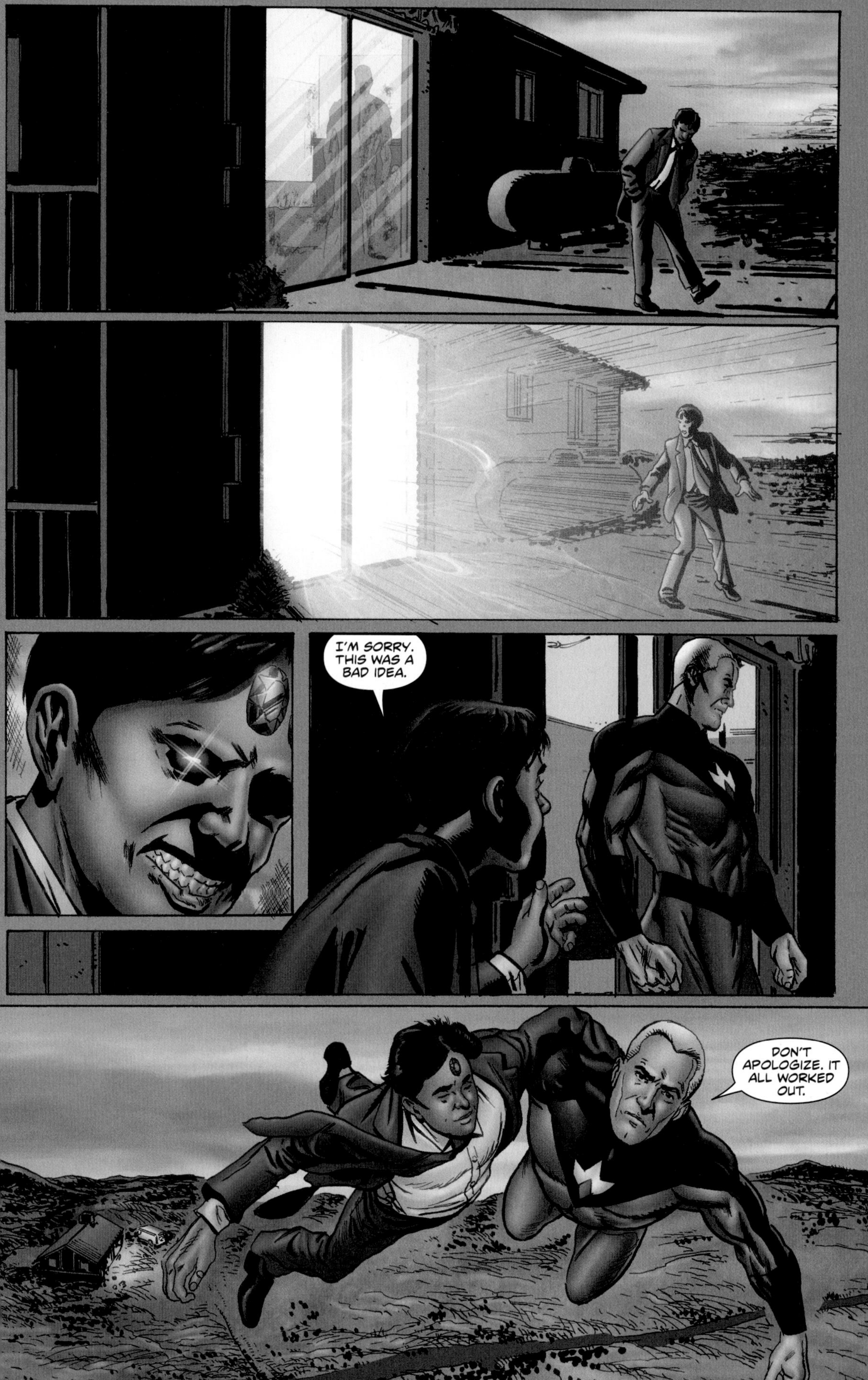
I'M SORRY. THIS WAS A BAD IDEA.
DON'T APOLOGIZE. IT ALL WORKED OUT.

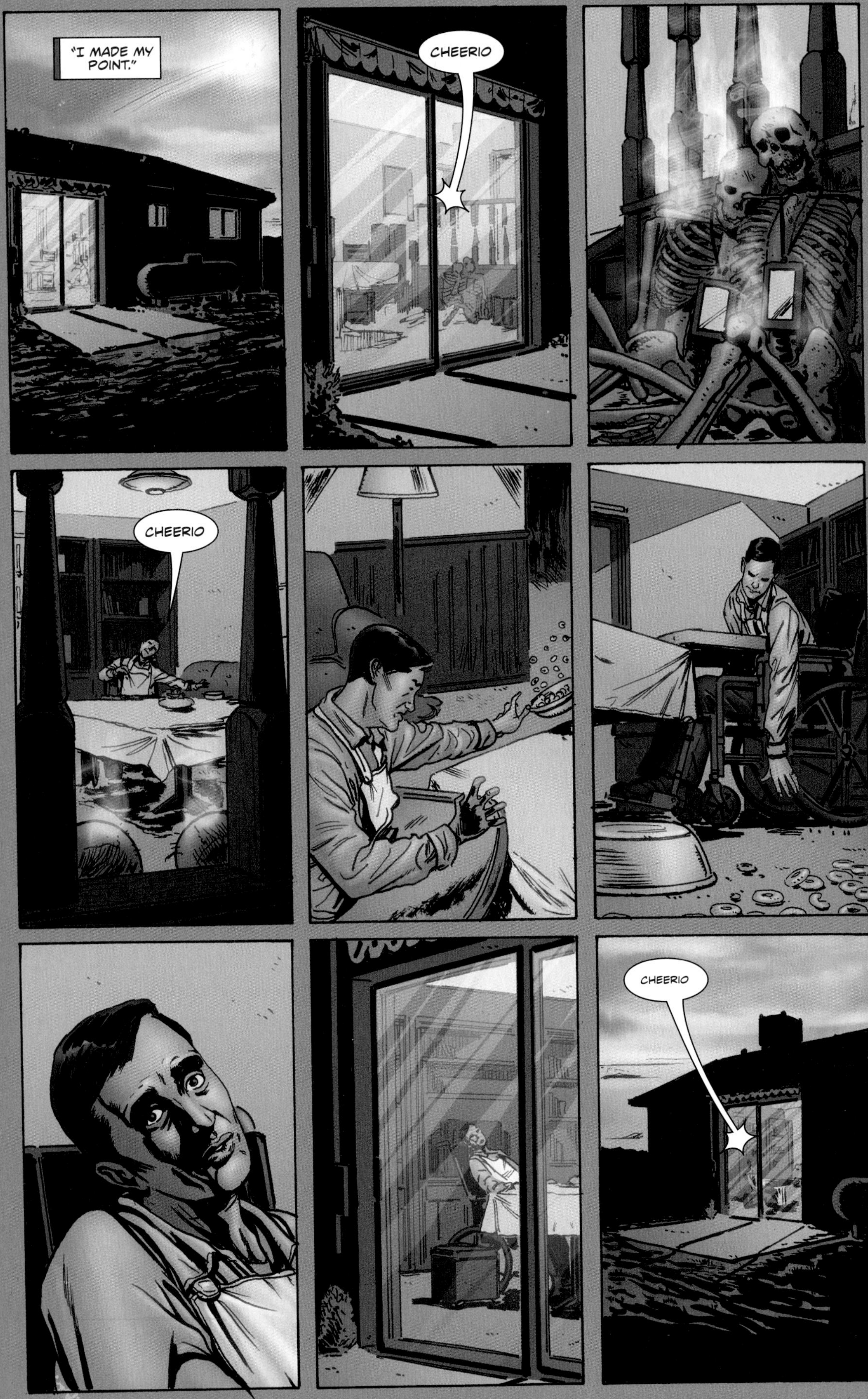
"I MADE MY POINT."
CHEERIO
CHEERIO
CHEERIO

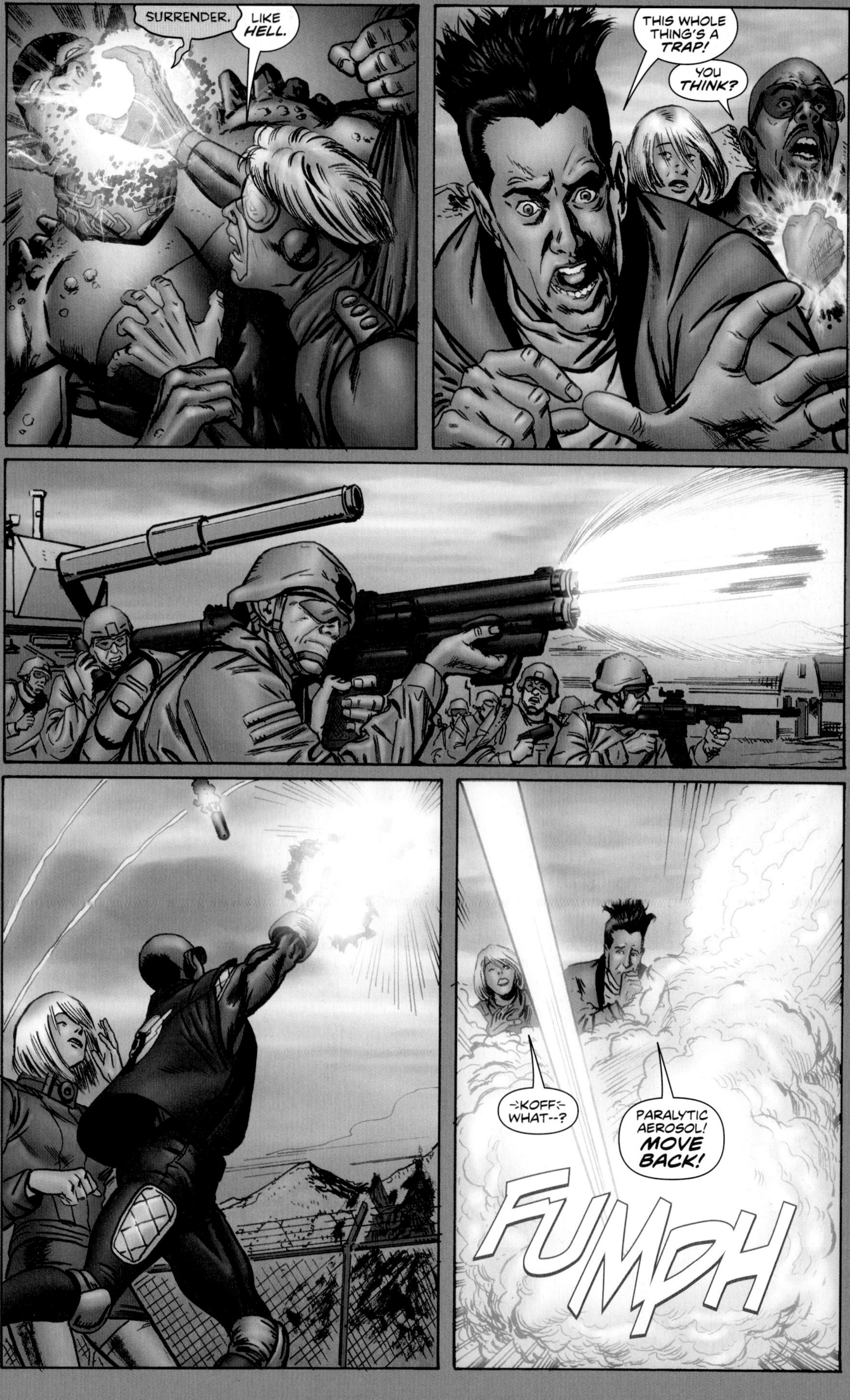
SURRENDER.
LIKE *HELL.*
THIS WHOLE THING'S A *TRAP!*
YOU *THINK?*
-KOFF- WHAT--?
PARALYTIC AEROSOL! **MOVE BACK!**
FUMPH

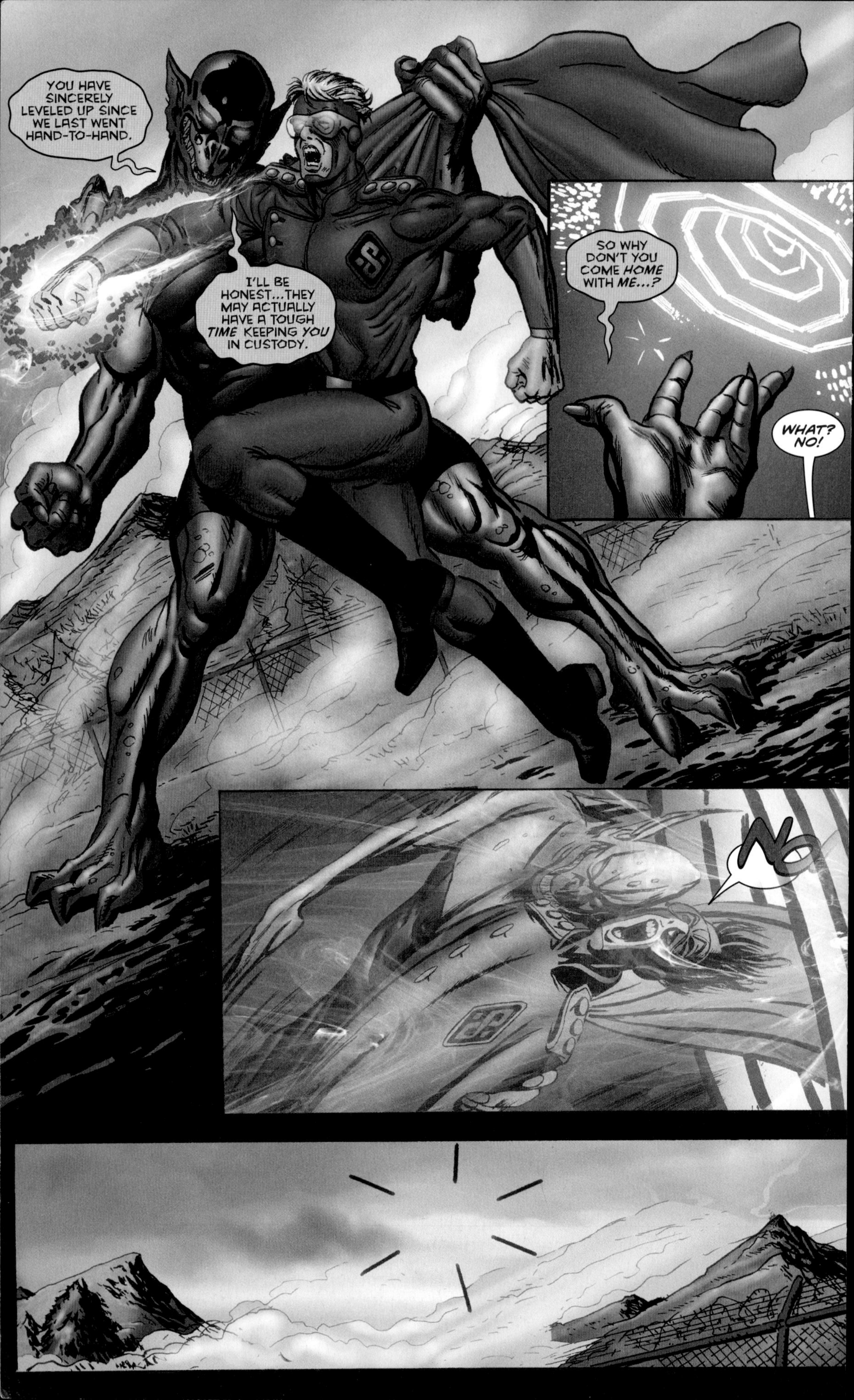
YOU HAVE SINCERELY LEVELED UP SINCE WE LAST WENT HAND-TO-HAND.
I'LL BE HONEST...THEY MAY ACTUALLY HAVE A TOUGH TIME KEEPING YOU IN CUSTODY.
SO WHY DON'T YOU COME HOME WITH ME...?
WHAT? NO!
NO

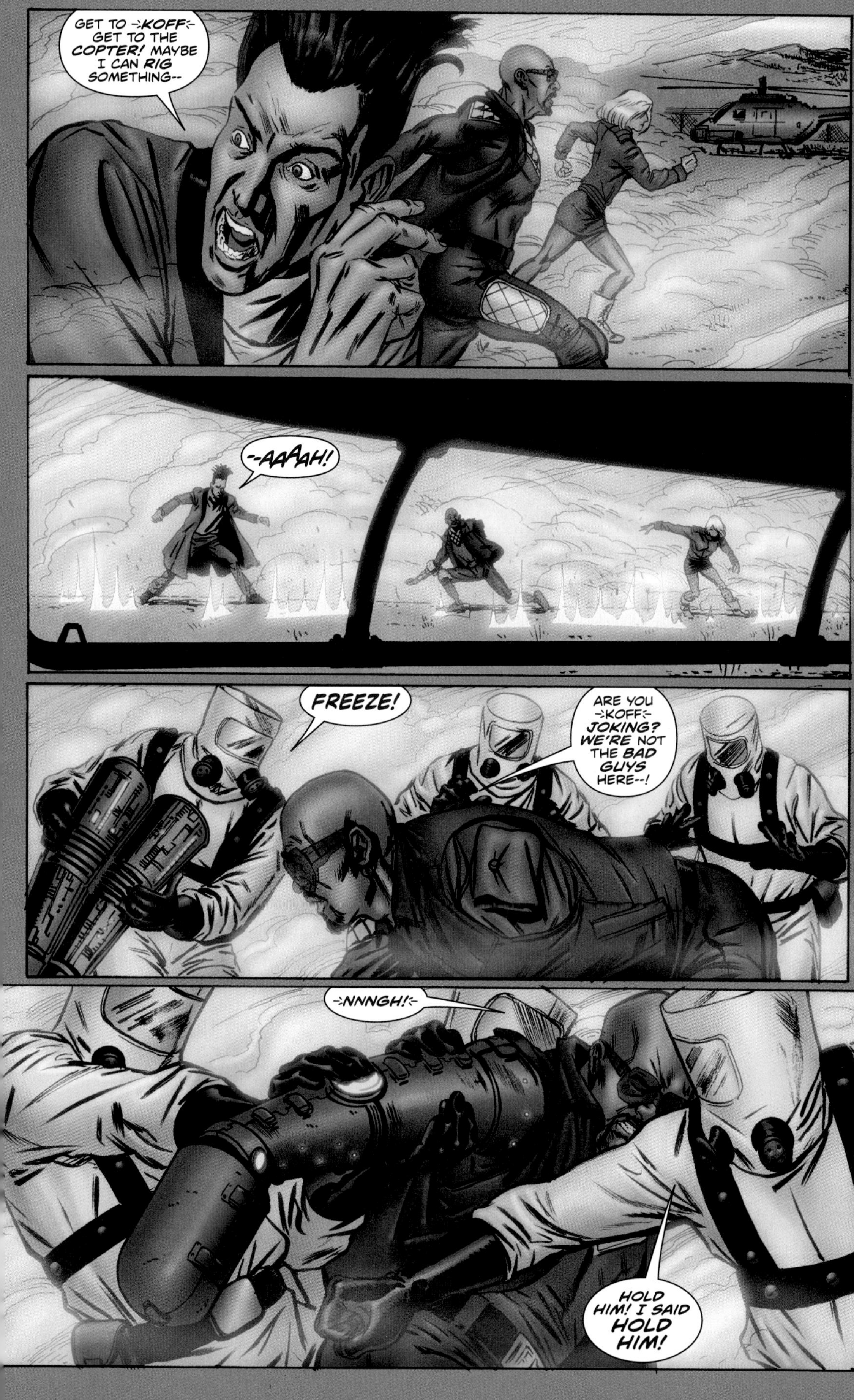
GET TO -KOFF- GET TO THE COPTER! MAYBE I CAN RIG SOMETHING--
--AAAAH!
FREEZE!
ARE YOU -KOFF- JOKING? WE'RE NOT THE BAD GUYS HERE--!
-NNNGH!-
HOLD HIM! I SAID HOLD HIM!

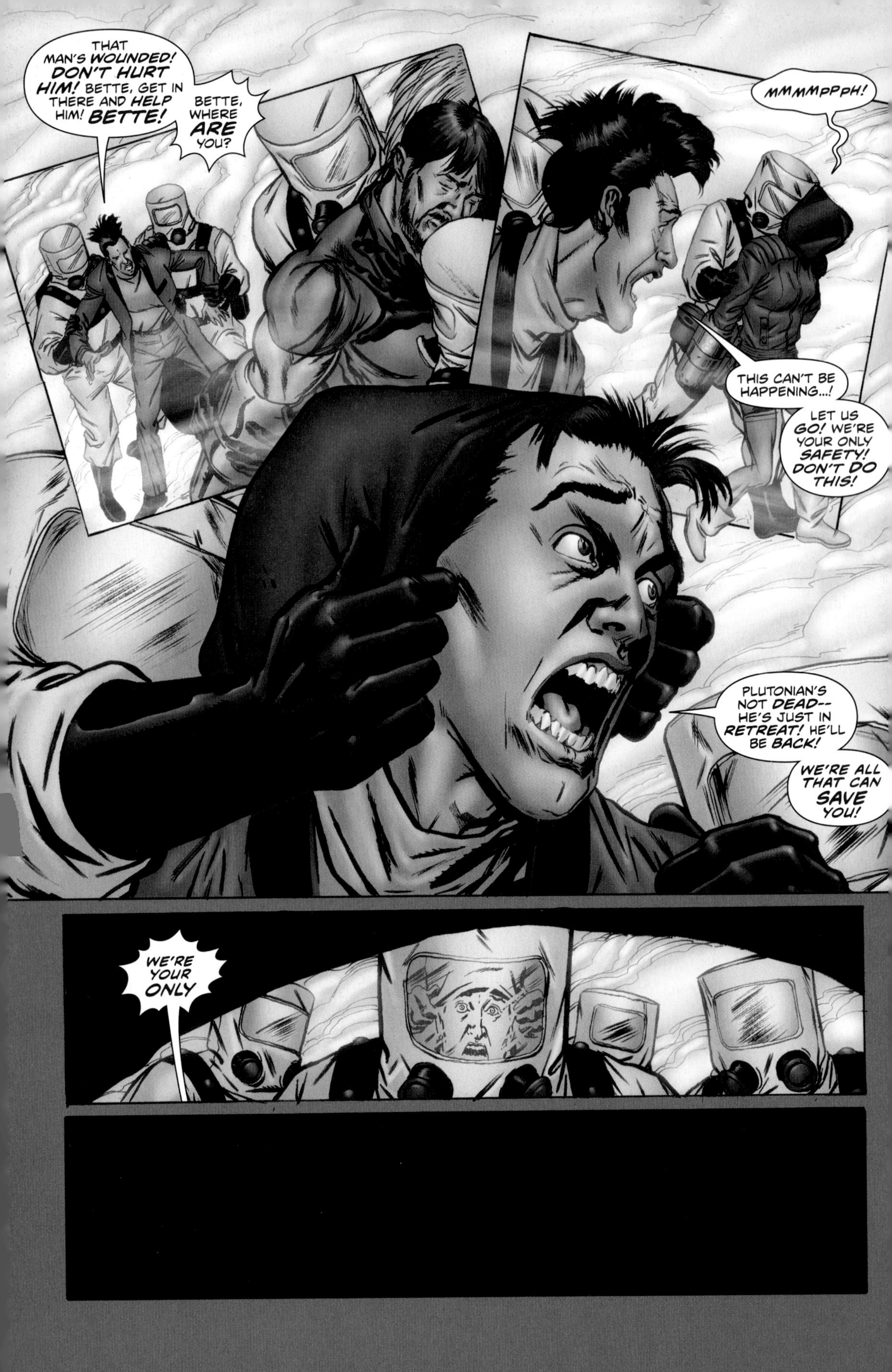

THAT MAN'S WOUNDED! DON'T HURT HIM! BETTE, GET IN THERE AND HELP HIM! BETTE!
BETTE, WHERE ARE YOU?
MMMMPPPH!
THIS CAN'T BE HAPPENING...!
LET US GO! WE'RE YOUR ONLY SAFETY! DON'T DO THIS!
PLUTONIAN'S NOT DEAD--HE'S JUST IN RETREAT! HE'LL BE BACK!
WE'RE ALL THAT CAN SAVE YOU!
WE'RE YOUR ONLY

To be continued...

COVER GALLERY

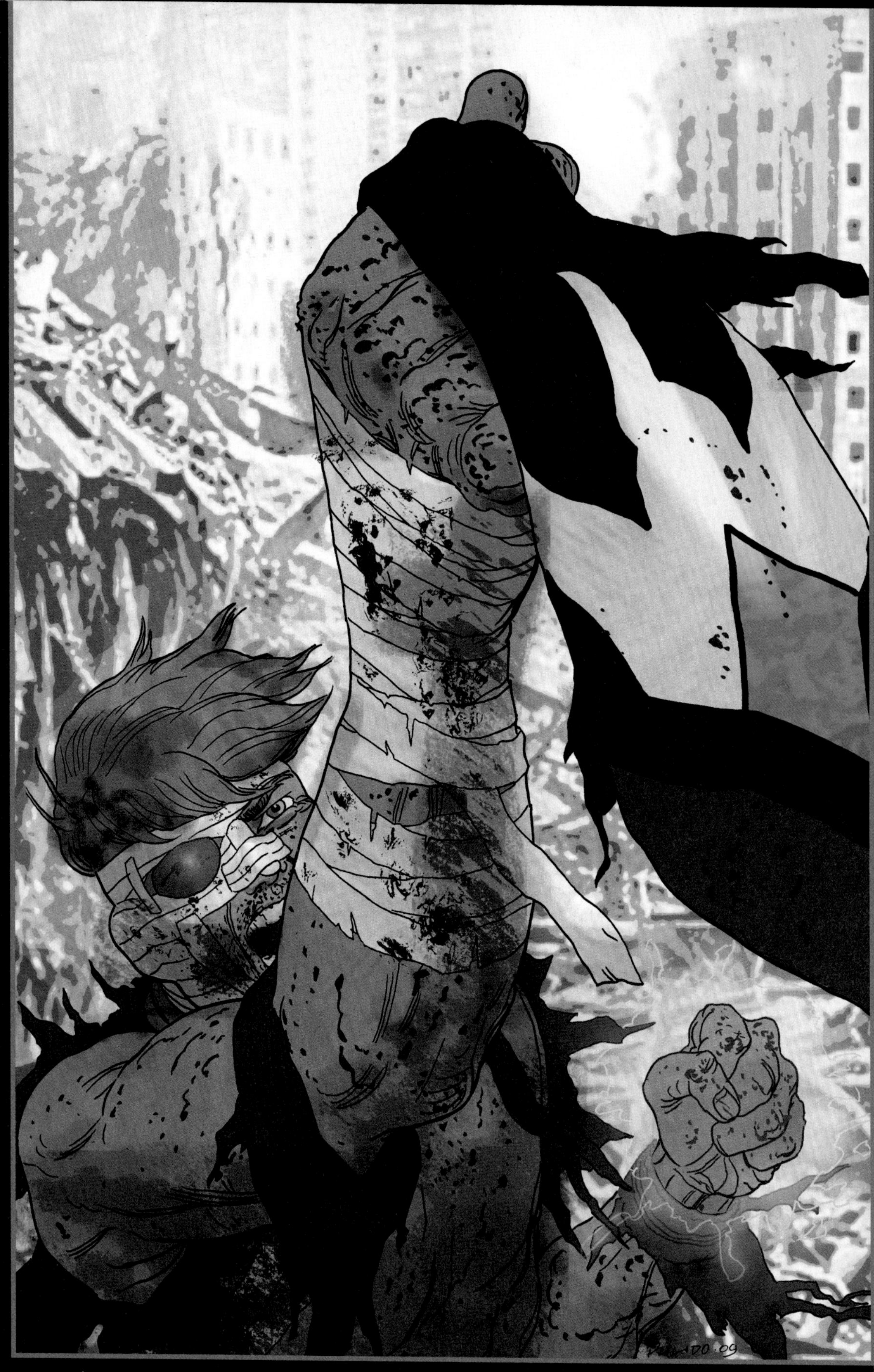

COVER 9A: JAVIER PULIDO

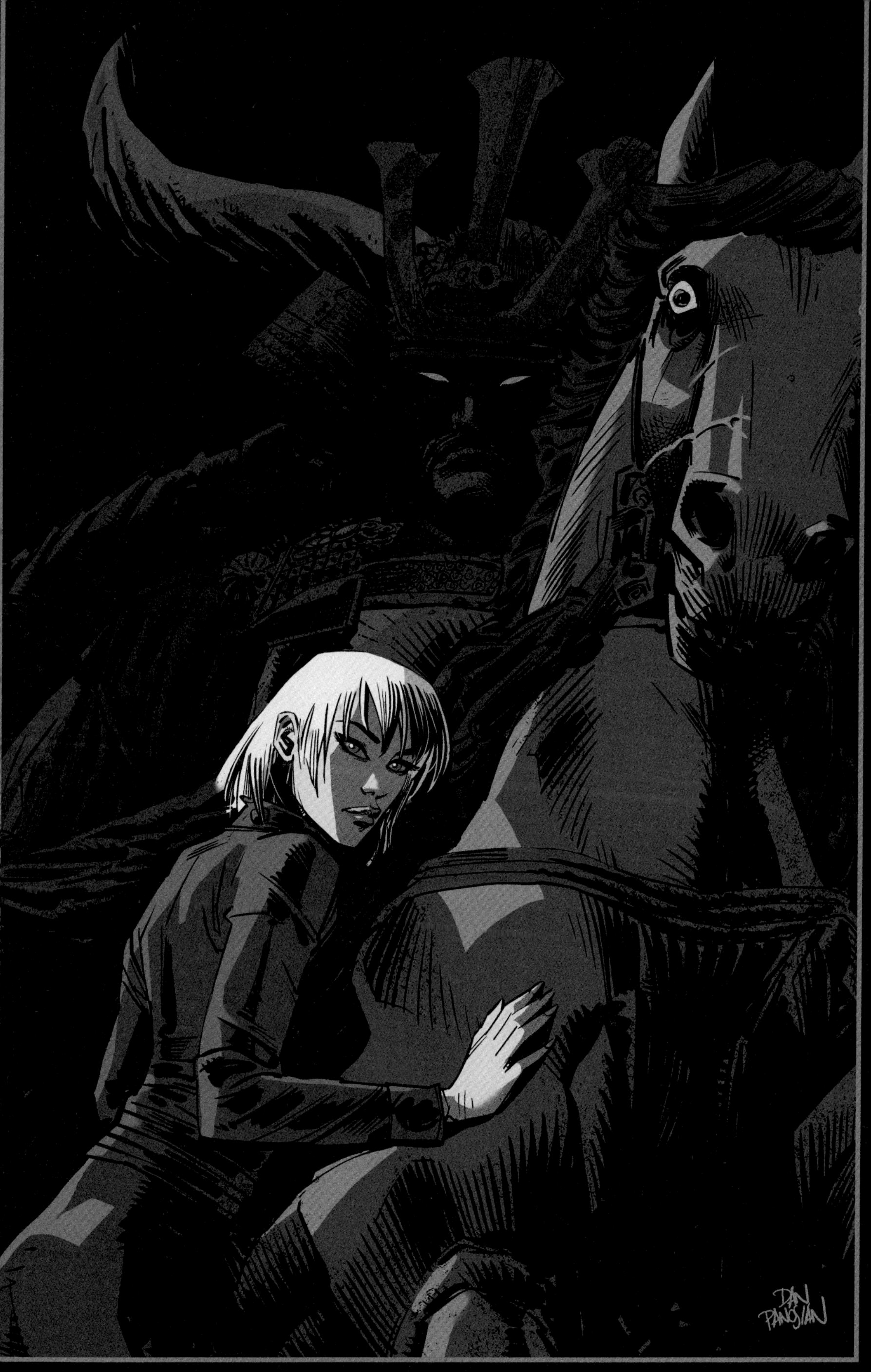
DAN PANOSIAN

COVER 9B: DAN PANOSIAN

BY JEFFREY SPOKES

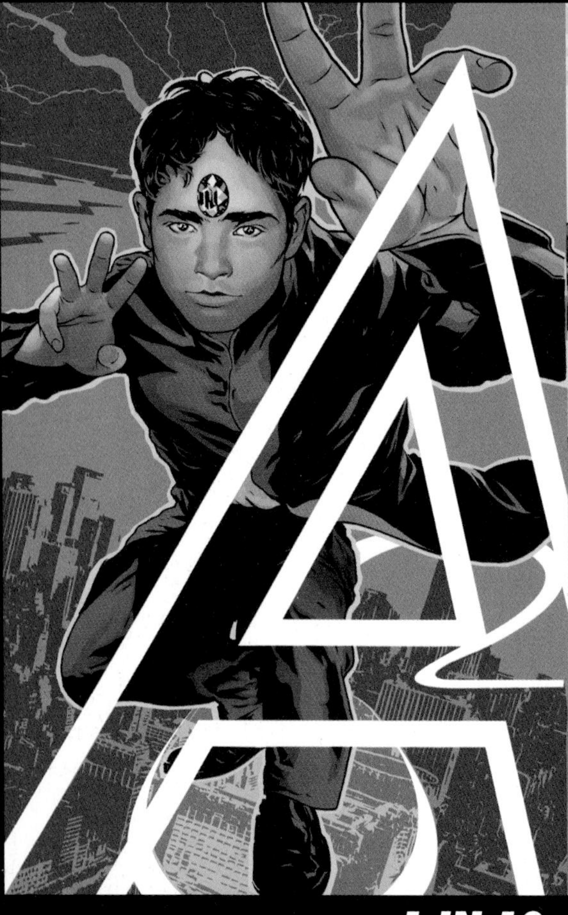

1 IN 10

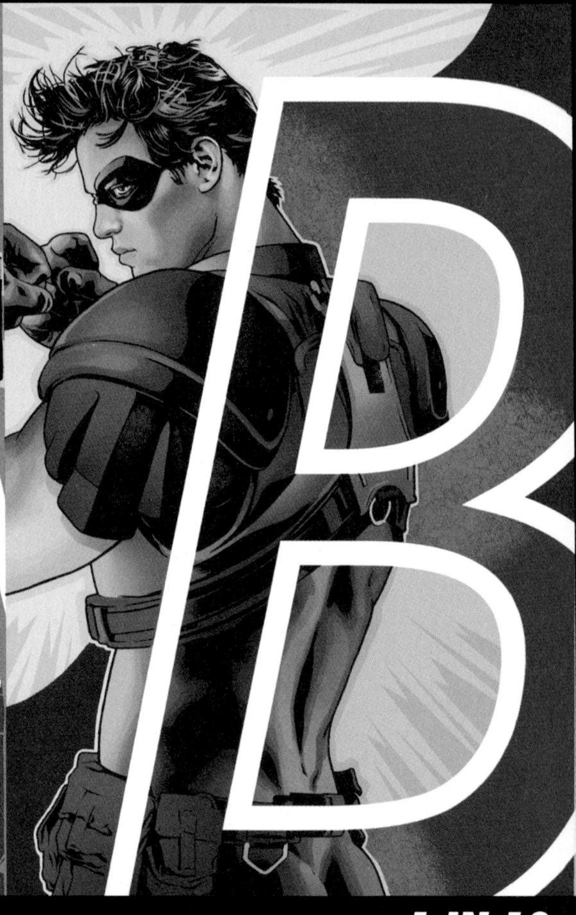

1 IN 10

COVERS 9-12

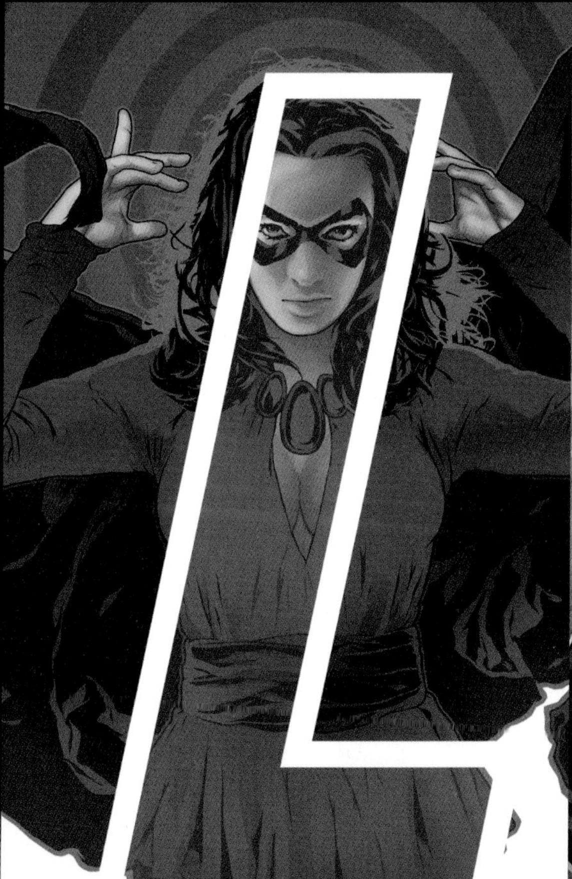

1 IN 10

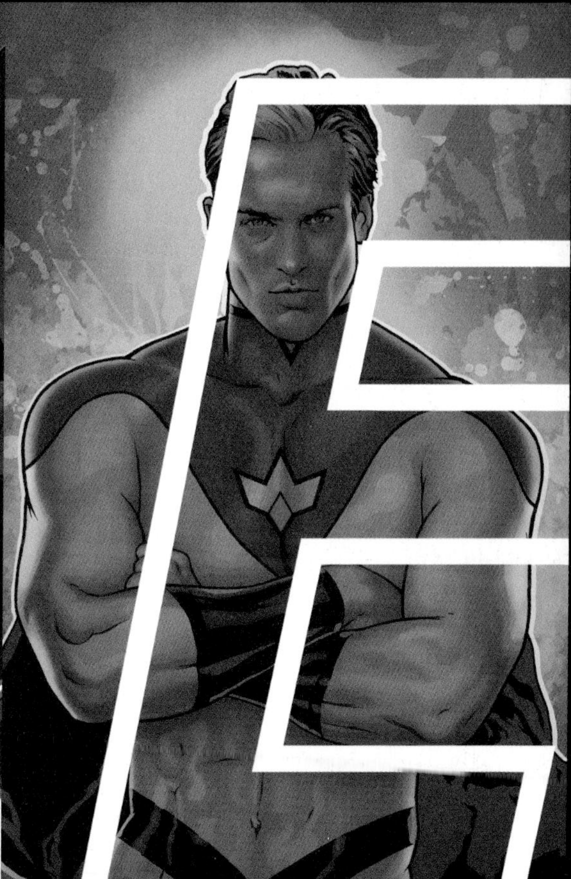

1 IN 10

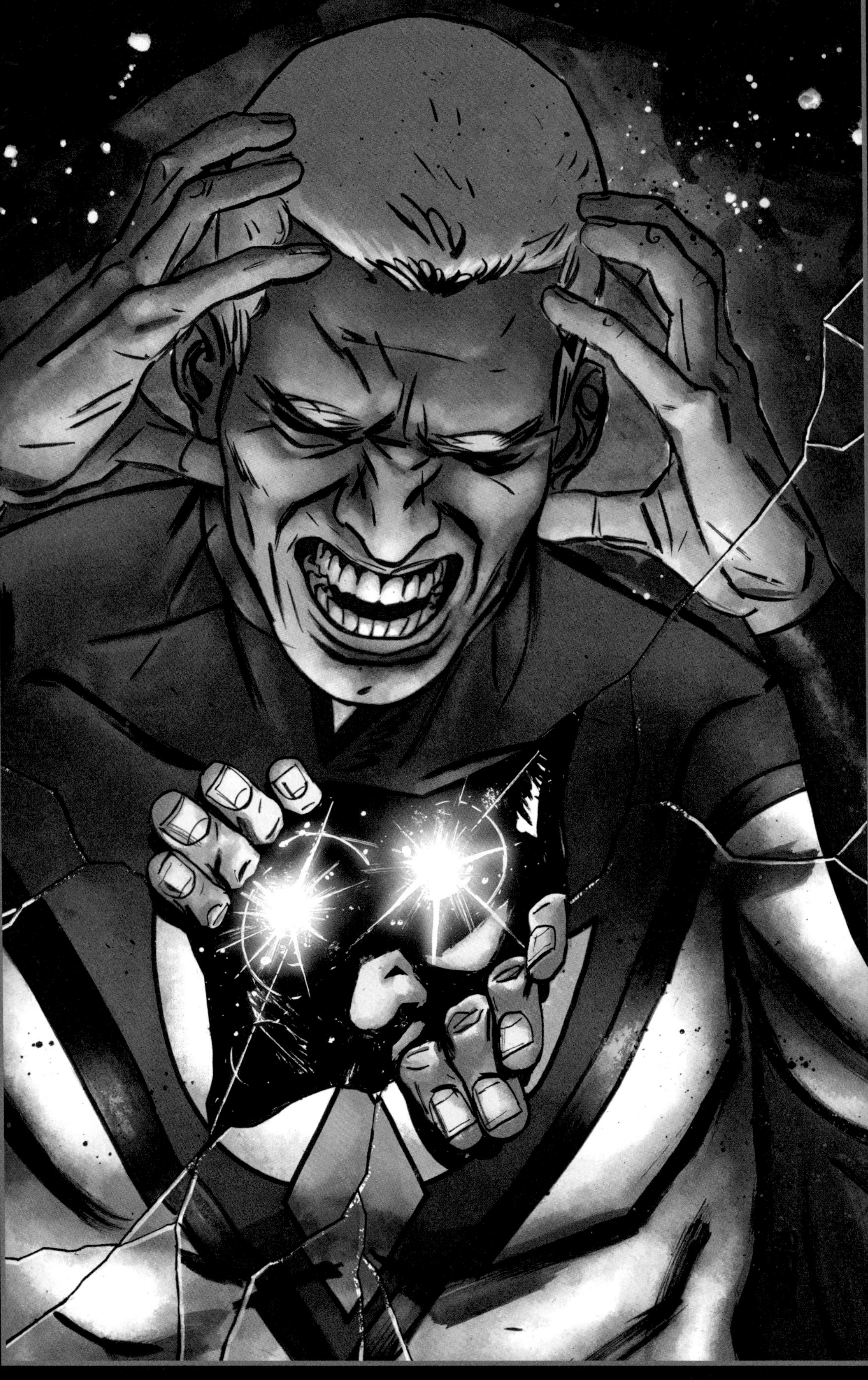

COVER 10A: **PAUL AZACETA**

COLORS: NICK FILARDI

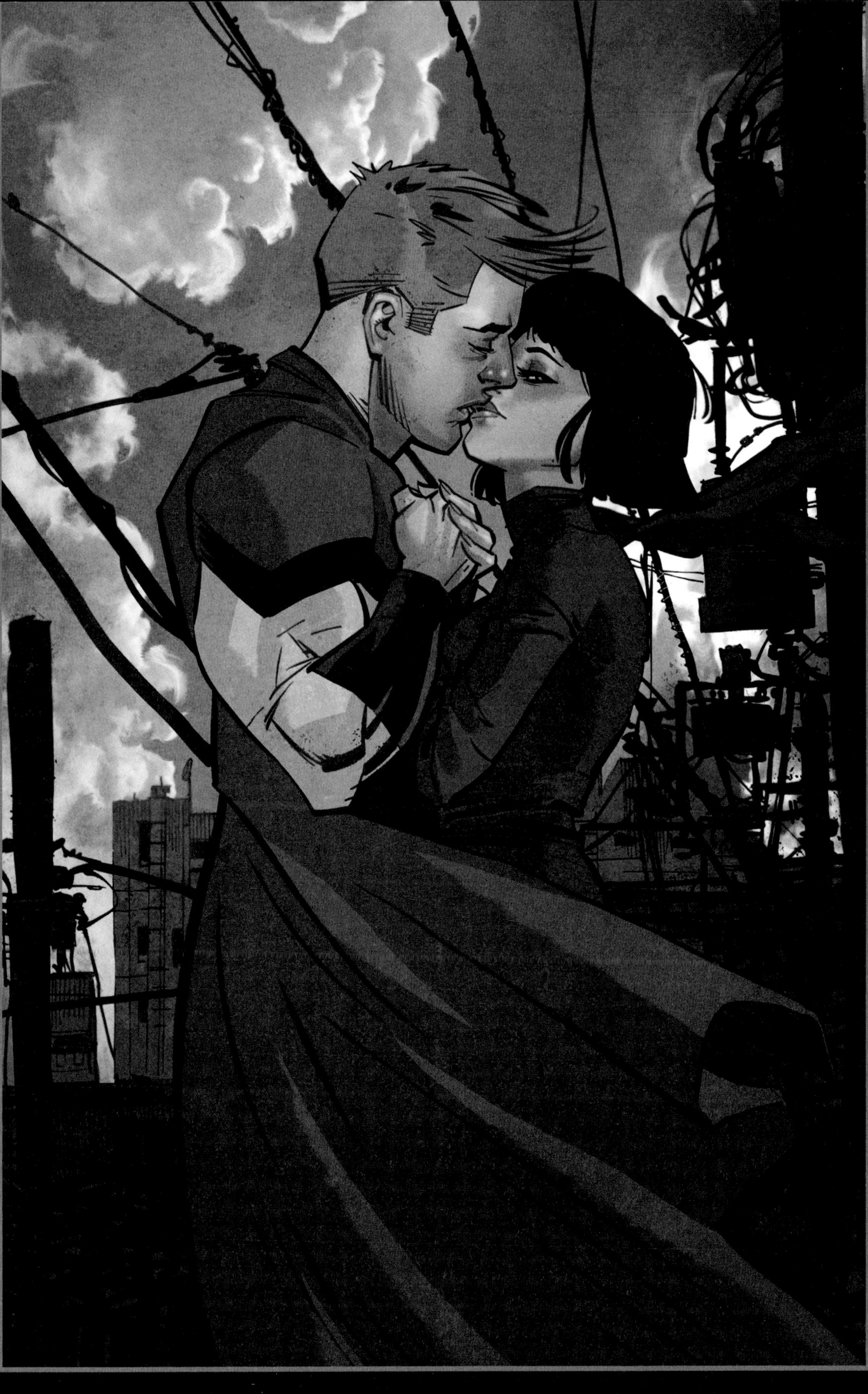

COVER 10B: DAN PANOSIAN

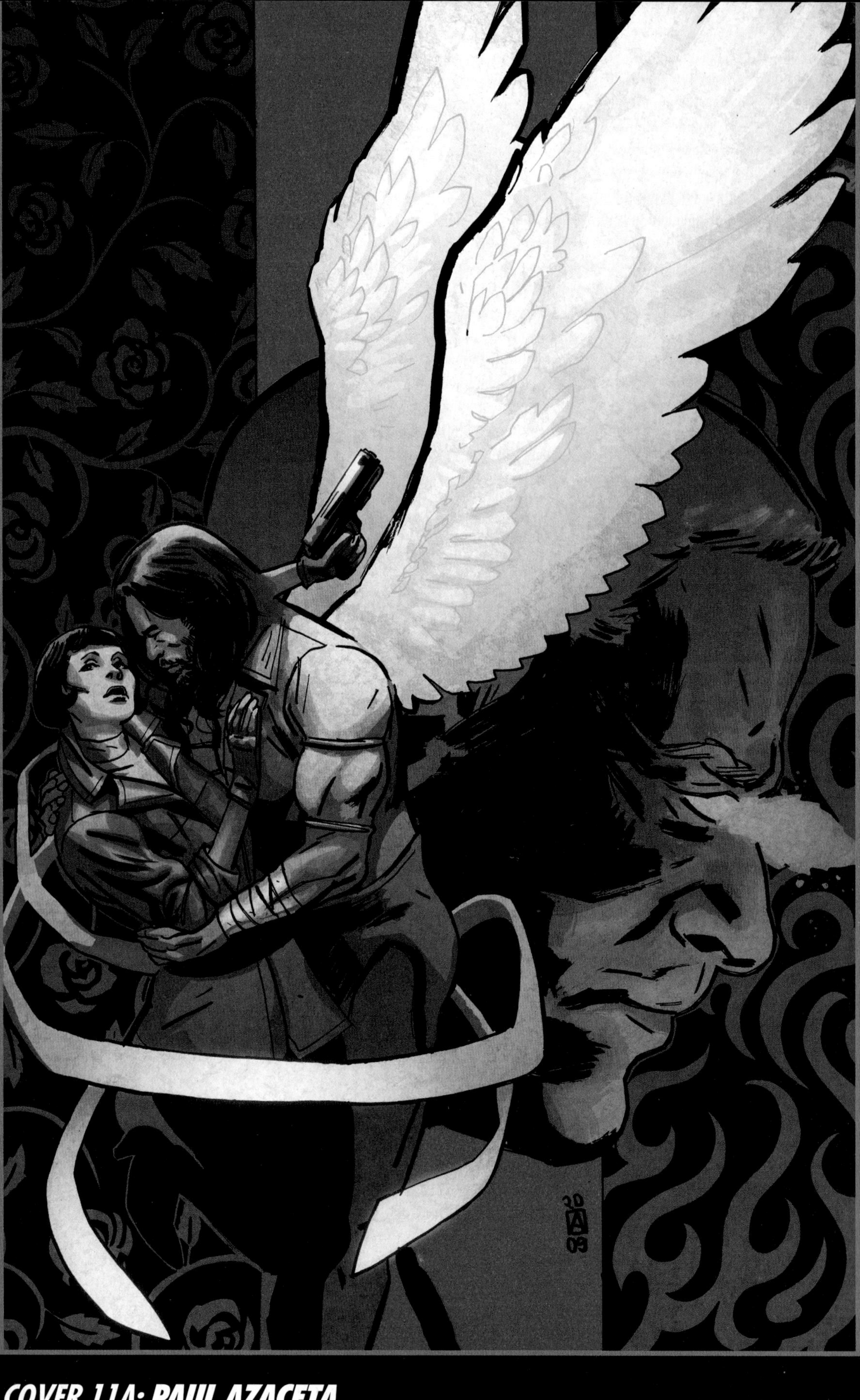

COVER 11A: PAUL AZACETA

COLORS: NICK FILARDI

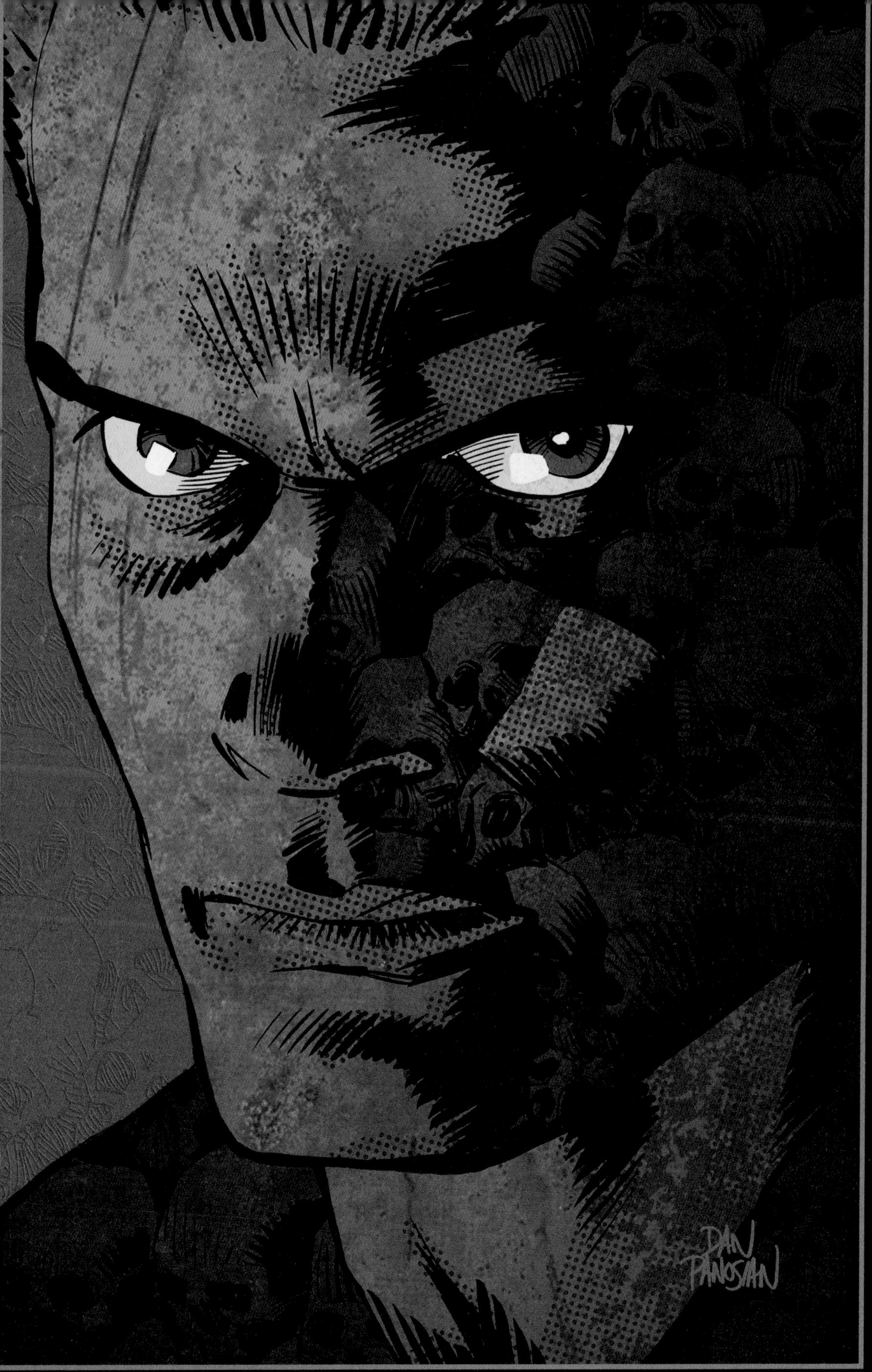
DAN PANOSIAN

COVER 11B: **DAN PANOSIAN**

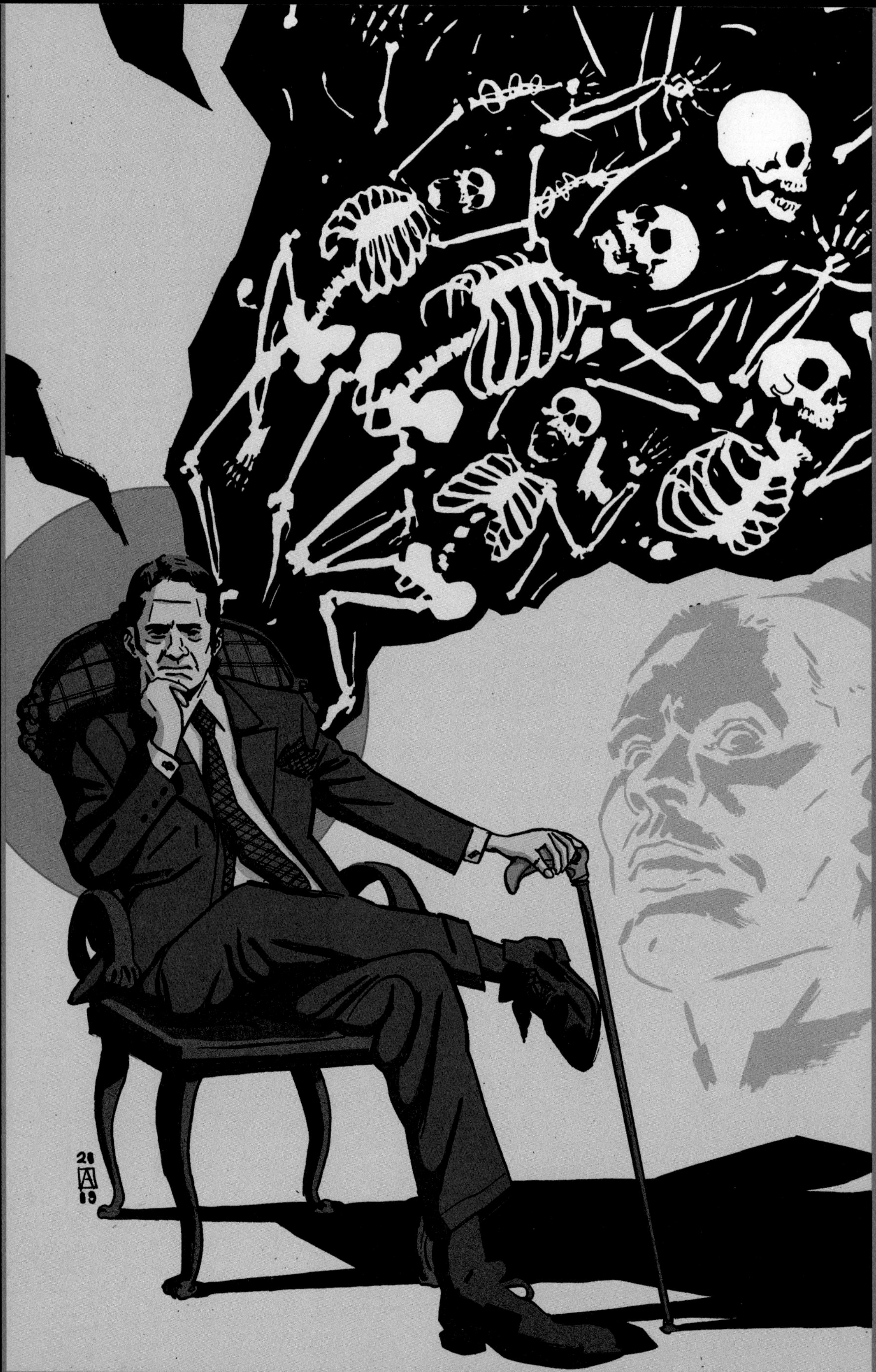
20
A
09

COVER 12A: PAUL AZACETA

COLORS: ANDREW DALHOUSE

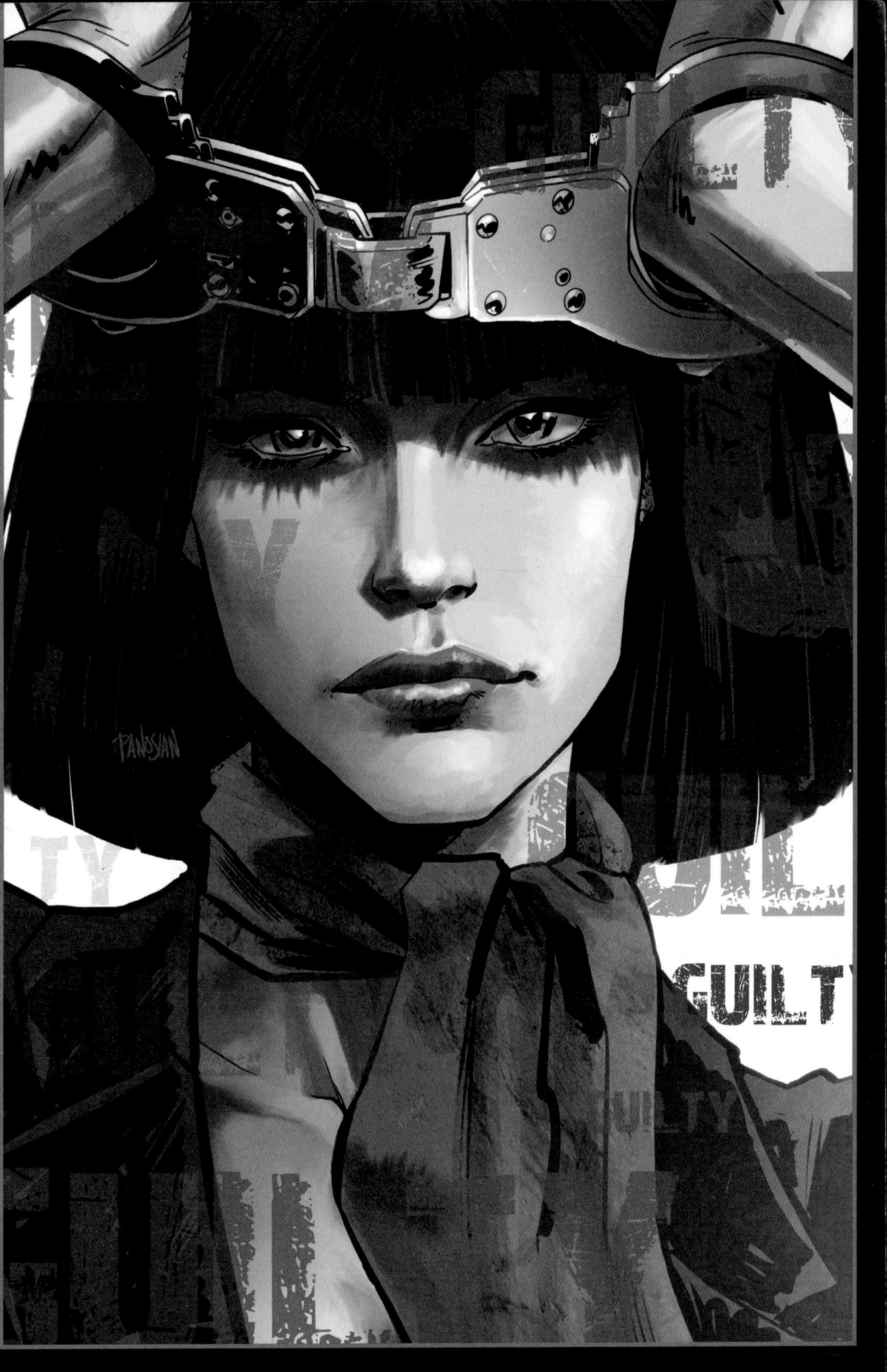
PANOSIAN
GUILTY
GUILTY

COVER 12B: DAN PANOSIAN

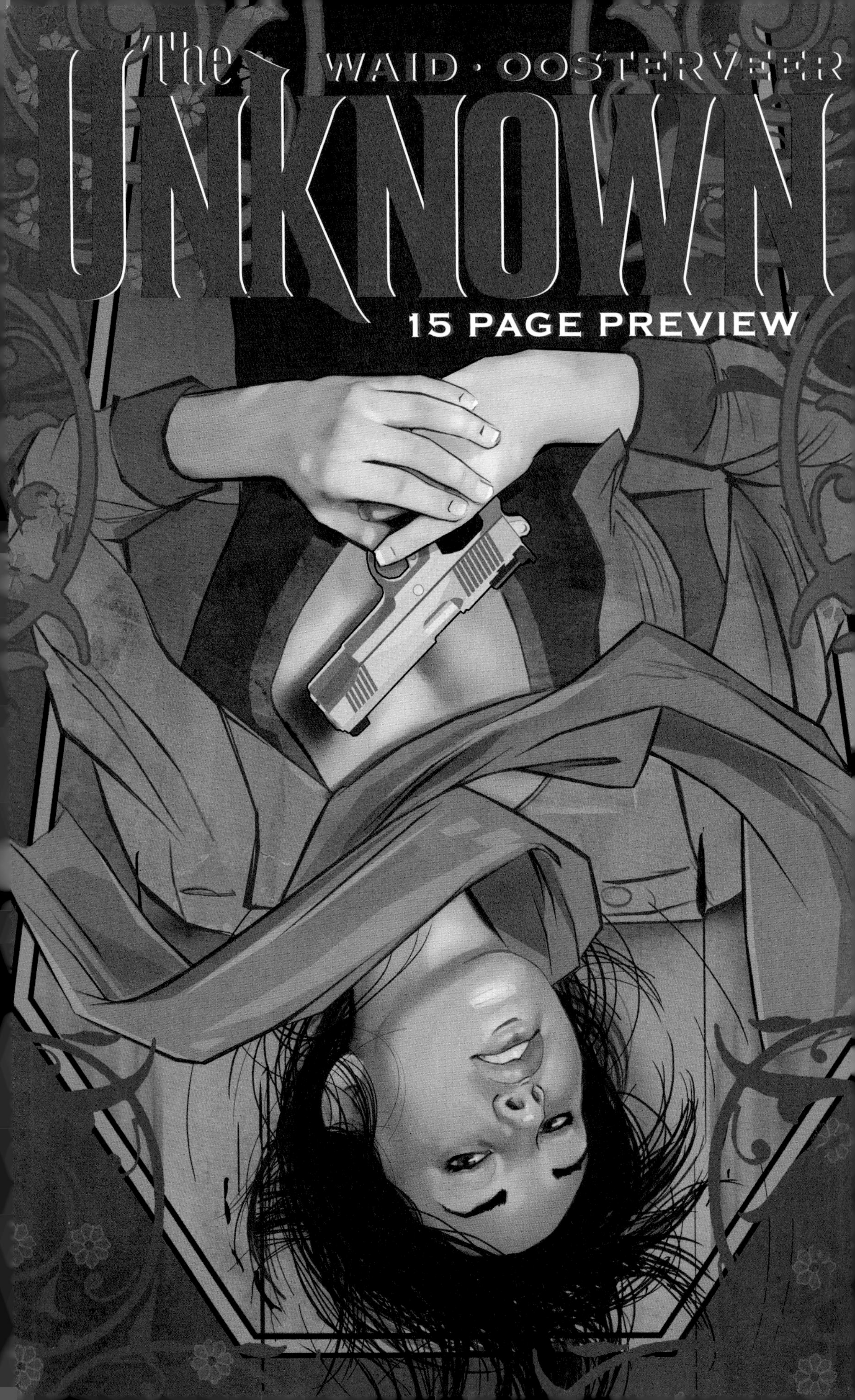
The UNKNOWN
WAID · OOSTERVEER
15 PAGE PREVIEW

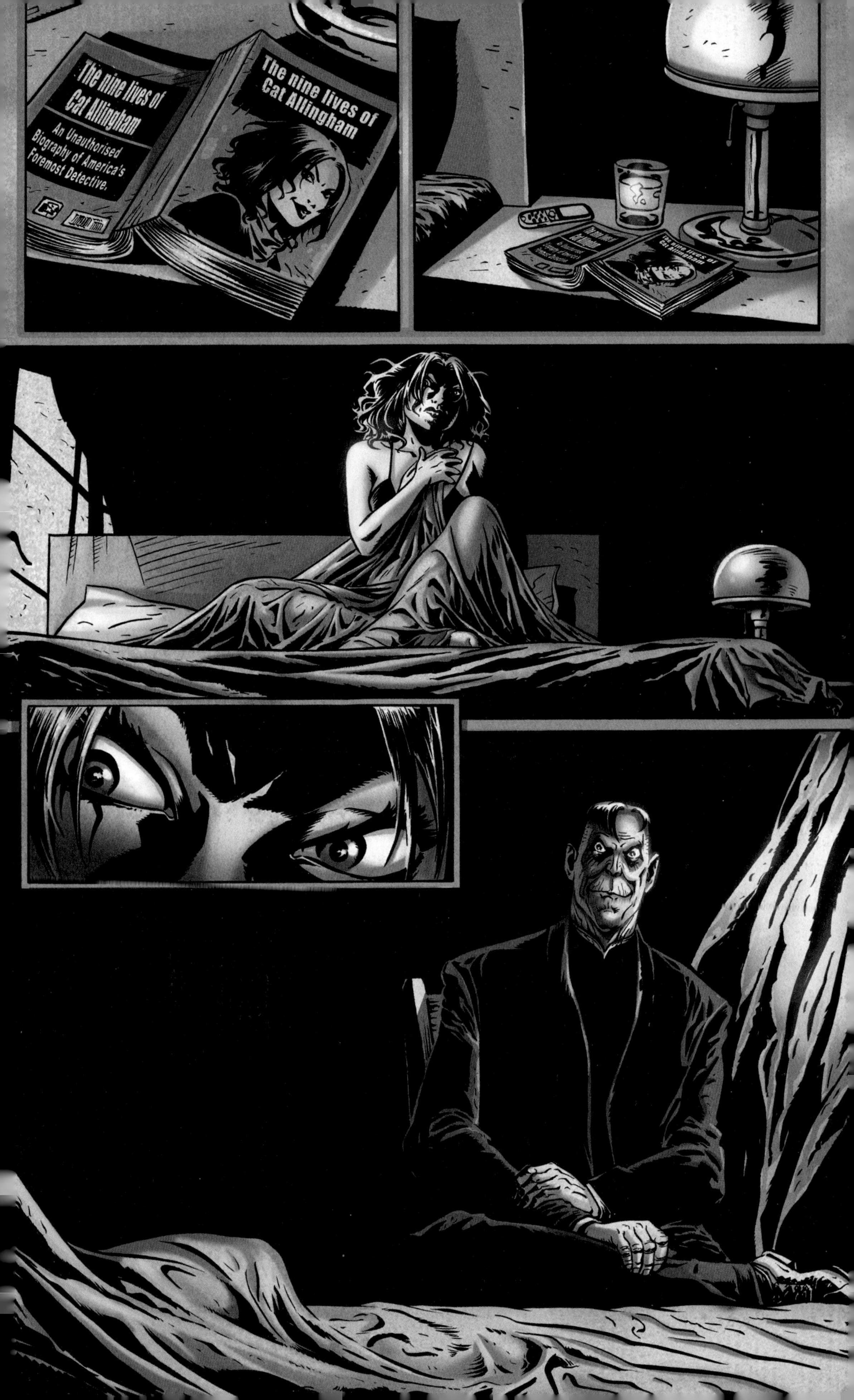
The nine lives of Cat Allingham
An Unauthorised Biography of America's Foremost Detective.
The nine lives of Cat Allingham

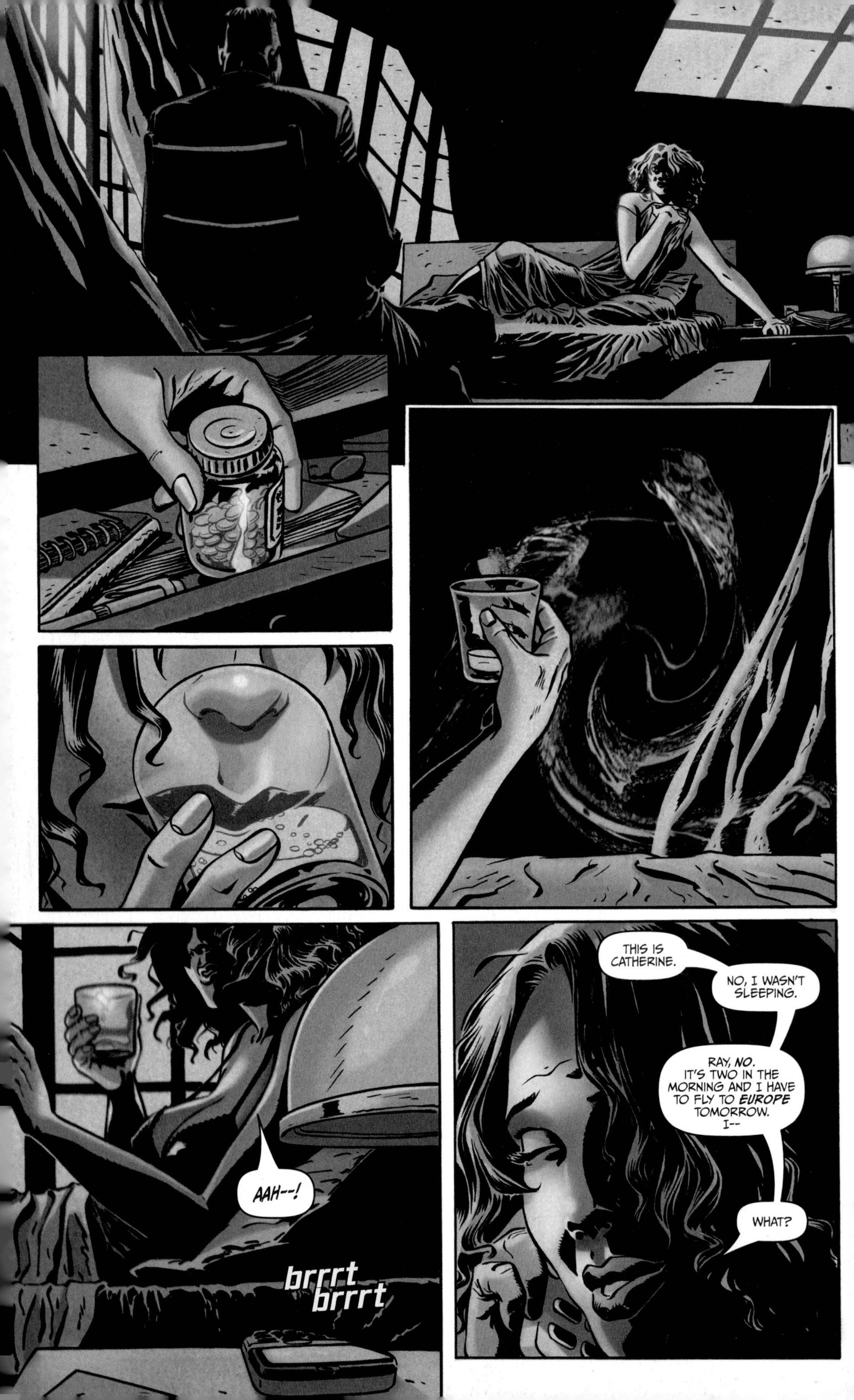
AAH--!
brrrt
brrrt
THIS IS CATHERINE.
NO, I WASN'T SLEEPING.
RAY, NO. IT'S TWO IN THE MORNING AND I HAVE TO FLY TO EUROPE TOMORROW. I--
WHAT?

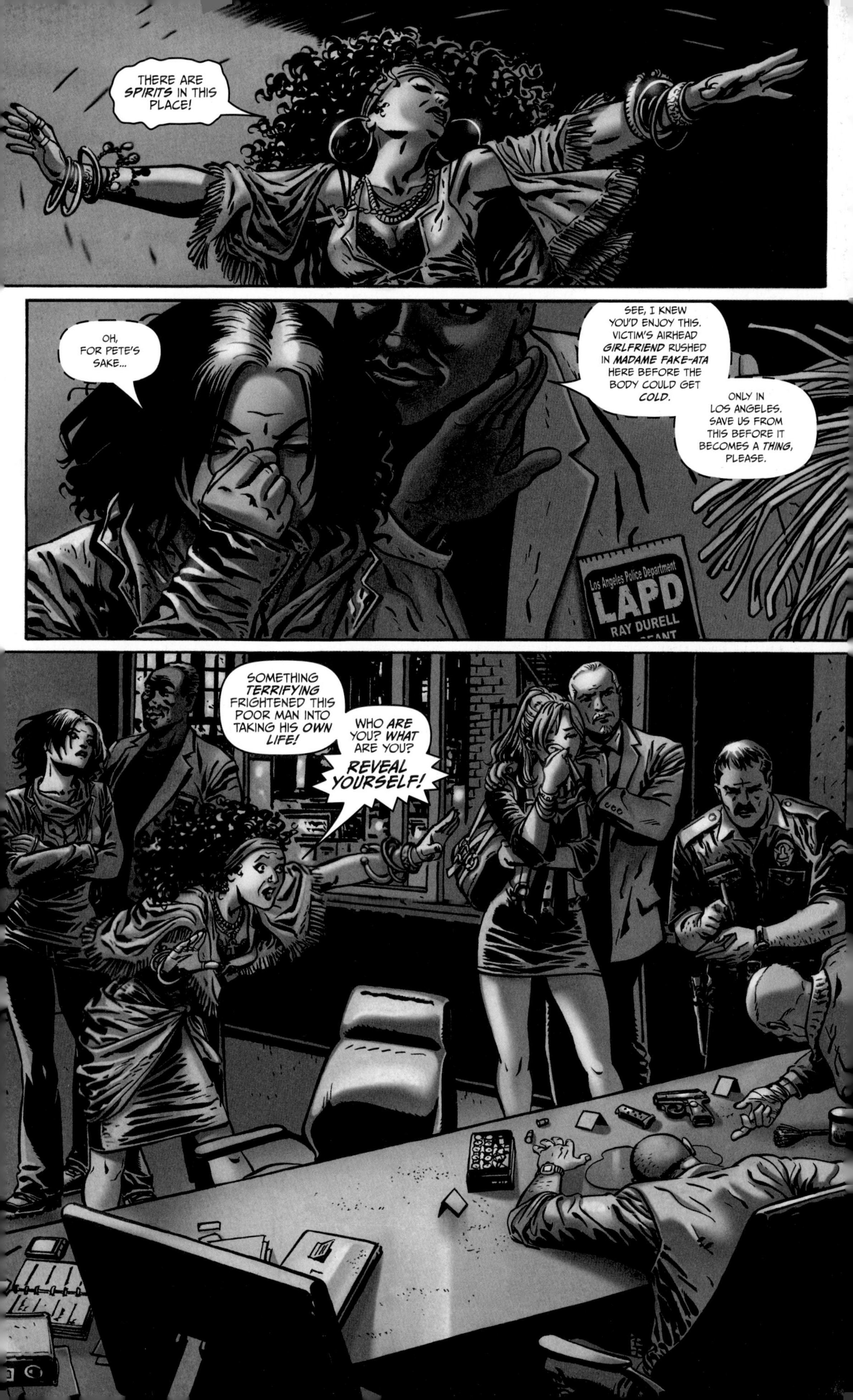
THERE ARE *SPIRITS* IN THIS PLACE!
OH, FOR PETE'S SAKE...
SEE, I KNEW YOU'D ENJOY THIS. VICTIM'S AIRHEAD *GIRLFRIEND* RUSHED IN *MADAME FAKE-ATA* HERE BEFORE THE BODY COULD GET *COLD*.
ONLY IN LOS ANGELES. SAVE US FROM THIS BEFORE IT BECOMES A *THING*, PLEASE.
Los Angeles Police Department
LAPD
RAY DURELL
SOMETHING *TERRIFYING* FRIGHTENED THIS POOR MAN INTO TAKING HIS *OWN LIFE!*
WHO *ARE* YOU? *WHAT* ARE YOU?
REVEAL YOURSELF!

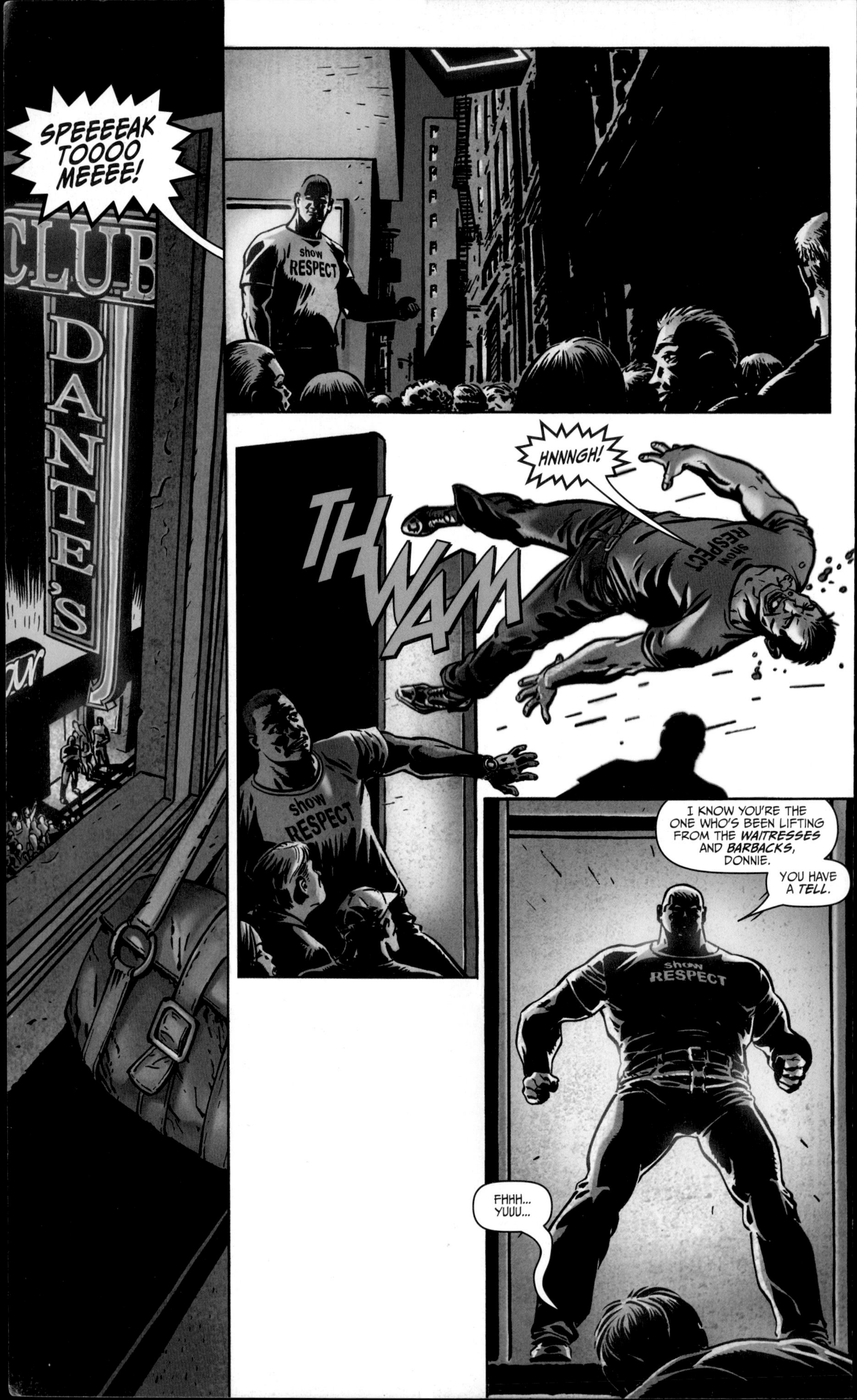
SPEEEEAK TOOOO MEEEE!
CLUB DANTE'S
show RESPECT
HNNNGH!
THWAM
show RESPECT
show RESPECT
I KNOW YOU'RE THE ONE WHO'S BEEN LIFTING FROM THE WAITRESSES AND BARBACKS, DONNIE.
YOU HAVE A TELL.
show RESPECT
FHHH... YUUU...

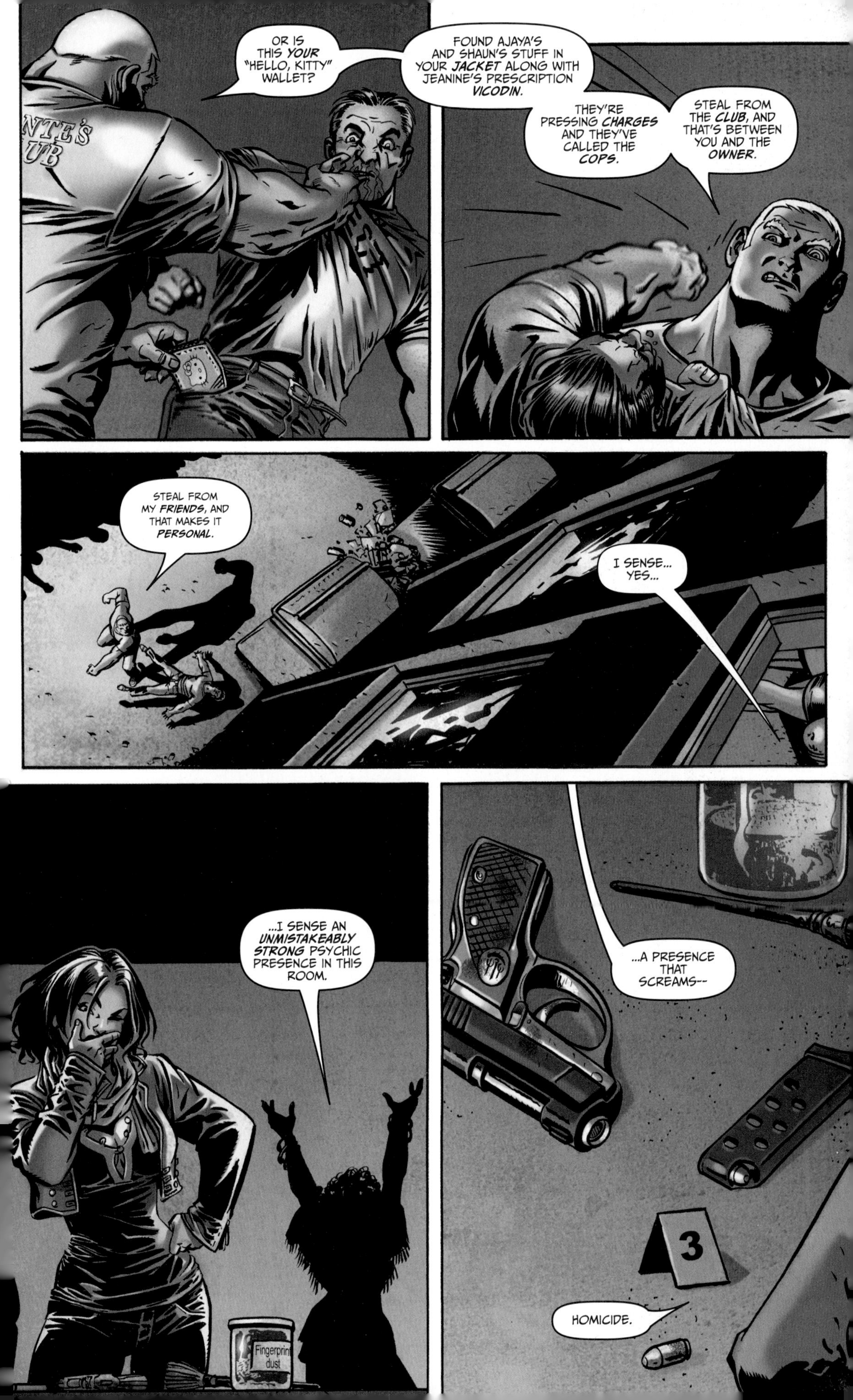
NTE'S
UB
OR IS THIS YOUR "HELLO, KITTY" WALLET?
FOUND AJAYA'S AND SHAUN'S STUFF IN YOUR JACKET ALONG WITH JEANINE'S PRESCRIPTION VICODIN.
THEY'RE PRESSING CHARGES AND THEY'VE CALLED THE COPS.
STEAL FROM THE CLUB, AND THAT'S BETWEEN YOU AND THE OWNER.
STEAL FROM MY FRIENDS, AND THAT MAKES IT PERSONAL.
I SENSE... YES...
...I SENSE AN UNMISTAKEABLY STRONG PSYCHIC PRESENCE IN THIS ROOM.
Fingerprint dust
...A PRESENCE THAT SCREAMS--
3
HOMICIDE.

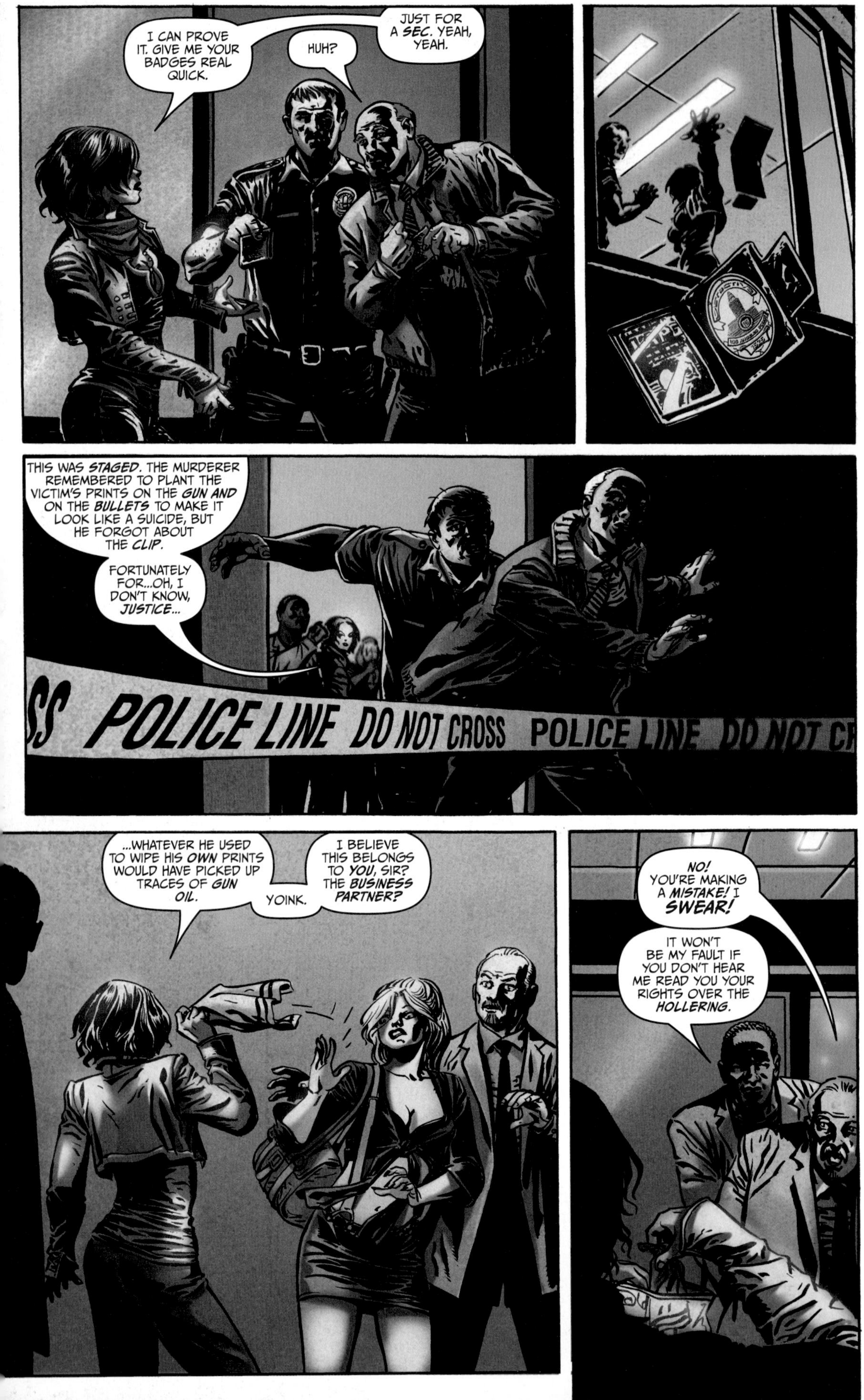
I CAN PROVE IT. GIVE ME YOUR BADGES REAL QUICK.
HUH?
JUST FOR A SEC. YEAH, YEAH.
THIS WAS STAGED. THE MURDERER REMEMBERED TO PLANT THE VICTIM'S PRINTS ON THE GUN AND ON THE BULLETS TO MAKE IT LOOK LIKE A SUICIDE, BUT HE FORGOT ABOUT THE CLIP.
FORTUNATELY FOR...OH, I DON'T KNOW, JUSTICE...
POLICE LINE DO NOT CROSS POLICE LINE
...WHATEVER HE USED TO WIPE HIS OWN PRINTS WOULD HAVE PICKED UP TRACES OF GUN OIL.
YOINK.
I BELIEVE THIS BELONGS TO YOU, SIR? THE BUSINESS PARTNER?
NO! YOU'RE MAKING A MISTAKE! I SWEAR!
IT WON'T BE MY FAULT IF YOU DON'T HEAR ME READ YOU YOUR RIGHTS OVER THE HOLLERING.

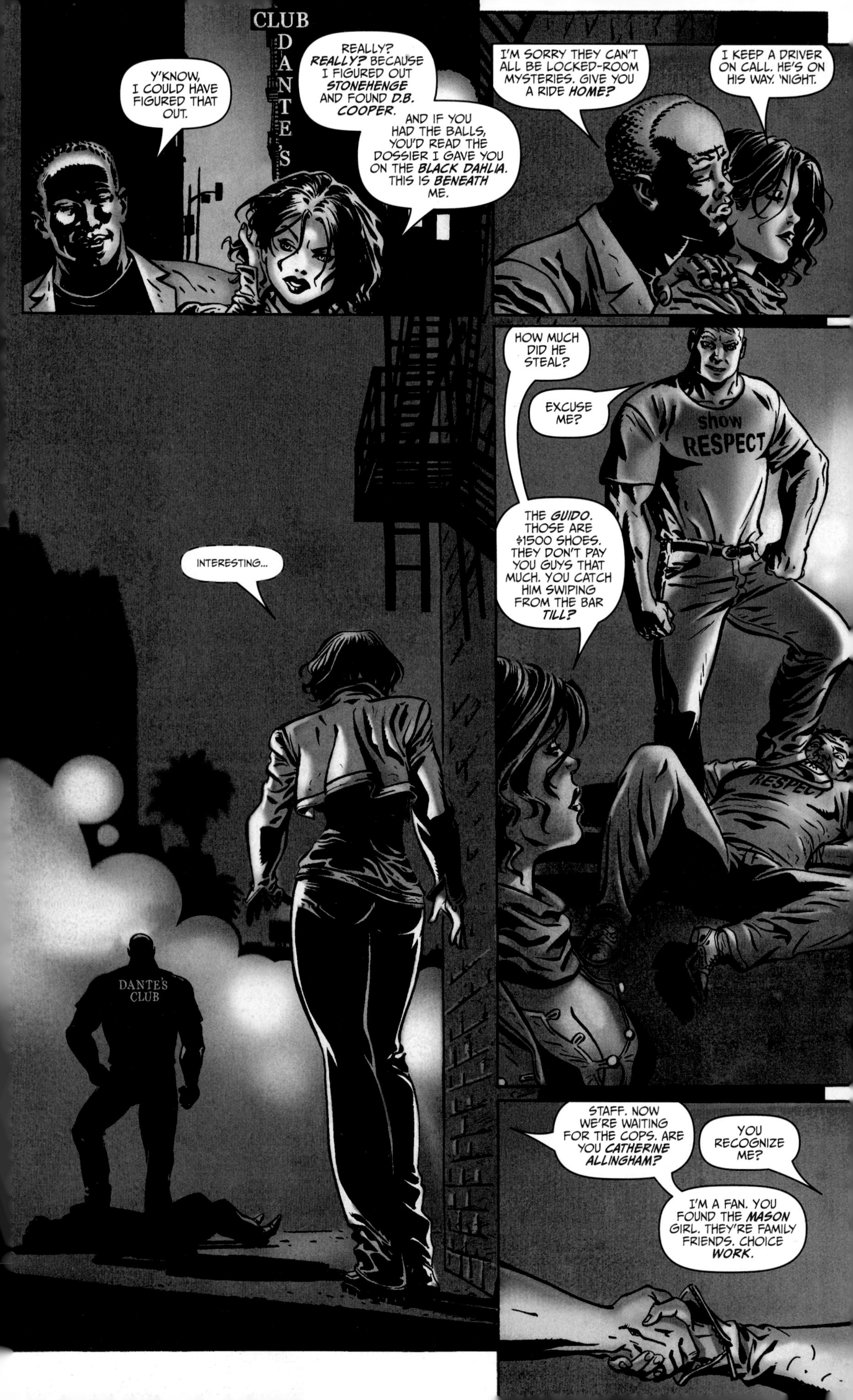
CLUB DANTE'S
Y'KNOW, I COULD HAVE FIGURED THAT OUT.
REALLY? REALLY? BECAUSE I FIGURED OUT STONEHENGE AND FOUND D.B. COOPER.
AND IF YOU HAD THE BALLS, YOU'D READ THE DOSSIER I GAVE YOU ON THE BLACK DAHLIA. THIS IS BENEATH ME.
I'M SORRY THEY CAN'T ALL BE LOCKED-ROOM MYSTERIES. GIVE YOU A RIDE HOME?
I KEEP A DRIVER ON CALL. HE'S ON HIS WAY. 'NIGHT.
INTERESTING...
DANTE'S CLUB
HOW MUCH DID HE STEAL?
EXCUSE ME?
show RESPECT
THE GUIDO. THOSE ARE $1500 SHOES. THEY DON'T PAY YOU GUYS THAT MUCH. YOU CATCH HIM SWIPING FROM THE BAR TILL?
RESPECT
STAFF. NOW WE'RE WAITING FOR THE COPS. ARE YOU CATHERINE ALLINGHAM?
YOU RECOGNIZE ME?
I'M A FAN. YOU FOUND THE MASON GIRL. THEY'RE FAMILY FRIENDS. CHOICE WORK.

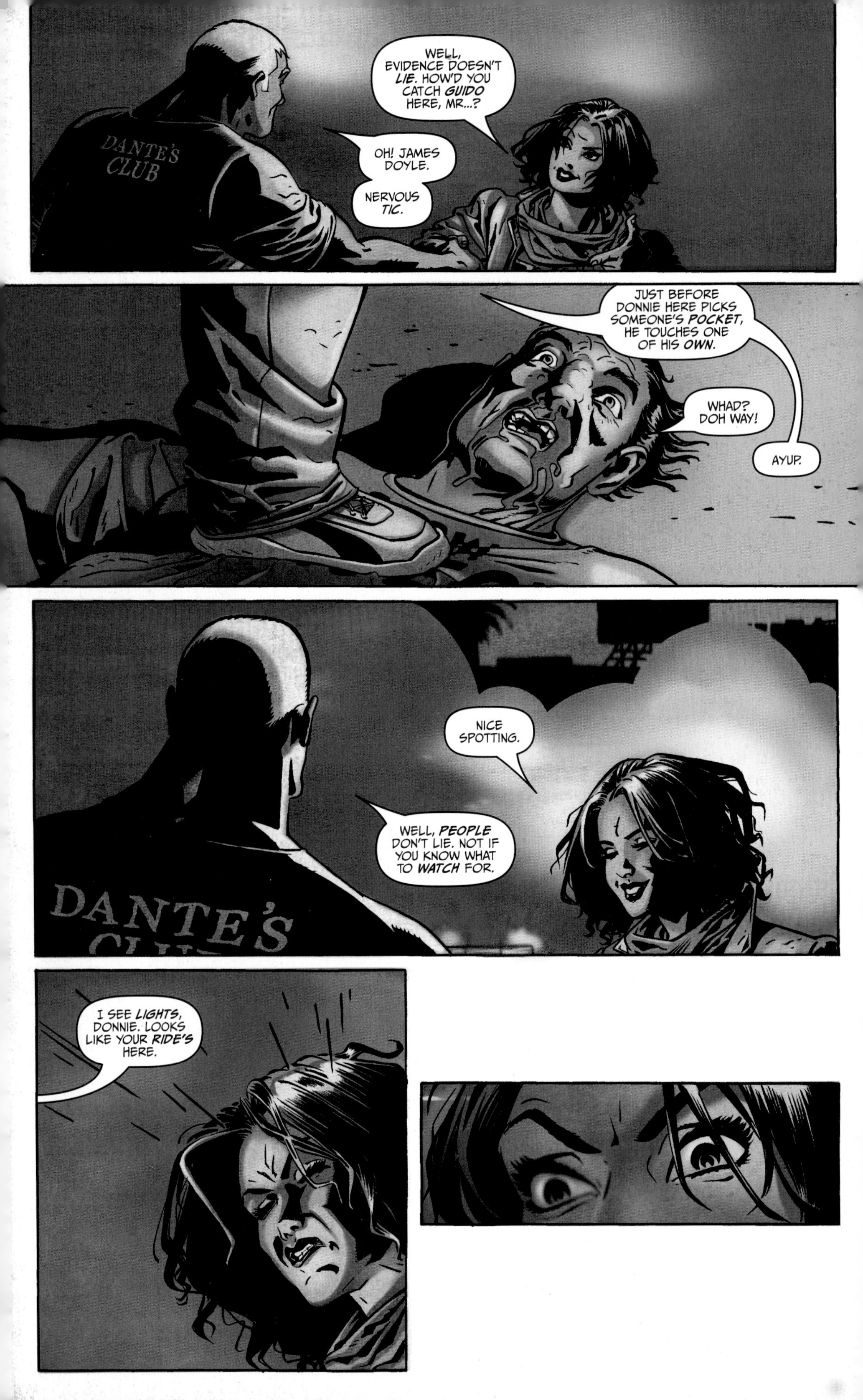
WELL, EVIDENCE DOESN'T LIE. HOW'D YOU CATCH GUIDO HERE, MR...?
OH! JAMES DOYLE.
NERVOUS TIC.
DANTE'S CLUB
JUST BEFORE DONNIE HERE PICKS SOMEONE'S POCKET, HE TOUCHES ONE OF HIS OWN.
WHAD? DOH WAY!
AYUP.
NICE SPOTTING.
WELL, PEOPLE DON'T LIE. NOT IF YOU KNOW WHAT TO WATCH FOR.
DANTE'S
I SEE LIGHTS, DONNIE. LOOKS LIKE YOUR RIDE'S HERE.

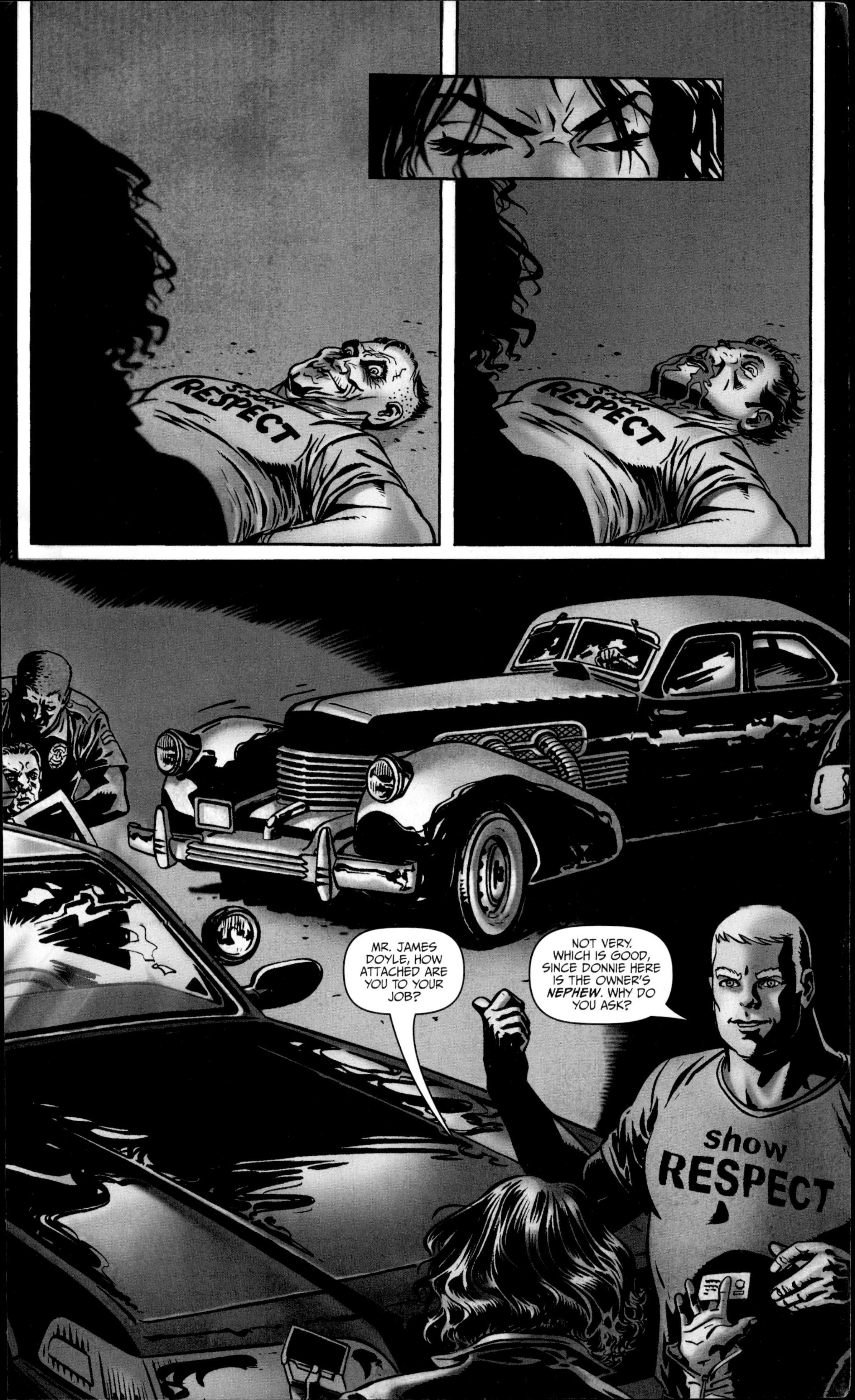
show
RESPECT
show
RESPECT
MR. JAMES DOYLE, HOW ATTACHED ARE YOU TO YOUR JOB?
NOT VERY. WHICH IS GOOD, SINCE DONNIE HERE IS THE OWNER'S NEPHEW. WHY DO YOU ASK?
show
RESPECT

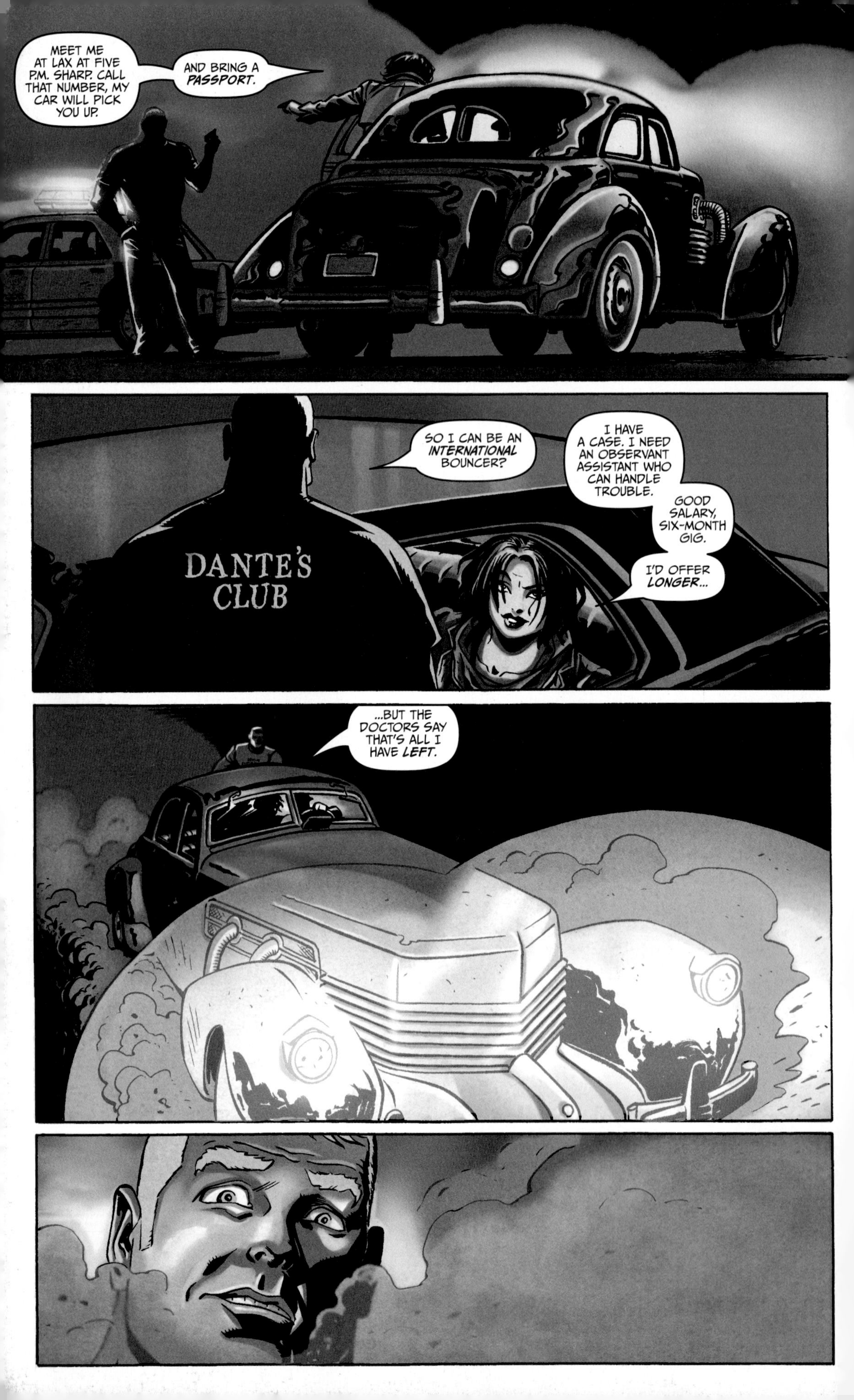
MEET ME AT LAX AT FIVE P.M. SHARP. CALL THAT NUMBER, MY CAR WILL PICK YOU UP.
AND BRING A *PASSPORT*.
SO I CAN BE AN *INTERNATIONAL* BOUNCER?
DANTE'S CLUB
I HAVE A CASE. I NEED AN OBSERVANT ASSISTANT WHO CAN HANDLE TROUBLE.
GOOD SALARY, SIX-MONTH GIG.
I'D OFFER *LONGER*...
...BUT THE DOCTORS SAY THAT'S ALL I HAVE *LEFT*.

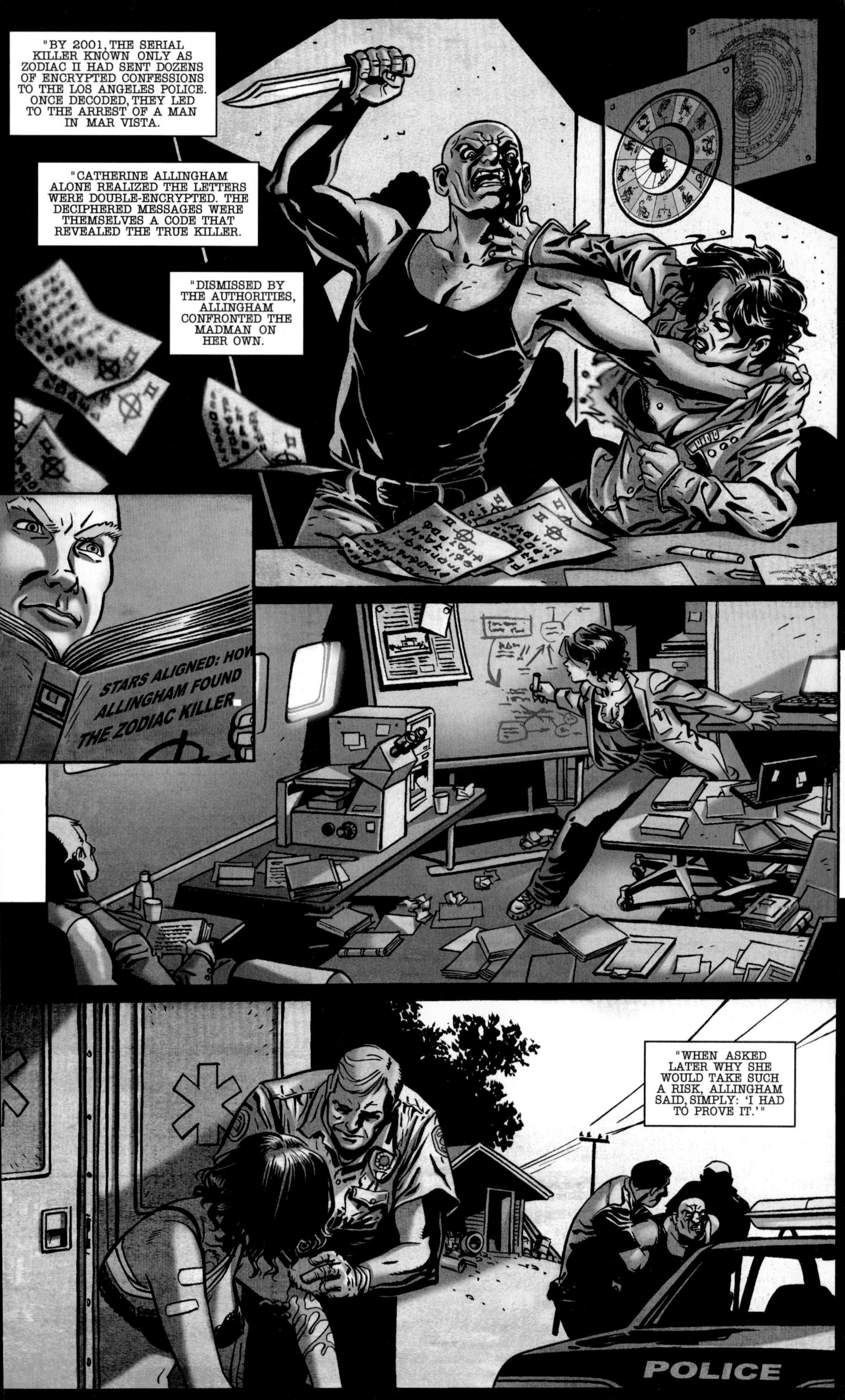
"BY 2001, THE SERIAL KILLER KNOWN ONLY AS ZODIAC II HAD SENT DOZENS OF ENCRYPTED CONFESSIONS TO THE LOS ANGELES POLICE. ONCE DECODED, THEY LED TO THE ARREST OF A MAN IN MAR VISTA.
"CATHERINE ALLINGHAM ALONE REALIZED THE LETTERS WERE DOUBLE-ENCRYPTED. THE DECIPHERED MESSAGES WERE THEMSELVES A CODE THAT REVEALED THE TRUE KILLER.
"DISMISSED BY THE AUTHORITIES, ALLINGHAM CONFRONTED THE MADMAN ON HER OWN.
STARS ALIGNED: HOW ALLINGHAM FOUND THE ZODIAC KILLER
"WHEN ASKED LATER WHY SHE WOULD TAKE SUCH A RISK, ALLINGHAM SAID, SIMPLY: 'I HAD TO PROVE IT.'"
POLICE

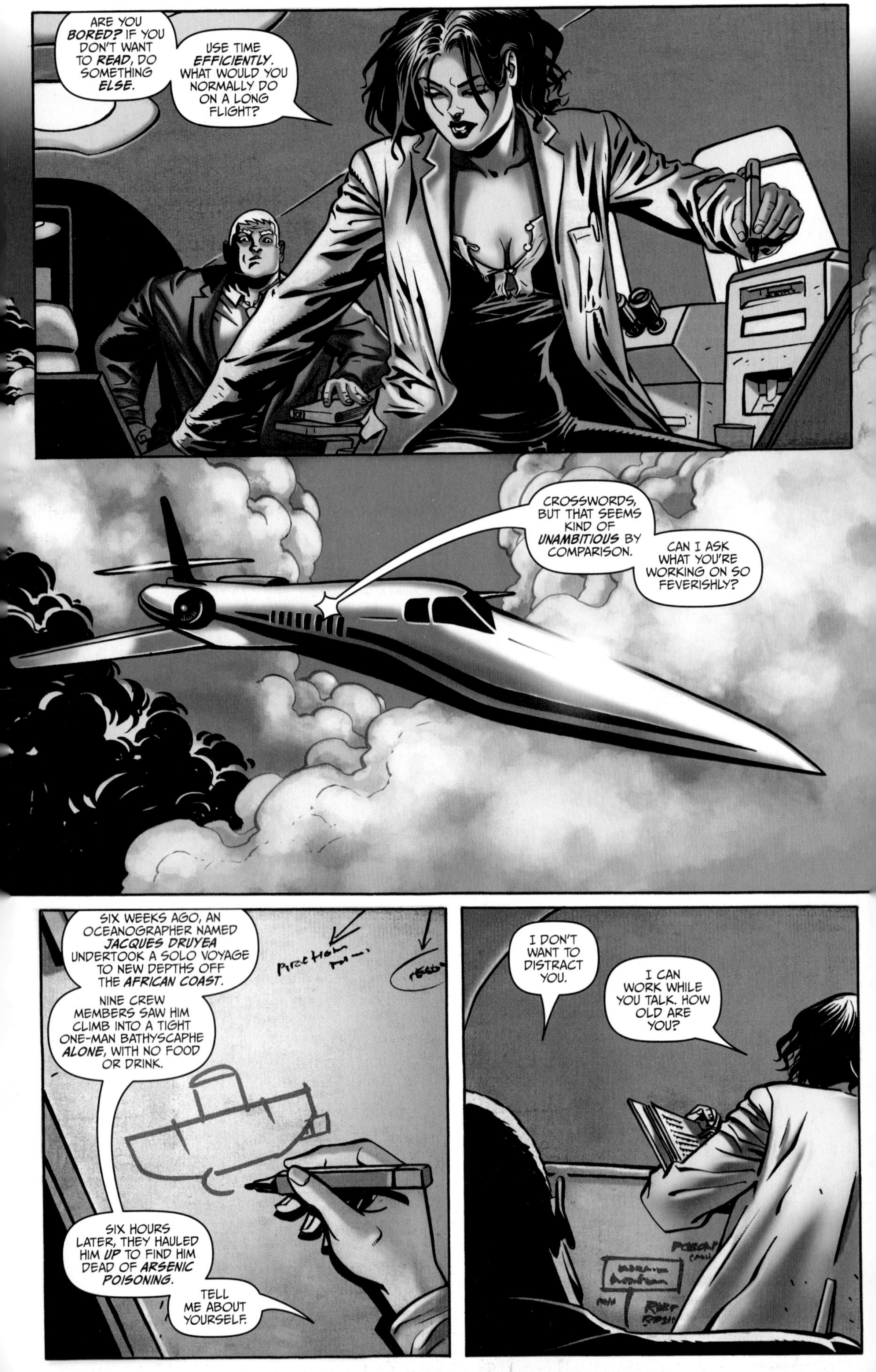
ARE YOU *BORED?* IF YOU DON'T WANT TO *READ*, DO SOMETHING *ELSE*.
USE TIME *EFFICIENTLY*. WHAT WOULD YOU NORMALLY DO ON A LONG FLIGHT?
CROSSWORDS, BUT THAT SEEMS KIND OF *UNAMBITIOUS* BY COMPARISON.
CAN I ASK WHAT YOU'RE WORKING ON SO FEVERISHLY?
SIX WEEKS AGO, AN OCEANOGRAPHER NAMED *JACQUES DRUYEA* UNDERTOOK A SOLO VOYAGE TO NEW DEPTHS OFF THE *AFRICAN COAST*.
NINE CREW MEMBERS SAW HIM CLIMB INTO A TIGHT ONE-MAN BATHYSCAPHE *ALONE*, WITH NO FOOD OR DRINK.
SIX HOURS LATER, THEY HAULED HIM *UP* TO FIND HIM DEAD OF *ARSENIC POISONING*.
TELL ME ABOUT YOURSELF.
I DON'T WANT TO DISTRACT YOU.
I CAN WORK WHILE YOU TALK. HOW OLD ARE YOU?

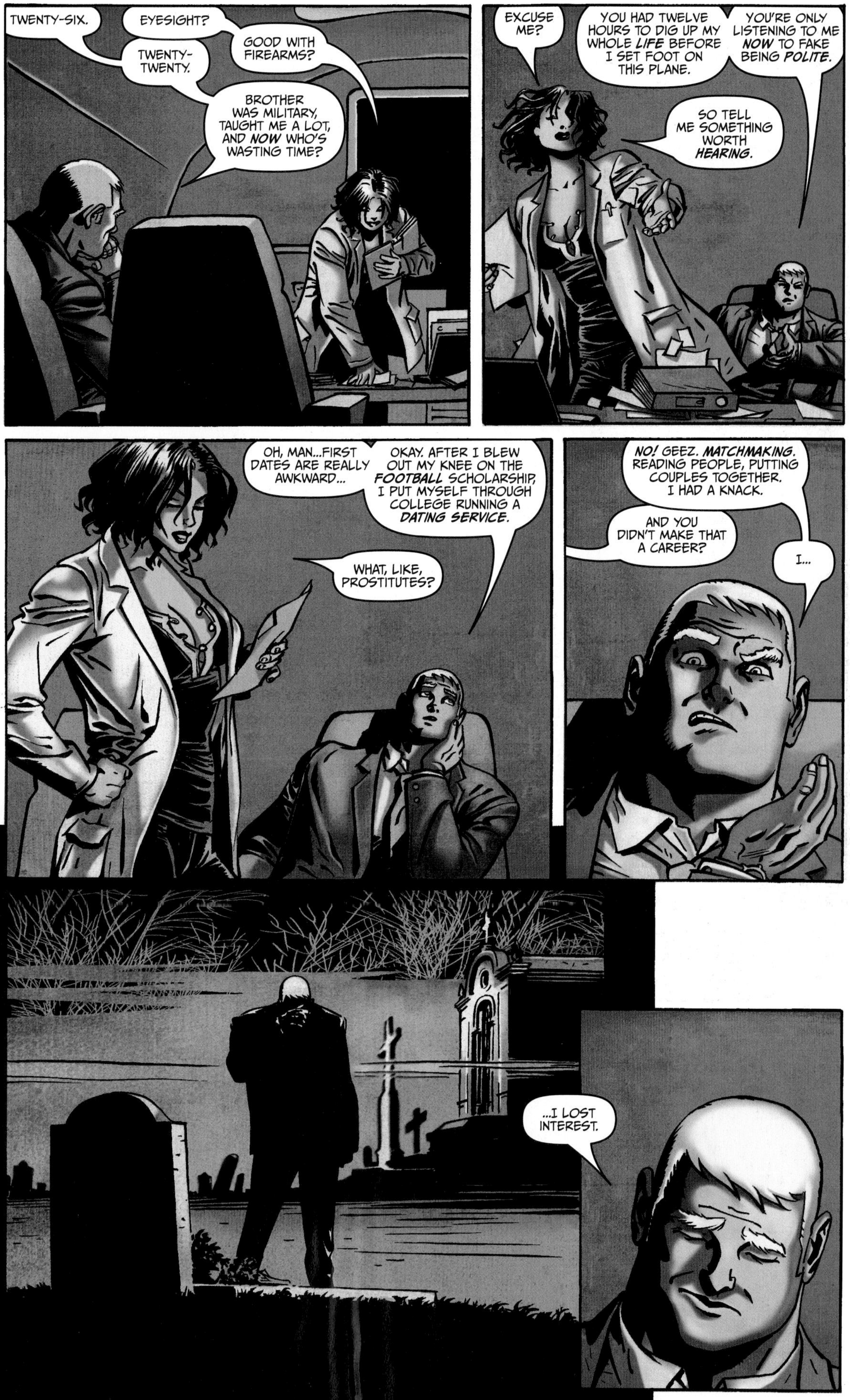
TWENTY-SIX.
EYESIGHT?
TWENTY-TWENTY.
GOOD WITH FIREARMS?
BROTHER WAS MILITARY, TAUGHT ME A LOT, AND NOW WHO'S WASTING TIME?
EXCUSE ME?
YOU HAD TWELVE HOURS TO DIG UP MY WHOLE LIFE BEFORE I SET FOOT ON THIS PLANE.
YOU'RE ONLY LISTENING TO ME NOW TO FAKE BEING POLITE.
SO TELL ME SOMETHING WORTH HEARING.
OH, MAN...FIRST DATES ARE REALLY AWKWARD...
OKAY. AFTER I BLEW OUT MY KNEE ON THE FOOTBALL SCHOLARSHIP, I PUT MYSELF THROUGH COLLEGE RUNNING A DATING SERVICE.
WHAT, LIKE, PROSTITUTES?
NO! GEEZ. MATCHMAKING. READING PEOPLE, PUTTING COUPLES TOGETHER. I HAD A KNACK.
AND YOU DIDN'T MAKE THAT A CAREER?
I...
...I LOST INTEREST.

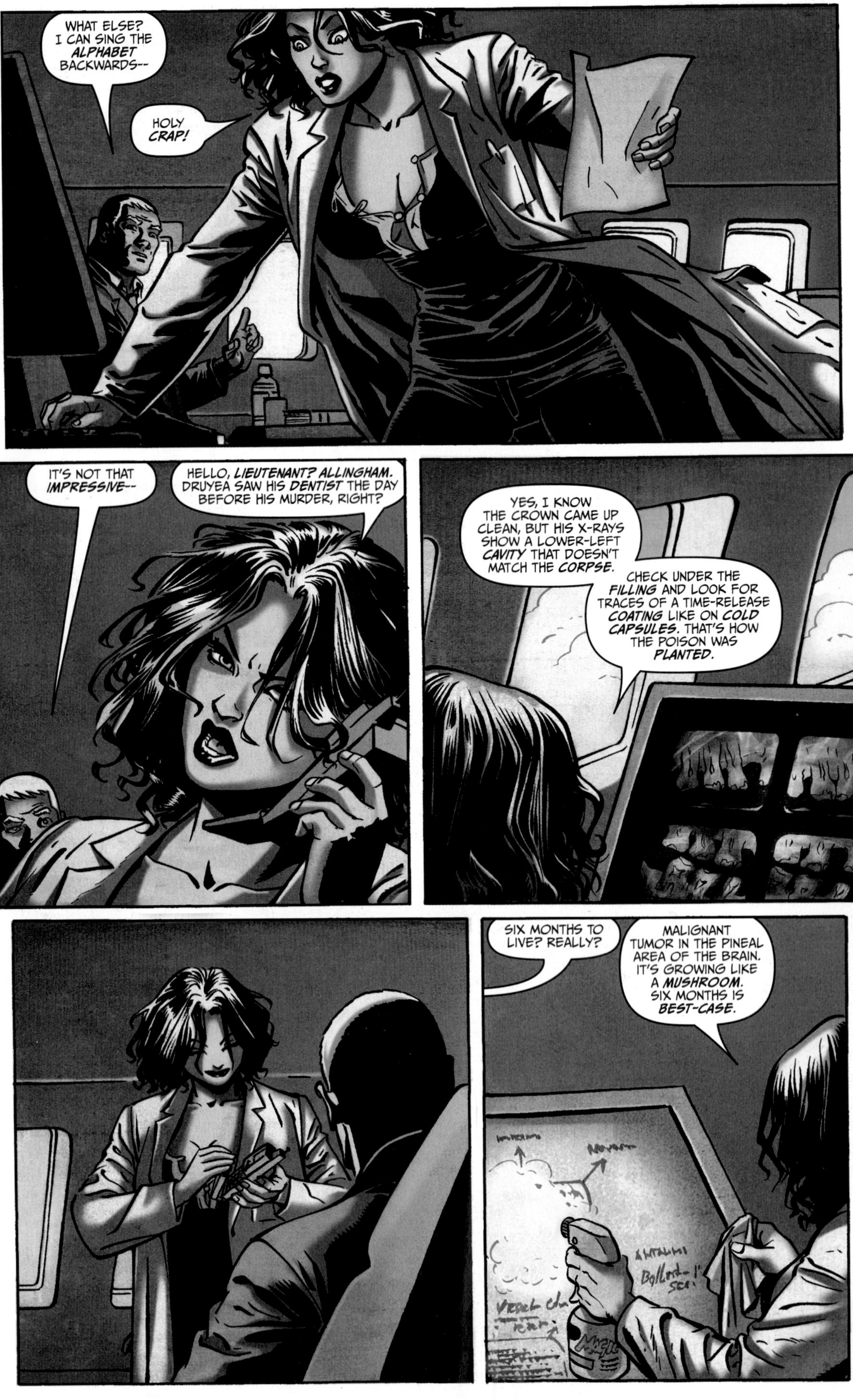
WHAT ELSE? I CAN SING THE ALPHABET BACKWARDS--
HOLY CRAP!
IT'S NOT THAT IMPRESSIVE--
HELLO, LIEUTENANT? ALLINGHAM. DRUYEA SAW HIS DENTIST THE DAY BEFORE HIS MURDER, RIGHT?
YES, I KNOW THE CROWN CAME UP CLEAN, BUT HIS X-RAYS SHOW A LOWER-LEFT CAVITY THAT DOESN'T MATCH THE CORPSE.
CHECK UNDER THE FILLING AND LOOK FOR TRACES OF A TIME-RELEASE COATING LIKE ON COLD CAPSULES. THAT'S HOW THE POISON WAS PLANTED.
SIX MONTHS TO LIVE? REALLY?
MALIGNANT TUMOR IN THE PINEAL AREA OF THE BRAIN. IT'S GROWING LIKE A MUSHROOM. SIX MONTHS IS BEST-CASE.

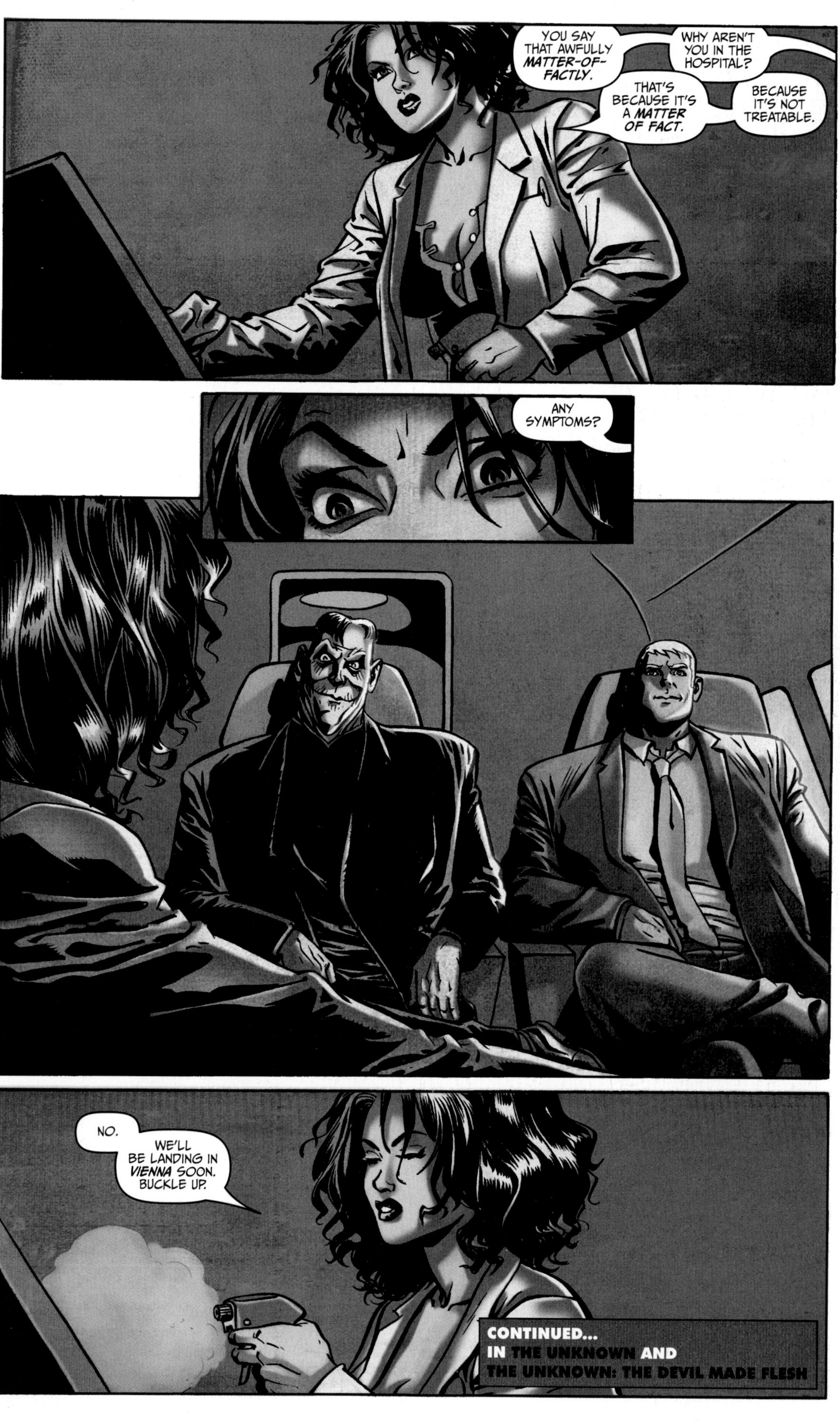
YOU SAY THAT AWFULLY *MATTER-OF-FACTLY*.
THAT'S BECAUSE IT'S A *MATTER OF FACT*.
WHY AREN'T YOU IN THE HOSPITAL?
BECAUSE IT'S NOT TREATABLE.
ANY SYMPTOMS?
NO.
WE'LL BE LANDING IN *VIENNA* SOON. BUCKLE UP.
CONTINUED...
IN THE UNKNOWN AND
THE UNKNOWN: THE DEVIL MADE FLESH

IRREDEEMABLE

VOLUME 4

SUMMER 2010